Protectionism, Exchange Rates and the Macroeconomy

J.L. FORD AND S. SEN

Basil Blackwell

© J. L. Ford and S. Sen 1985

First published 1985

Basil Blackwell Ltd
108 Cowley Road, Oxford OX4 1JF, UK

Basil Blackwell Inc.
432 Park Avenue South, Suite 1505,
New York, NY 10016, USA

British Library Cataloguing in Publication Data

Ford, J.
  Protectionism, exchange rates and the macroeconomy.
  1. Free trade and protection
  I. Title   II. Sen, S.
  382.7   HF1713

  ISBN 0-631-14352-1

Library of Congress Cataloging in Publication Data

Ford, J. L.
  Protectionism, exchange rates, and the macroeconomy.

  Bibliography: p.
  1. Free trade and protection – Protection. 2. Foreign exchange problem. 3. Economic policy. I. Sen, S.
  (Somnath) II. Title.
  HF1713.F65 1985   382.7'3   85-4043
  ISBN 0-631-14352-1

Typeset by Unicus Graphics Ltd, Horsham
Printed in Great Britain by The Camelot Press Ltd, Southampton

Protectionism, Exchange Rates
and the Macroeconomy

For Margaret and Saadet

Contents

Audi partem alteram

Preface

The current depressed state of the world economy, inevitably, has rejuvenated discussion of protectionism. The move towards a system of freely floating exchange rates, has heightened the role of the exchange rate in the world economy. By way of contrast, of course, it has sought to make the economies of the world more interdependent.

Whilst there is, and indeed always has been, a powerful protectionist lobby in the USA, most Western governments seem to be adamant that such policies are beggar-my-neighbour and should not be adopted by any of them. In that regard they are echoing the latest pronouncement by GATT (December 1984) urging governments not to succumb to protectionist policies. However, the pressure is there and there can be no doubt that developing countries, affected by the world recession, are adopting, or have adopted, protectionist policies. Some of those policies are not overtly protectionist; that is, they do not all involve the imposition of tariffs or the setting of import quotas, they often take the form of subsidies to import-competing and export industries (e.g. in Taiwan, Hong Kong and Singapore).

There seems little doubt, though, that the move to a world of flexible exchange rates is here to stay. It is difficult to envisage a return to fixed exchange rates given the complexion of most Western governments.

However, one suspects that further moves towards protectionism cannot be ruled out. Naturally, systematic moves along that road would be likely to lead to an abandonment of flexible exchange rates. But the resort to protectionist policies by less developed countries, 'small open economies', in fact, is likely to be intensified, and for macroeconomic purposes. Furthermore, any protectionist policy will have to be implemented in a regime of freely fluctuating exchange rates. That is a key issue, deserving the attention of academic economists.

There is a small, and rapidly growing literature, on that matter: the effects on the macroeconomy, largely for small open economies, of protectionism under flexible rates of exchange. The overwhelming view is that in a variety of macroeconomic models protectionism will be harmful to output and employment; at the very best it can have neutral effects on them.

The springboard for the discussion in almost every aspect of the literature is the seminal paper by Robert Mundell (1961). Inevitably, the paradigm that he developed has shaped the formulation for the extensions that have been made since that date; and it has been accorded a central role in key surveys of the work in the area, the major one being that of Paul Krugman (1982).

In this monograph we have endeavoured to consider the macroeconomic effects of protectionism under flexible exchange rates in as systematic a way as possible at the analytical level. We have tried to accomplish that task in a scholarly fashion in that we have provided some exegesis of existing literature, dissected it critically and extended it to produce alternative and new findings. The prominence of Mundell's paper and the description of it means that we make constant reference to it and, naturally, to Krugman's survey. Both of those articles are of major importance, in different ways, to the development of the literature in this area: but they form, as it were, our Aunt Sallies, and by the nature of things we are critical of them.

However, we hope that our contribution appears to be more than just a demolition exercise on the Mundellian models. In any event the negative conclusions they offer on the wisdom of protectionist policies are feasible, but they are not unique conclusions.

In preparing this manuscript we have been assisted and encouraged in a number of ways; accordingly, we would like to extend our thanks to several individuals. We begin with the anonymous readers of the first draft of the manuscript. That was a lengthy and very much a first draft with countless rough edges: we are grateful to them for their remarkable tolerance in wading through that draft and for providing many perceptive comments of both a specific and a general nature. Peter Neary also was kind enough to cast a general eye over the manuscript and, although he may have his reservations about the form of macromodels used in international trade, his overview was so generous that it too encouraged us to push ahead rapidly with the production of a revised version of the manuscript. The essential ingredients of chapter 2 were presented to the European Meeting of the Econometric Society at Madrid in September 1984, and we are grateful to Ronald Jones, the Chairman of the Session, for his comments. We are thankful for the interest that Wynn Godley has shown in this book. He is naturally concerned that macroeconomic models can be constructed that provide a rationale for his strongly held view in favour of protectionism. We have also benefited from discussions with several colleagues at Birmingham and elsewhere, especially with David Dickinson, Michael Driscoll, Stan Metcalfe, Prasanta Pattanaik and Saadet Deger. But none of these, of course, should be held responsible for any errors of omission or of commission in the completed version of this book.

We now turn to two special plaudits. The first is to Ralph Bailey, our Computer Officer, who performed all of the computing and numerical analysis required to produce the simulation results we have reported in chapters 2 and 8. Those in chapter 2 are especially crucial in providing conclusive support for our analytical results; and in chapter 8 they help determine results that are unobtainable by analytical methods. Much hard work and ingenuity went into the derivation of those results and we are heavily indebted to him.

The second special thank you is to our secretary, Miss Marilyn Mansell. As always, no matter how complex the manuscript or how bad the handwriting, she is able to produce a first-class typed version of it in a quite staggeringly short length of time; and the only errors are those of a technical nature that we have made, for even the grammar and spelling have been corrected. Words just cannot express her qualities adequately; and as an expression of gratitude to her, 'thank you' also seems inadequate. But we say it all the same.

Finally, we would like to acknowledge the assistance, kindness and courtesy extended to us by the editorial staff of Basil Blackwell during the production of this book and for all the care that they have lavished on it. In particular, we offer our thanks to Norma Whitcomb, copy-editor, Jacqueline McDermott, who compiled the index, and especially to Sue Banfield who, as Senior Desk Editor, co-ordinated the whole enterprise.

1
The Open Economy and the Effects of Economic Policy: an Introduction

The past decade has seen a stubborn persistence of international economic recession, with conventional demand management policies being regarded as inadequate for reversing the continual slowdown in economic growth. As a consequence discussions have focused increasingly on the use of commercial policy to protect and thus to raise domestic output. The effects of real supply shocks on the international economic system during the past few years have intensified the interest in protectionism. Whether import controls at an aggregate level can be used to reduce unemployment and raise national output has likewise emerged as a major policy concern. In this book we wish to reconsider this subject analytically, and to demonstrate under what conditions general tariffs or general quotas can boost domestic production.

It took a long while before macroeconomic models were widened to embrace fully the presence of a foreign trade sector. But once they were, the literature on open economy macromodels grew at a phenomenal pace. However, in giving consideration to economic policy within the context of an open economy, the predominant, but by no means sole, emphasis in the journals and the textbooks, has been placed on the role of the traditional policy types, monetary and fiscal policy. Much attention has been devoted to the role of the exchange rate, and to the question of fixed versus flexible exchange rates, in the framework of an open economy. Indeed, the modern literature on the theories of the determination of the exchange rate, the optimal exchange rate and its dynamic path, especially in the in-vogue topic of the overshooting of the exchange rate, is now voluminous (see Krueger (1983) for an outstanding book length survey).

1

The amount of coverage given, by way of contrast, to the role of commercial policy in open economy macromodels is minimal. That form of policy relies on the use of controls on imports through the medium of a general tariff (*ad valorem* or specific) or of a quota on the quantity of imports that will be permitted to enter the country. Controls on imports via the imposition of a general tariff might not, in fact, lead ultimately to a reduction in imports. The initial impact of the general tariff might only be of such a nature. The expenditure switching between overseas and home-produced goods that is induced by the price increase imposed immediately on the domestic cost of importables can have multiple effects thoughout the economy to such an extent that, via the income effect on imports, imports become greater in the new equilibrium than they were in the free-trade situation.

Although there is a relative paucity of references, on the responsiveness of the macroeconomy to the implementation of active commercial policy by a government, in the literature, this is largely, one suspects, because the presumption is that in a world of fixed exchange rates, commercial policy will merely be another branch of Keynesian stabilization policies, and as such there will exist a concatenation of economic conditions under which such a policy can have an impact, in the short and/or long run, on the aggregate level of output and employment in the economy. In a world of fixed exchange rates, there will exist no automatic mechanism by which the balance of payments will be equilibrated. With only discrete changes (devaluation or upvaluation) of the exchange rate between currencies occurring and then only when balance of payments positions (deficits or surpluses) become severe, governments have to adopt other policies to remove the imbalances and to countervail the effects on output, employment and inflation that have arisen as a consequence of the payments imbalances.

Thus, if a particular country is in balance of payments deficit with falling output and rising unemployment, unless it devalues its currency, it can only resort to conventional fiscal and monetary policies to rectify the imbalance. Its control over its own monetary policy is restricted by the assumption of fixed exchange rates, and the fiscal stance that it would adopt would be one of deflation if the balance of payments deficit were to be removed. But, at least the short-run consequences of such a budgetary position will be that they aggravate the unemployment problem. In situations such as these it would be an obvious temptation for governments to alter their strategy and to introduce import controls of one form or another; this, as we know, was the pattern adopted by governments in their 'beggar-my-neighbour' policies of the 1930s. Such policies have the obvious attraction that they can, even if only initially, improve the balance of payments position and protect domestic output and employment.

Of course, at the level of the world economy, there are inherent dangers in the adoption of general tariffs by many countries that dominate world trade, as was witnessed again in the 1930s. The obvious threat of competitive retaliation is ever present; and ultimately it will lead to an ever-diminishing value of world trade, income and employment. But for small countries, or perhaps the old major trading countries (such as the UK in the 1930s), the strategy can be successful;[1] however, it might not even then be an optimal one, because devaluation or a package of policy options might dominate it. *But*, if adjustment of the exchange rate is ruled out, *ex hypothesi*, then a move to inhibit imports (at least as a first step) can, depending upon the elasticities of the home country's import demand and the 'rest of the world's' demand for the home country's exports, lead to an improvement in the balance of payments and to a boost in economic activity.[2]

It is on the situation of commercial policy in the context of flexible or freely floating exchange rates that most of the journal literature has concentrated, with the first explicit commentary being contained in Mundell's (1961) now classic paper, which itself built on the outstanding, wide-ranging article of 'flexible exchange rates' by Laursen and Metzler (1950); and which perhaps has a forerunner in the work of Sohmen (1958), which was expanded in Sohmen's classic *Flexible Exchange Rates* (1969). If the exchange rate is permitted, by the government, to adjust fully, at all times, to alterations in the demand for and supply of foreign exchange, then the balance of payments will always be in balance; so the move to a regime of flexible exchange rates removes one constraint on the government's conduct of macroeconomic policy. There is then no necessity to introduce protectionist-orientated commercial policy for balance of payments purposes; and if there should be unemployment, resort can be had to conventional monetary policy (over which the government does have control, in principle, under flexible exchange rates) and/or fiscal policy to remedy it.

Under fixed exchange rates, the introduction of commercial policy is advocated precisely because of the fixity (except at discrete time intervals) of the exchange rate. The argument is that allowing the exchange rate to adjust continuously will render commercial policy otiose. Indeed, it appeared to be a natural step to argue that because a flexible exchange rate would remove any balance of payments difficulties, the imposition of tariffs/quotas might worsen the situation; whilst not being able to affect the natural equilibrating mechanisms provided by a flexible exchange rate, they might have a detrimental effect on domestic output and employment (and reduce both exports and imports within a 'balanced' balance of payments).

The literature since the 1960s has thus provided an additional argument to those traditionally advanced in support of flexible exchange rates (see Friedman (1953), ch. 6, and for an up-dated survey, Johnson (1972), ch. 8). They can offer a powerful argument against 'protectionism': it is likely to be self-defeating even for a small country, reducing its output/employment, and probably its 'welfare'. It is likely to provoke retaliation because it will reduce the home country's import demand, and hence the exports of those with whom it trades; the subsequent multiplier effects are likely to drag down their level of economic activity so encouraging (fruitless) competitive retaliation.

Indeed, these propositions emerge in a much stronger and more definitive form in the literature. Almost without exception the open economy macromodels that have been used to analyse the role of commercial policy in a world of flexible exchange rates have reached the conclusion that they have negative effects in the short run and often in the long run on total output and employment in the economy. Usually only in the long run do the models generate the weaker result of neutrality. With only one type of model (that where there is a financial system consisting of at least two assets, money and 'bonds' that can be held across countries) is there any possibility that commercial policy can be of any assistance to the government's stabilization strategy with floating exchange rates.

Our purpose in this book is to provide a critical and comprehensive analysis of the role and efficacy of commercial policy (predominantly of general tariffs) in the kinds of models that have been used in the literature in the last twenty years or so. In doing so, we shall demonstrate that the conclusions of the literature, and especially of that which relies totally on Mundell (1961) as its antecedent, are not valid universally. Commercial policy can stimulate output and employment in aggregate even with flexible exchange rates. That proposition will be demonstrated intuitively, by formal analysis and by simulation studies. The models we shall use do also offer some refinements and extensions to those found in the literature; and, in particular, we utilize a truly dynamic open economy model based on the Phillips curve (or the Lucas supply hypothesis) in a form that has been used extensively by Turnovsky (1977). One of the conclusions we obtain suggests that retaliation by other countries to the 'home country's' imposition of a general tariff will not necessarily be forthcoming; the home country's imports from the 'rest of the world' can, in fact, increase in the new equilibrium attained by the economy after it has absorbed the impact of the tariff. Our analyses will be conducted largely in a world of freely floating exchange rates. This is because the real world is one which can now be characterized as one of flexible rather than of fixed exchange rates and because the negatory effects of protectionism have been generated in the literature for a regime of flexible exchange rates. However, in small measure we refer occasionally to results attainable for fixed exchange rates or set out our models to permit the findings to be derived for fixed exchange rates if the reader so wishes (see, for example, chapter 8).

Likewise, although the emphasis in this book is placed on commercial policy we will, where appropriate, examine the relative effects on the macroeconomy of monetary policy, fiscal policy and commercial policy. We will also consider whether conventional demand management policies can be aided by commercial policy.

As we proceed we will operate with models which gradually increase in complexity, from a simple static model without an explicit money sector to a dynamic model with a financial sector; from models with fixed to fully flexible prices. The models branch out logically from each other; and they largely follow the development of the literature. In a sense, although the conclusions we have reached largely contradict and extend those in the literature, this monograph offers a kind of synthesis of the literature. But it also adds refinements to the structure of existing models and it provides a fully-specified dynamic macroeconomic model for the analysis of protectionism.

Despite the fact that the models we employ increase in complexity in a coherent fashion, the various models are not nested uniquely within the most general model, namely the dynamic, flexi-price model (of chapter 8). Therefore, it has not proved feasible to begin with that model and develop the others as special cases, through the imposition of particular exclusion restrictions on behavioural parameters or economic variables. But this is not surprising since changing a model's structure alters its causal mechanism; so that the 'new' model has to be specified *de novo*, and solved on its own terms. In any event, to develop our argument systematically we would have had a preference for the layout of model structure we have utilized: this permits us to enucleate inconsistencies and inadequacies in the existing literature. Let us turn then to consider the contents of each of the ensuing chapters.

We commence, in chapter 2, with the 'demand creates its own supply' Mundellian–Keynesian macromodel for a *small* open economy. All of the models in the book will be alleged to apply to such economies; the standard conventions will be adopted that there will be only one other country – the world – which is the aggregate of all other nations, and which is designated 'the rest of the world'. The Mundellian model represents the first formal model structure that was designed to consider the efficacy of utilizing commercial policy for the attainment of macroeconomic objectives in a world of flexible exchange rates. The model consists only of a real sector; there is no explicit money sector of any kind, and hence the model abstracts from capital movements. It also assumes away any formal government intervention through the operation of fiscal policy. It is very much a minimal model which focuses attention on the demand for the infinitely elastic supply of domestic output, with the balance of trade equation appearing, of necessity, to determine, *ceteris paribus*, the rate of exchange between currencies.

That Mundellian model has featured as the framework in many of the inquiries into the value of commercial policy under floating exchange rates. But several extensions have been made to it. The simplest development of it involves the addition of a domestic money market, which trades in money and bonds. The monetary version of the model is set out in chapter 4 but its framework is extended to include capital mobility. The intervening chapter, chapter 3, presents some brief exposition, in the light of the Mundellian model, of the use of a general quota as the instrument of commercial policy, rather than the general tariff.

The first three chapters are all founded on models of the fix-price variety, and the methodology employed to exploit the efficacy of commercial policy is that of comparative statics. In chapter 5 we consider the monetary version of the Mundellian model with capital mobility, by the method of pseudo-dynamics which is used to permit the price of domestically-produced goods to vary, whilst the money wage remains fixed.

A natural extension of chapter 5 is the amplification of the money market to include trading in domestic and foreign (rest of the world) money and bonds across both frontiers. This 'portfolio' version of the model is the subject of chapter 6. Chapters 2 to 4 employ a fix-price assumption; chapters 5 and 6 permit some dynamic adjustment of the price of domestic goods to be present. So it is again a natural progression for us to consider a model wherein there is explicit flexibility of the price of the domestically-produced (basket of) goods accompanied by flexibility of domestic money wages. By explicit flexibility of the domestic price level we mean that we posit a price-setting equation that holds for all periods rather than rely on a pseudo-dynamic equation to generate changes in that price level. But, since the general view these days is that in the real world, whilst prices and money wages are flexible (even if, as in the Keynesian description, wages are so only in the upward direction), the activity of trade unions has led to a situation in which real wages are rigid. The literature that has assessed whether it is worthwhile to impose a general tariff (or a quota) where there is real wage resistance has arrived at the firm conclusion that it is not. In view of the fact that in many real world open economies real wage rigidity is likely to prevail, we consider the part that could be played in such a world by commercial policy in chapter 7. It is the general opinion of the Cambridge Economic Policy Group (CEPG) that in such conditions macroeconomic stabilization policies *must* include the adoption of (initially) trade-restricting devices; devices which, in the aftermath of their introduction might well produce an increase in the home country's imports. The CEPG propositions are given some consideration in the course of chapter 7.

The most natural selection for the final model in the book is one which is truly dynamic (and not based upon pseudo-dynamics), has wages and prices potentially flexible (including the possibility that real wages are rigid), includes the essence of the 'portfolio model' and allows free mobility of financial capital between countries. Chapter 8 contains such a model, which besides emphasizing the notion of perfect capital mobility, which is a state to which Western economies have moved, pays attention to the expected depreciation of the exchange rate (through the expected interest rate parity condition across countries) and so allows for the possibility of rational expectations in the formation of that expectation.

In each of these differing models the primary objective is to evaluate the feasibility of using commercial policy to boost macroeconomic activity. But concomitant issues figure throughout the chapters, such as the final response of imports to a general tariff. However, those issues are not dealt with in each and every chapter; otherwise the discussion would assume far too much of a taxonomic structure. We have tried to offer at least some variety in our analysis. Yet there must, obviously, be the recurring concern with the impact on economic activity of commercial policy.

The questions then that we seek to answer, in different parts and to varying degrees in this book in the context of a domestic/ rest of the world economic structure, are these:

1 Will there be any kind of small open economy macromodel in which a general tariff can have beneficial effects on output and employment?

2 Will the introduction of a general quota on the level of imports affect the domestic economy in the same way as would the general tariff?

3 Must a general tariff levied by the home country lead inevitably to a decline in the quantity of its imports in the new equilibrium?

4 Will the flexibility in the determination of prices and of money wages have any part to play in determining the macroeconomic value of commercial policy?

5 Will monetary and/or fiscal policy have a more beneficial effect on the macroeconomy than the levying of a general tariff?

6 Can monetary and/or fiscal policy be employed alongside commercial policy to raise the latter's effectiveness?

7 Is it possible that the implementation of monetary and/or fiscal policy to stimulate the economy can be more successful if there is already a general tariff on imports?

8 Will the success or otherwise of commercial policy depend upon whether it is seen as being a temporary or a permanent feature of the government's strategy?

9 Can commercial policy be successful in a dynamic world and also provide stability to the time profiles of output and employment?

10 Do the methods used by the government to raise and disburse the revenue from a general tariff (or a quota) have any bearing on its ultimate impression on the macroeconomy?

11 Can the tariff-imposing country's level of 'welfare' be improved by the general tariff?

12 What part, if any, do the concepts of the maximum revenue and optimum tariff, developed in the pure theory of international trade (its GE macroformat) have to play in the success or otherwise of a general tariff in the context of the macroeconomy?

These are important issues, predominantly for the conduct of economic policy. We shall see that in regard to some of the more major questions, such as 1 and 7, there will be a concatenation of circumstances in all of the alternative models we examine, that will produce affirmative answers. But, the precise qualitative and quantitative answers to most of the issues raised will be conditioned by particular conditions. That is not surprising since we are all well aware that economics is a discipline where altering assumptions can alter conclusions; or as Joan Robinson (1964) put it more poignantly, it is a discipline where 'we cannot get a knock-down answer'. However, the overriding conclusion is that the prevailing orthodoxy is not the embodiment of universal truth: flexible exchange rates do not necessarily cause protectionism to engender detrimental effects on the macroeconomy. Protectionism *per se* can ameliorate output and employment and its presence can assist conventional demand management policies to do likewise.

Notes

1 Much interest has always been shown in the general tariff introduced by the UK in 1932, but the recent macroeconomic trends in the world, especially in the 'developed' countries, have intensified that interest. There is dispute about the consequences of the tariff but the work of economists suggests that they were favourable (see the most recent study by Eichengreen (1979)); the researches of those who might be classified as economic historians *per se*, raise doubts about the benefit of the general tariff (see, for example, Capie (1983)). We comment on the tariff in chapter 2 and we demonstrate how the observed movements in macroeconomic variables and the overshooting of the exchange rate that occurred could be explained.

2 For a 'descriptive' analysis of trade controls and the balance of payments, see Johnson (1972, ch. 6), which, though partly dated, is still one of the best surveys of the theory of the balance of payments.

2
Tariffs in a Mundellian – Keynesian Model

2.1 *Introduction*

The macroeconomic effects of protection, implemented by a general tariff or import quota, have become a topical policy issue. The subject has generated considerable controversy and discussion in the political economy arena. Possibly as a consequence of that situation, increasing attention has been devoted to the implications for the macroeconomy of commercial policy. The literature is still relatively small; and it is predominantly founded on a world of freely floating exchange rates. The reasons for that bias are probably two-fold. The first reason is that there exists a general presumption that under fixed exchange rates it will be possible for protection to produce beneficial real macroeconomic effects; and the second, more important, reason is that governments have moved increasingly to the introduction of flexible exchange rates. Exchange rates are not always permitted to adjust according to 'market forces' but we are witnessing a situation where the major trading countries in the world are operating loosely 'managed floats'; and on occasions in recent periods (*vide* the UK and the USA in the summer and autumn of 1984), we have seen freely floating rates (as far as we, outside observers, can ascertain).

The overwhelming view in the literature, indeed we might say, apart from exceptions in the most minor of ways, the unanimous opinion in the literature is that commercial policy, envisaged as protectionism, through the imposition of a general tariff or of a general import quota, should not be given a moment's thought by the practitioners of macroeconomic policy. At the best it will have neutral effects on output and employment; but, at the worst, and almost invariably, it will produce negative repercussions on those real magnitudes.

The seminal paper that propounded that contractionary view was that of Mundell (1961). Despite the fact that his discussion of commercial policy under flexible exchange rates, in section V of his paper, amounted to no more than a page or so, it has become the cornerstone of almost all of the subsequent analysis on this topic. His conclusion was that commercial policy (defined as 'any policy which restricts imports or promotes exports without directly affecting the level of saving or investment' (Mundell, 1961, p. 54)) and hence a non-retaliatory tariff, will have adverse consequences for output and employment, in a world of flexible exchange rates. Tariffs lead to a current account surplus, an appreciation of the exchange rate, a lowering of the domestic price level and a *reduction* of output and employment in long-run equilibrium.

In spite of early scepticism regarding Mundell's results, recent analysis has come full swing in accepting his conclusions even with a large number of extensions to the basic model. Tower (1973), Chan (1978), Eichengreen (1981) and Krugman (1982) all demonstrate formally that a non-retaliatory general tariff is contractionary from a macroeconomic point of view, in the sense that it reduces aggregate output and increases unemployment. Eichengreen (1981) shows that there might be short-run beneficial effects of tariffs but even these are counterbalanced by long-run adverse effects. One of the major purposes of this book is to show that these results are not universally valid and there may be plausible situations where tariffs may increase national output in long-run equilibrium, within the confines of the various paradigms that have been developed, but especially within the basic Mundellian framework.

It seems apposite at this point to quote what Keynes (1936) had to say on this matter when he was reviewing his earlier opinion regarding the debate on protectionism prior to the imposition of the general tariff of 1932:

> During the fiscal controversy of the first quarter of the present century I do not remember that any concession was ever allowed by economists to the claim that protection might increase domestic employment. It will be fairest perhaps to quote, as an example, what I wrote myself. So lately as 1923, as a faithful pupil of the classical school who did not at that time doubt what he had been taught and entertained on this matter no reserve at all, I wrote: 'If there is one thing that Protection can *not* do, it is to cure Unemploy-

ment ... There are some arguments for Protection, ... But the claim to cure Unemployment involves the Protectionist fallacy in its grossest and crudest form.' So absolutely overwhelming and complete has been the domination of the classical school. (Keynes, 1936, p. 344)

Our critique of the contemporary orthodoxy is also motivated by this Keynesian point of view.

In this chapter we shall utilize the Mundellian (Keynesian) model to analyse the macroeconomic implications of a general tariff imposed by a small open economy under flexible exchange rates. The chapter is divided into a number of sections. Since consistent specification of the tariff-ridden model is crucial for many of the results, the next section deals with this issue in some detail. Section 2.3 analyses the Laursen–Metzler effect which plays an important role in the Mundellian model and its implications should be made clear at the outset. These give us the background. A critical exegesis of Mundell's celebrated paper is essential to put the analysis in proper perspective. This is done in section 2.4. The next section then analyses the conditions under which aggregate output (and thus employment) may increase, within the framework of internal and external balance. Recent discussion on terms of trade effects on expenditure (Obstfeld, 1982; Svensson and Razin, 1983; Persson and Svensson, 1984) has focused on the difference between temporary and permanent changes in the relative price of importables and home goods. Section 2.6 gives a macroeconomic representation of these issues. A brief discussion on dynamics and some illustrative numerical simulation results on discrete tariff changes and their possible expansionary role are presented in the last two sections.

We have also provided an appendix to this chapter which tries to give a microfoundation to the Laursen–Metzler effect and shows within an intertemporal optimizing model why it is possible to get counterintuitive results. The method is similar to Obstfeld (1982), though with very different assumptions.

2.2 *Consistent Specification of the Model*

The model used is of the basic Keynesian type, based on Mundell's (1961) classic paper which in turn draws on the earlier work of Laursen and Metzler (1950) and Harberger (1950). Though simple, it has been the basic framework in which the macroeconomic implications of commercial policy have been generally examined and most of the contractionary results derived. Since a number of alternative formulations are possible, it is important to specify the various components consistently. In particular, the valuation problem is crucial since potentially the model has three prices, that of the home good, foreign good and the general price level (cost of living index, an aggregate price of the 'basket' of goods).

The salient features of the model are as follows. The government is assumed to perform no specific role in the economy; and its activities only need to be considered when commercial policy is implemented, say, via the imposition of an *ad valorem* tariff on the price of imports. Then the government's budget constraint is of the simplest kind since it is hypothesized that it collects the tariff revenue and distributes all of the revenue to the private sector by means of transfer payments. It is assumed that there are no capital flows in the model; so the balance of payments is equated with the balance of trade. Since expenditure on domestic and foreign goods by the economy is assumed to be independent of a rate of interest, the role of the money market is ignored. It is also assumed that the model is fix-price except for the exchange rate; and so the domestic price level and the import price level are normalized at unity (in the respective domestic currencies). Equilibrium in the model is then attained when expenditure equals income (internal balance: IS schedule) and the value of exports equals the value of imports (external balance: BP schedule). The exchange rate r is freely floating and is determined, along with domestic output, by these two schedules.

Equilibrium in the domestic economy or internal balance may be represented by the equality of aggregate supply and demand of domestic output V. Letting D be the demand for domestic output by domestic residents, we have

$$V = D + X \tag{2.1}$$

where X is exports. Since the price of the domestic product is set at unity, $p_d = 1$, equation (2.1) also implies that nominal demand and supply are equal. A more conventional formulation is to rewrite (2.1) in the form of an expenditure–income balance. In a situation where the government imposes an *ad valorem* tariff t, we have from (2.1)

$$V = D + r(1 + t)I + X - r(1 + t)I \tag{2.2}$$

where I is the volume of imports and $r(1 + t)$ is the domestic price of imports; r being the exchange rate defined as the units of domestic currency required to purchase a unit of foreign currency (thus r is measured as domestic currency divided by foreign currency units). The domestic terms of trade is defined as

$$p = r(1 + t) \frac{p_f}{p_d} = r(1 + t) \tag{2.3}$$

(because we recall that the *own* currency prices of the foreign good p_f and of the domestically produced basket p_d are unity).

Absorption measured in terms of home good is A so that (2.2) can be written as follows, since $A \equiv D + r(1 + t) I$

$$V = A + X - rI - rtI \tag{2.4}$$

or

$$V + R = A + X - rI \tag{2.5}$$

where $R = rtI$ is of course the tariff revenue. Since tariff revenues are all redistributed to domestic residents, the left-hand side of (2.5) is disposable income. Therefore equation (2.5) is the familiar condition that disposable income is equal in equilibrium to absorption plus trade balance. Note again that A or absorption is the sum of expenditure by residents on consumption C and investment I^n of both home and foreign goods, with government expenditure G set equal to zero. Finally, nominal disposable income or (under the assumption that $p_d = 1$), disposable income in terms of home goods, is

$$y = V + rtI \tag{2.6}$$

Economic intuition is better revealed, however, if all variables are measured in 'real' terms. Since expenditure (or absorption) is now on a 'basket' of goods (domestic and foreign), the 'consumer price index' (or more appropriately the 'absorption price index') is defined as

$$P = \phi(p_f^*, p_d) \tag{2.7}$$

where p_f is the foreign price of the foreign good. Given that $p_f^* = r(1 + t) p_f = r(1 + t)$ in the presence of a tariff, we have

$$P = \phi(r(1 + t), 1) \tag{2.8}$$

A specific version of (2.8) is

$$P = (r(1 + t))^\delta = r^\delta (1 + t)^\delta = p^\delta \tag{2.9}$$

δ being the share of imports in expenditure. According to Samuelson and Swami (1974), equation (2.9) represents a true, ideal, cost of living index.

Real disposable income now becomes

$$Y = \frac{y}{P} = \frac{V + trI}{P} \tag{2.10}$$

Internal balance or domestic equilibrium embodied in (2.5) can now be stated as

$$Y = A^* + \frac{B}{P} \tag{2.11}$$

where $A^* = A/P$ and $B = X - rI$, the balance of trade. A^* is absorption measured in terms of the basket of goods, thus it is *real* absorption. Equation (2.11) is particularly appropriate since it stresses the openness of the economy, specifically the presence of two separate aggregated goods. If we now define 'hoarding' as the difference between disposable income and absorption, then real hoarding H is

$$H = Y - A^* \tag{2.12}$$

and internal balance implies

$$H = \frac{B}{P} \tag{2.13}$$

or hoarding must be equal (in equilibrium) to the trade balance. Given the definition of absorption, $A = C + I^n + G$, $G = 0$, and that saving is equal to disposable income minus consumption, hoarding is essentially saving minus investment. In the absence of investment, therefore, hoarding would be equivalent to saving.

The conditions for internal balance, accordingly, can be stated in these alternative forms: the demand for domestic output equals supply (equation (2.1)); the current account balance equals saving minus investment (hoarding) as in equation (2.13); or the trade balance is equal to income minus absorption (equation (2.11)). For a consistently specified general equilibrium model it is immaterial which formulation we use. However, convenience and heuristic understanding of the model dictate our preference for one formulation over another. In this chapter we shall generally use the condition given by (2.13).[1] Further discussion of these issues will be found in section 2.4.

The determinants of the absorption or hoarding functions, naturally, are of key importance. Mundell assumed, following Laursen–Metzler and Harberger, that real absorption was governed by real disposable income thus

$$A^* = A^*(Y) \tag{2.14}$$

so that using (2.12)

$$H = Y - A^*(Y) = H(Y) \tag{2.15}$$

In nominal terms, since $A^* = A/P$, $Y = y/P$, we get

$$A = PA^*\left(\frac{y}{P}\right) = p^\delta A^*\left(\frac{y}{p^\delta}\right) \tag{2.16}$$

so that nominal absorption (or alternatively absorption measured in terms of home goods, since $p_d = 1$) can be expressed as

$$A = A(y, p) \tag{2.17}$$

The signs of the derivatives $A_1^* = \partial A^*/\partial Y$, etc. form the essence of the Laursen–Metzler effect and this we leave until the next section.

We now turn to external balance. This requires

$$X = rI \Rightarrow B = 0 \tag{2.18}$$

Assume that exports depend on the terms of trade faced by the economy in world markets. Thus

$$X = X(r) \tag{2.19}$$

Specification of the import function is more problematical. If investment is equal to zero and absorption consists only of consumption expenditure, then a simple optimizing model for the aggregate consumer would predict that

$$I = \tilde{I}(A, p) \tag{2.20}$$

In other words, the volume of imports depends on aggregate expenditure A in nominal terms, as well as the relative price $p = r(1 + t)$. The Slutsky substitution effect then tells us that (see Bhagwati and Johnson, 1961)

$$\tilde{I}_1 I + \tilde{I}_2 < 0 \tag{2.21}$$

This inequality is essential for an analysis of the impact of tariffs, as we shall see later on. Further, using (2.17), (2.20) can be written as

$$I = \tilde{I}(A(y, p), p) \tag{2.22}$$

or

$$I = I(y, p) = I(V + rtI, p) \tag{2.23}$$

where a similar inequality to (2.21) can be established. Disposable income y affects absorption or consumption expenditure A which in turn determines imports, given relative prices p.

However, with positive investment, it is not clear what the relation between imports and income (which includes domestic output V) should be. It is possible that the import demand function may be reflecting some input–output considerations, particularly if intermediate imported inputs are being used to produce the national product. Consider the case analysed by Findlay and Rodriguez (1977). Capital K and labour L are used to produce domestic value added Q. Thus

$$Q = F(K, L) \tag{2.24}$$

Q is then used with intermediate inputs imported from abroad I to produce gross output V

$$V = V(Q, I) \tag{2.25}$$

From (2.24) and (2.25) we get

$$V = V(F(K, L), I) \tag{2.26}$$

For given K and L, (2.26) can be inverted to get an import (demand) function of the type

$$I = I(V) \tag{2.27}$$

Comparing (2.23) and (2.27), it is seen that though they look very similar (for given p and $t = 0$), there are fundamental differences in the formulations. In particular, $\partial I / \partial V$ is an income effect term from demand theory in (2.23), while it is an input–output term in (2.27).

We shall be using the most general form of the import function

$$I = I(V + trI, p) \tag{2.28}$$

with a strict caveat that the derivatives of these functions are essentially reflecting many different types of factors and should be treated with caution. Specifically, inequalities such as (2.21) may be inappropriate and should not be used with abandon (as they have been in the macrotariff literature) to justify specific results. We would expect that $I_1 > 0$, $I_2 < 0$, but not much more a priori. However, in our analysis of the Mundellian model we shall use this assumption since we wish to follow closely the canonical argument on contractionary tariffs. But its specific role will be explicitly pointed out wherever it appears.

External balance is now given by

$$X(r) = rI(V + trI, r(1 + t))$$ (2.29)

where imports are valued at the world terms of trade r. Internal balance is specified as

$$H\left(\frac{V + trI}{P}\right) = \frac{B}{P}$$ (2.30)

and

$$P = r^{\delta}(1 + t)^{\delta}$$ (2.31)

In principle δ is a variable itself (dependent on relative prices) but in this chapter we follow tradition and assume it to be a constant. Equations (2.29)–(2.31) give a coherently specified basic Keynesian model, which can be used to analyse the effect of a change in tariff t on output V, as well as the exchange rate r.

2.3 The Laursen–Metzler Effect

In the previous section, real absorption (in terms of the basket of goods consisting of importables and home goods) was made a function of real income (see equation (2.14)). We have

$$A^* = A^*(Y)$$ (2.14′)

or

$$A = p^{\delta} A^*\left(\frac{y}{p^{\delta}}\right)$$ (2.16′)

It is assumed following standard Keynesian procedure that

$$0 < A_1^* < 1$$ (2.32)

It is also clear from (2.16′) that absorption measured in home goods is a function of income also measured in home goods and relative price

$$A = A(y, p)$$ (2.17′)

However, A_1 and A_2 are not independent of each other and the relation between these two partial derivatives, as well as their signs, have been christened the Laursen–Metzler effect (hereafter called L–M). From (2.16')

$$\frac{\partial A}{\partial y} = A_1^* = A_1$$

(2.33)

$$\frac{\partial A}{\partial p} = \delta p^{\delta-1} A^* + p^\delta A^* y (-\delta) p^{-\delta-1}$$

so that

$$\frac{p}{A} \frac{\partial A}{\partial p} = \delta \left(1 - \frac{y}{A} A_1 \right)$$

(2.34)

Equation (2.34) tells us that the elasticity of absorption (measured in home goods or in nominal terms with $p_d = 1$) with respect to price is equal to one minus the elasticity of absorption with respect to income y, multiplied by the share of imports in absorption. Note now that *if* there is trade balance ($X - rI = 0$) and (disposable) income is equal to absorption, then (2.34) becomes

$$\frac{p}{A} \frac{\partial A}{\partial p} = \frac{pI}{A} (1 - A_1)$$

(2.35)

or

$$A_2 = \frac{\partial A}{\partial p} = I(1 - A_1)$$

(2.36)

A_2 is expected to be positive provided $A_1 < 1$. Thus we have absorption measured in home goods rising with an increase in the relative price of imports with respect to the price of home goods.

Another implication of the L–M effect is that real hoarding is positively related to real income. Thus

$$H = Y - A^*(Y) = H(Y)$$

(2.37)

and

$$\frac{\partial H}{\partial Y} = H_1 = 1 - A_1^* > 0$$

(2.38)

where, remember, Y is real disposable income, that is in terms of the basket of goods. It is this positive propensity of real hoarding (or real saving) that has been exploited by authors from Mundell to Krugman to get the aforementioned negative relation between tariffs and aggregate output.

The L–M effect *per se* is, however, a thin reed on which to base the strong conclusion regarding contractionary tariffs. The major problem of the specifications (2.36) or (2.38) is that they are *ad hoc*, and not based on any optimizing foundation. In particular, intertemporal factors are ignored in the formulation, but without them a *saving* function is not easy to construct. A recent spate of papers (Obstfeld, 1982; Svensson and Razin, 1983; Persson and Svensson, 1984) have criticized the L–M effect, and shown under plausible conditions that absorption may go *down* with a rise in relative price ($A_2 = \partial A/\partial p < 0$), alternatively hoarding (saving) or the current account may decrease with an increase in real income. Within an explicit intertemporal model it is intuitively clear why the sign of these derivatives may be ambiguous. Essentially a (relative) price change will cause consumption (expenditure) smoothing, taking the whole future stream of income, spending, saving and discount rates into account. Depending on various factors, almost any eventuality is feasible.

Essentially, there are three effects that determine the behaviour of absorption consequent on a price change. First, we have a direct effect, by which a rise in price induces absorption to rise. Secondly, there is a wealth or income effect; a price rise will reduce the present (discounted) value of income stream and reduce absorption. Thirdly, there are intertemporal and within-period substitution effects, which may go either way. Clearly, the final outcome is uncertain and depends on a variety of factors, particularly the rate of time preference used as a discounting factor. In the appendix to this chapter, using an optimizing model, we have demonstrated how expenditure (absorption) can decline or rise consequent on an increase in p. The upshot of that discussion is that we must be careful before putting a heavy reliance on the L–M effect, as it is defined in the orthodox literature.

Finally, it may be noted that the hoarding function representation of the L–M effect (2.37) and (2.38) is relatively free from some of the problems mentioned above. The only point that needs to be clarified is whether H_1 is positive or negative. There are no other difficulties similar to those with the A function and the relationship between A_1 and A_2. This is another justification for utilizing the hoarding specification in what follows.

2.4   *The Mundellian Model: Critical Exegesis*

As discussed in section 2.2, a consistently specified Mundellian model would have internal balance specified by the equality of disposable income and expenditure plus the current account balance. Alternatively, we have real hoarding as equal to the real balance of trade (payments). Thus

$$H\left(\frac{V + trI}{P}\right) = \frac{B}{P} \tag{2.39}$$

$$B = X(r) - rI \tag{2.40}$$

$$I = I(V + trI, p) \tag{2.41}$$

$$p = r(1 + t) \tag{2.42}$$

$$P = p^\delta \tag{2.43}$$

Balance of payments equilibrium or external balance obtains when

$$X = rI \tag{2.44}$$

The original Mundell (1961) paper is very loosely structured and it is only in the appendix to it that anything approaching a formal specification of the internal and external balance schedules is attempted. The statement is that equation (2.1) produces a relationship between V and r; the implicit assumption being that I depends upon V and r (via the terms of trade) and that absorption and hoarding depend upon real disposable income. It is then argued that the internal balance schedule must be positively sloped in (V, r) space. With exports implicitly assumed to be dependent upon r (via the terms of trade) the external balance line is also judged to be positively sloped in (V, r) space:

> [The internal balance] schedule has a positive slope because an increase in output creates an excess supply of goods and services, while an increase in the price of foreign exchange creates an excess demand for goods and services; consequently, an increase in output must be associated with an increase in the price of foreign exchange for excess demand to return to zero. Similarly, the [external balance] schedule traces the locus of exchange rates and output along which the balance of payments is in equilibrium. This curve also has a positive slope because an increase in the price of foreign

exchange improves the balance of payments while an increase in income worsens it, and this means that increases in the price of foreign exchange must be accompanied by increases in output if the balance of payments is to remain constant. (Mundell, 1961, p. 510).

This is the argument that is repeated in all the literature and is incorporated in Krugman's (1982) survey of the area. Krugman, in line with the now standard portrayal of open-economy macro-models, offers a specification of the behavioural equations in the model that follow those which are implied in Mundell's own, extremely cursory, analysis of the output effects of commercial policy. On that foundation the view that both the internal and external balance lines are positive sloped cannot be gainsaid.

Consider the initial case of zero tariffs. Putting $t = 0$, take total differentials of (2.39) using (2.40) to (2.43) to get

$$\frac{dr}{dV}\bigg|_{IB} = (H_1 + rI_1)\bigg/ \left(X_1 - rI_2 - I - \frac{\delta B}{r} + H_1\frac{\delta V}{r} \right) \qquad (2.45)$$

where we have also used the fact that

$$\frac{dP}{P} = \frac{\delta}{r}\frac{dr}{r} \qquad (2.46)$$

The Marshall–Lerner condition states that

$$\frac{\partial B}{\partial r} > 0 \Rightarrow X_1 - rI_2 - I > 0 \qquad (2.47)$$

However, this is insufficient to sign the slope of the internal balance (IB) line from (2.45). Only in the neighbourhood of general equilibrium where $B = 0$ is dV/dr for the IB schedule positive. Mundell implicitly acknowledges this when he states 'an increase in output must be associated with an increase in the price of foreign exchange for *excess demand to return to zero* (our italics) (Mundell, 1961, p. 510). However, in the general case there is no supposition that internal balance will always be positively sloped. Be that as it may, we also assume that the IB line is upward sloping.

The slope of the external balance line (EB) is

$$\frac{dr}{dV}\bigg|_{EB} = \frac{rI_1}{X_1 - I_2r - I} \qquad (2.48)$$

which, using the Marshall–Lerner condition and $I_1 > 0$, is always positive. The relative slopes of IB and EB cannot be compared a priori from (2.45) and (2.48). However, if we have a dynamic model which specifies

$$\dot{V} = \theta_1 \frac{A + B - V}{P}$$

$$= \theta_1 \left(\frac{B}{P} - H \right); \quad \theta_1 > 0 \tag{2.49}$$

($\dot{V}$ is the time derivative of output, thus output increases when there is an excess demand for output) as well as

$$\dot{r} = \theta_i (rI - X); \quad \theta_i > 0 \tag{2.50}$$

(exchange rate rises or domestic currency depreciates when there is a balance of trade deficit), then the stability conditions for the dynamical system (2.49), (2.50) require that the IB line is steeper than the EB line. This is because the determinant of the Jacobian for the dynamic model given by (2.49) and (2.50) needs to be positive[2]

$$|J| = \begin{vmatrix} -(H_1 + rI_1) & X_1 - rI_2 - I - \dfrac{\delta B}{r} + H_1 \dfrac{\delta V}{r} \\ rI_1 & -(X_1 - I_2 r - I) \end{vmatrix} > 0$$

In terms of equations (2.39) and (2.44), putting $t = 0$ and given the underlying assumptions in the model, it can be represented in Mundellian fashion by figure 2.1. The zero tariff equilibrium is given by E.

Now suppose that the government imposes a tariff, which we may imagine it does in an attempt to increase domestic output by inducing expenditure switching by domestic residents from imports to domestic goods. The usual interpretation of the consequences of the tariff for the IB and EB schedules, and hence for output V, is that provided by Krugman (1982), namely:

> Now suppose the tariff rate is increased, starting from zero. Clearly, this shifts the external balance schedule down by improving the trade balance at any r. It also shifts the internal balance schedule down, which we can demonstrate by the following argument: at an unchanged rate of exchange, the effects of the tariff in raising the price level

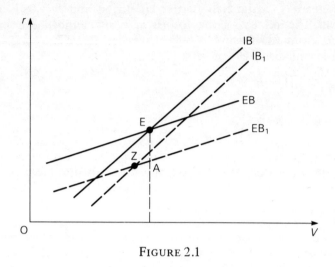

FIGURE 2.1

and the revenue cancel out, leaving real income and hence hoarding unchanged. Since the trade balance is improved, there is an excess demand for domestic output at that point, showing that the internal balance line must have shifted down.

But it will not shift down by as much as the external balance line. Consider point A [in figure 2.1]. At that point output and the trade balance are the same as at the initial position [E]. *But real income and hence real hoarding are higher than originally because the terms of trade have improved.* There is an excess of domestic output, showing that the internal balance line lies somewhat to the left. The result then is that output drops. (Krugman, 1982, pp. 144–6; our italics)

Thus, for Krugman the final equilibrium position will be a point such as Z on the new (dotted) IB and EB schedules (IB$_1$ and EB$_1$). The argument Krugman has used is a paraphrase of that contained in Mundell's (1961) seminal paper, which has been used ever since then to demonstrate that output falls when a (small) tariff is imposed, or there is a further small increase in an already existing tariff.

At this point we comment on Krugman's analysis of the reasons for the rightward shift of the IB schedule once a tariff is imposed, or an already existing tariff is increased. It is, indeed, not always the case that, at any given exchange rate, the introduction (or raising) of the tariff will leave real disposable income unchanged for a given level of output. Consider the definition of real disposable income

$$Y = \frac{V + trI}{r^\delta(1 + t)^\delta} \tag{2.51}$$

Let us start from an initial tariff rate of zero. Thus the initial nominal disposable income is V. Given r, the proportional change in the numerator of (2.51) is trI/V or the tariff revenue as a proportion of V. On the other hand, the proportional change in the denominator is $(\delta \, dt)$ or $(r(1 + t) It/A)$, where $t = dt$ and δ is the value of imports as a ratio of absorption. Unless one assumes that $t = 0$ and $A = V$, the proportional changes in the numerator and denominator for given r (and V) will not be the same. In effect Y may change either way with a tariff. Thus it is not clear which way the IB line would move (Krugman, 1982). However, the analysis of the next section will permit us to prove *en passant*, under certain conditions, that IB must shift to the right.

What about the EB line? Tariffs, by raising the price of imports, will of course reduce imports. But redistributed tariff revenue will increase disposable income, and thus have a positive effect on output. If import demand is *only* for consumption purposes, then for a non-Giffen good, the Slutsky term tells us that the substitution effect will dominate and imports will in effect fall. We have, to maintain balance of trade,

$$rI(V + trI, r(1 + t)) = X(r) \tag{2.52}$$

so that for unchanged r

$$\frac{dV}{dt}\bigg|_r = \frac{-r(II_1 + I_2)}{I_1} > 0 \tag{2.53}$$

given that

$$II_1 + I_2 < 0 \tag{2.54}$$

Thus for any r, V rises with the tariff to preserve external balance; the EB line shifts down. However, given our previous discussion on the sign of the inequality in (2.54), some doubts still remain regarding the movement of the EB line too.

Let us assume, in effect, along with Mundell, Krugman and others, that IB does shift to the right on figure 2.1. (It is likely, incidentally, to exhibit a non-linear relationship between r and V; but again, along with the standard literature in the diagrammatic analysis, we shall preserve the assumption that it is linear.) Suppose that when the tariff is imposed the lines move to IB_1 and EB_1, the dotted lines on Figure 2.1. Consider then point A compared to point E.

It is correct that at point A the balance of payments is identical with that at E, being at a value of zero. Output V is kept the same at the two points. The argument is then that H, real hoarding, increases at A, compared with E, because of the improvement in the terms of trade. Hence there is an excess supply of output; to permit balance to be re-established in the market for domestic goods, output must fall. Therefore, equilibrium output must lie to the left of A along the new EB line.

In essence, this conclusion depends upon the basic proposition that real disposable income does rise at given V after a tariff has been introduced. Since, from (2.51), a tariff will increase the numerator of Y (real disposable income), the final outcome will depend on the behaviour of the denominator of the expression. Thus we could have a situation where the price level $P = r^\delta(1 + t)^\delta$ *falls* after the imposition of tariffs, thus the downward movement of the exchange rate outweighs the inflationary effect of the tariff. Alternatively, if P rises, the rise in nominal income ($\mathrm{d}y = trI = R$, the tariff revenue) more than offsets the deflationary effect of tariffs.

Recall that

$$Y = \frac{y}{P} = \frac{V + trI}{r^\delta(1 + t)^\delta} \tag{2.51}$$

From (2.42) and (2.43)

$$\frac{\mathrm{d}P}{P} = \delta\,\frac{\mathrm{d}r}{r} + \delta\,\mathrm{d}t \tag{2.55}$$

for initial tariff equal to zero. Thus

$$\frac{1}{P}\frac{\mathrm{d}P}{\mathrm{d}t} = \delta\left(1 + \frac{1}{r}\frac{\mathrm{d}r}{\mathrm{d}t}\right) \tag{2.56}$$

Furthermore, from (2.40) and (2.41) for given V and initial $t = 0$

$$\left.\frac{\mathrm{d}r}{\mathrm{d}t}\right|_V = -\left[\frac{-r^2(II_1 + I_2)}{X_1 - I - rI_2}\right] = \frac{r^2(II_1 + I_2)}{X_1 - I - rI_2} \tag{2.57}$$

which is negative given the Marshall–Lerner condition and *provided* $II_1 + I_2 < 0$. Substituting (2.57) in (2.56)

$$\frac{1}{P}\frac{dP}{dt} = \delta\left(\frac{r(X_1 - I + rII_1)}{X_1 - I - rI_2}\right) \tag{2.58}$$

Using the trade balance condition $X = rI$ and defining the price elasticity of exports to be

$$x = \frac{rX_1}{X} = \frac{X_1}{I} \tag{2.59}$$

we can rewrite (2.58) as

$$\frac{1}{P}\frac{dP}{dt} = \left(\frac{rI(x - 1 + rI_1)}{X - I - rI_2}\right) \tag{2.60}$$

(2.60) alerts us then to the possibility of the Metzler paradox (Metzler, 1949). Thus if the export elasticity is high enough such that the Metzler paradox does not obtain and we have

$$(x + rI_1) > 1 \tag{2.61}$$

then $(dP/dt) > 0$ and the aggregate price level rises with an increase in tariffs. Since the empirical validity of the export elasticity being greater than unity $(x > 1)$ is well verified, we assume henceforth that (2.61) holds. Thus P increases with a tariff in spite of the fall in r (if at all). On the other hand if r rises (given our earlier discussion of the sign of $II_1 + I_2$) from (2.57), then of course P *must* rise consequent on a tariff.

Now consider the second issue with reference to figure 2.1. At point A, the proportionate change in nominal income is the tariff revenue divided by initial income (which is in effect the level of output since initial tariff is equal to zero). Thus if

$$Y = \frac{y}{P} = \frac{V + trI}{P} \tag{2.62}$$

then consequent on tariffs

$$\frac{dy}{y} = \frac{trI}{V} = \frac{R}{V} \tag{2.63}$$

where $R = trI$. On the other hand, the proportional change in the price level is

$$\frac{dP}{P} = \delta\frac{dr}{r} + \delta\,dt \tag{2.64}$$

Remember δ is the share of imports in absorption and with trade balance $B = 0$, absorption is equal to disposable income. The value of δ *at the point A* is therefore

$$\delta = \frac{r(1 + t)I}{V + R} \tag{2.65}$$

Substituting (2.65) into (2.64) and noting $dt = t$

$$\frac{dP}{P} = \delta \frac{dr}{r} + \frac{r(1 + t)I}{V + R} \, dt$$

$$= \delta \frac{dr}{r} + \frac{R(1 + t)}{V + R} \tag{2.66}$$

Comparing (2.63) and (2.66), it is not unambiguous whether

$$\frac{dy}{y} \lessgtr \frac{dP}{P}$$

even if $dr/r < 0$ from (2.57). Thus there can be no clear supposition that real disposable income Y will rise when both y and P rise. There can be alternative possibilities depending on parameter values and the level of tariffs.

The valuation of δ is crucial. If δ is assumed to be valued at the point E, then $\delta = rI/V$, and (2.66) becomes

$$\frac{dP}{P} = \delta \frac{dr}{r} + \frac{R}{V} \tag{2.66'}$$

Comparing (2.63) and (2.66') it is clear that real disposable income $(dY/Y = dy/y - dP/P)$ will rise since r has fallen and $dr/r < 0$. In the canonical argument, given the Laursen–Metzler effect, this will raise hoarding H, the resultant excess supply causing output V to fall.

The failure to note that if the reference point in figure 2.1 has changed from E to A then δ should be evaluated at the latter point is quite important. In effect this eliminates the effect of the tariff revenue from (2.62). Since at final equilibrium hoarding H must be zero (see (2.30) and note that $B = 0$), the only effects that remain in the hoarding function are those emanating from V and r. Given that a tariff causes an initial appreciation of the currency and r falls, V must fall correspondingly to make hoarding equal to zero in equilibrium. The income (revenue) effects originating from tariffs cancel out; what remains is the price effect caused by exchange rate appreciation. As we shall see later, the crucial importance of the Slutsky term, in proving the existence of contractionary tariffs, can be traced back to this method of eliminating revenue from the hoarding function (albeit indirectly).

The situation in the traditional model is analogous to an autonomous change in, say, foreign price. Trade surplus (through Marshall–Lerner) will cause r to fall. But if output is kept at its initial level as in figure 2.1, then trade balance requires that r falls in exactly the same proportion as the foreign price. Thus at point A in this analysis $B = 0$, relative price is unchanged and P is the same as before. Therefore if δ is evaluated at the point E, in effect all the elements of the hoarding function are unchanged. V cannot therefore change since there is neither excess demand or supply. Price effects are neutral. If now there is a 'manna from heaven' transfer to increase nominal income y, then V will have to go *down* to maintain the aforementioned 'neutrality'. The standard presentation of the contractionary tariff argument is similar, and stems clearly from a wrong valuation of the share parameter δ.

Lastly, it should be emphasized that *even if* real disposable income rises, hoarding or saving may not rise if the Laursen–Metzler effect does not operate. The Mundell–Krugman argument rests on the fact that (a) tariffs raise real disposable income for given output and trade balance; (b) this in turn raises hoarding or savings; (c) rise in hoarding causes excess supply at given V, leading to a fall in output. We have shown that (a) may not hold if the model is dissected in detail. Further, (b) may not be appropriate given that the Laursen–Metzler effect rests on weak foundations (see the appendix to this chapter). Thus proposition (c) might not follow.

We must conclude that even in circumstances favourable to the standard analysis, the fact that real disposable income increases, and that H is a positive function of it, is not sufficient to guarantee a reduction in output in the tariff-ridden equilibrium position compared to the initial tariff-free equilibrium.

The utilization of the concept of hoarding can also lead to the familiar problems that arise from aggregation. In essence, the assumption that H is determined by real disposable income alone presents us with either an ambiguity or with some special aggregation conditions (Turnovsky, 1977). Why is this? Simply because we recall that imports I are posited to depend upon output V and the terms of trade (relative prices). We have I^n included in A

(absorption) along with C. Yet, somehow, V has become replaced by Y and the terms of trade, *per se*, have disappeared, as $C(.)$ and $I^n(.)$ are combined to produce $A(.)$ and hence $H(.)$.

The quote from Krugman and the figure he and we have used to examine the comparative statics results of the tariff on output follow Mundell's (1961) exposition almost to the letter. However, in line with the earlier work by Laursen and Metzler (1950) upon which he relied, and Harberger (1950), Mundell, as those who have followed him (and whose work is summarized by Krugman (1982)), uses *saving* rather than hoarding.

Mundell states that:

> To find out whether national output increases or decreases we need to know whether the [EB] schedule shifts downwards by more or less than the [IB] curve ... If output remains constant a fall in the price of foreign exchange would be required to restore external balance; the new exchange rate would have to be that indicated by a point such as [A] below [E]. But this change in the exchange rate relieves excess demand in the internal market equal to the change in the balance of payments *plus* its effect on the excess of income over expenditure. If we now assume that investment is unchanged, the higher level of real income due to the improved terms of trade is likely to increase saving and reduce expenditure ... The complete export multiplier, which takes into account changes in the exchange rate, is negative.[6] (Mundell, 1961, p. 515; italics original)

> Footnote 6): The validity of this conclusion depends upon the argument, due to Laursen–Metzler and Harberger, that saving is a positive function of the terms of trade, an argument to which I would subscribe. If the reader prefers to assume that saving is independent of the terms of trade the conclusions of the present paper would not be undermined since its purpose is only to show that commercial policy cannot be relied upon to improve employment, not that more *liberal* trade policies necessarily improve employment. (Mundell, 1961, ibid; italics original)

Thus, Mundell rests his case on the hypothesis that there will be an increase in real disposable income (since the terms of trade will improve) which will lead to an increase in saving and to a reduction in expenditure. Explicitly, this is a different hypothesis from that given by Krugman; but ultimately it amounts to Krugman's premise and it suffers from similar deficiencies.

Mundell relies for his hypothesis on the fact that saving will be a positive function of an amelioration in the terms of trade, in his case seemingly operating, through an improvement in real disposable income, on the previous work of Harberger (1950). It will be recalled that the latter's paper was devoted to a formal analysis of devaluation. The equations he put forward to account for the domestic demand for home goods and for imports had, as separate independent variables, real disposable income *and* relative prices (the terms of trade). Mundell, as with all those who have followed his approach and confirmed his negative conclusions on the macroeconomic value of a tariff, or commercial policies, only has the terms of trade effect entering his framework via the domestic price level and so influencing real disposable income. However, it must be reiterated that Mundell does not develop a formal model. Consequently, it is not clear what is the definition of real income he is using; and because he is attempting to embrace all types of trade-restricting policies under the portmanteau 'commercial policy', tariff revenue is not accorded explicit consideration.

2.5   Increases in Output in the Mundellian Model

Let us now consider formally the Mundellian model. We analyse a general formulation in the sense that imports are a function not only of output but also redistributed tariff revenues. Thus with a tariff, the equilibrium relations are given by

$$H\left(\frac{V + trI}{P}\right) = \frac{1}{P}(X(r) - rI) = \frac{B}{P} \qquad (2.67)$$

$$X(r) = rI \qquad (2.68)$$

$$I = I(V + trI, r(1 + t)) \qquad (2.69)$$

where $P = r^\delta(1 + t)^\delta$.

Let us now evaluate the effect of a general tariff on the supposition that the initial tariff rate is zero. Writing the conditions for internal and external balance in excess demand form we have, upon taking the differentials of those conditions, that the new equilibrium will be attained when

$$d\frac{B}{P} - dH = 0 \tag{2.70}$$

$$dX - r\,dI - I\,dr = 0 \tag{2.71}$$

From equations (2.67)–(2.69) these equations become, with $y = V + trI = V + R^3$

$$(-rI_1 - H_1)\,dV + \left(X_1 - I - rI_2 - \frac{\delta B}{r} + \frac{H_1\delta y}{r}\right)dr$$

$$= [r^2(I_1 I + I_2) + \delta B + H_1 rI - H_1\delta y]\,dt \tag{2.72}$$

$$(rI_1)\,dV + (rI_2 + I - X_1)\,dr = -r^2(I_1 I + I_2)\,dt \tag{2.73}$$

The Jacobian of the system (2.72), (2.73) is

$$J = \begin{bmatrix} -rI_1 - H_1 & X_1 - I - rI_2 - \dfrac{\delta B}{r} + \dfrac{H_1\delta y}{r} \\[2mm] rI_1 & rI_2 + I - X_1 \end{bmatrix} \tag{2.74}$$

Given the relative slopes of the IB and EB lines, the determinant $|J|$ is positive. This is the stability requirement of the model.

Solving for the effect of the general tariff on output we have

$$\frac{\partial V}{\partial t} = \frac{1}{|J|}\begin{vmatrix} r^2(II_1 + I_2) + \delta B + H_1 rI - H_1\delta y & X_1 - I - rI_2 - \dfrac{\delta B}{r} + \dfrac{H_1\delta y}{r} \\[2mm] -r^2(I_1 I + I_2) & I + rI_2 - X_1 \end{vmatrix}$$

$\partial V/\partial t$ is evaluated at equilibrium where $B = 0$. Also disposable income y is equal to absorption (expenditure). Since δ is the value of imports as a proportion of absorption which equals y, and since y contains the tariff revenue, imports are valued at the tariff-ridden price. Thus $\delta y = r(1 + t)I = rI + R$. All partial derivatives are evaluated at the initial equilibrium since for marginal changes we do not expect any differences in magnitude. All variables are evaluated at the post-tariff position since to do otherwise would imply that there is no tariff. In particular, we have been careful *not* to set $R = 0$, since this would eliminate the expansionary income effect of tariffs. Therefore we get

$$\frac{\partial V}{\partial t} = \frac{1}{|J|}\begin{vmatrix} r^2(II_1 + I_2) - H_1 R & (X_1 - I - rI_2) + H_1 I + \dfrac{H_1 R}{r} \\[2mm] -r^2(II_1 + I_2) & I + rI_2 - X_1 \end{vmatrix}$$

$$= \frac{H_1}{|J|} \ [Ir^2(II_1 + I_2) + R(X_1 + rII_1 - I)] \tag{2.75}$$

We already know that $|J| > 0$ by stability. Further, $H_1 > 0$ on the assumptions of the Laursen–Metzler condition. If we now *assume* that $(II_1 + I_2) < 0$, or that the import income relation is purely that for a consumer good and therefore the substitution effect must be negative, the first term in brackets in (2.75) is negative. But the sign of the second term is not clear a priori, and this opens up the possibility that it can be positive, thus making it possible to have a positive tariff effect on output.

Noting that at equilibrium $X = rI$, we have

$$(X_1 - I) = I(x - 1) \tag{2.76}$$

where x is the price elasticity of exports. So

$$\frac{\partial V}{\partial t} = \frac{H_1}{|J|} \ [r^2(II_1 + I_2) + RI(x - 1 + rI_1)] \tag{2.77}$$

A necessary condition for $\partial V/\partial t$ to be positive is that

$$x - 1 + rI_1 > 0$$

that is the Metzler paradox should not hold. This is of course not sufficient. On the other hand, with the Metzler paradox occurring we definitely have a fall in output after the imposition of tariffs. The reason is clear as discussed in the previous section. With the Metzler paradox, P falls; thus disposable income *must* rise for a given output, causing hoarding (saving) to rise, the consequent excess supply of output pulling down the equilibrium output. However, on empirical grounds, the paradox can be ruled out (Houthakker and Magee, 1969; Krugman, 1982) and the final effect on output is unclear. This therefore contradicts the established paradigm that tariffs *must* reduce output in a simple Keynesian model. We note that for the case of fixed r, $dV/dt = -r(I_1 I + I_2)/I_1$; which is uniquely positive if the Slutsky condition holds.

What about the exchange rate? Using (2.72) to (2.74) we have

$$\frac{\partial r}{\partial t} = \frac{H_1[r^2(II_1 + I_2) + rI_1 R]}{|J|} \tag{2.78}$$

Again the direction of the movement of the exchange rate is not at all clear and, depending on the tariff revenue R, we can have a situation where the exchange rate *increases* after a tariff is imposed.

We can also show, after some tedious algebra, that the volume of imports can fall or rise after the imposition of tariffs. The expression for this turns out to be

$$\frac{\partial I}{\partial t} = (X_1 - I)\frac{H_1[r(II_1 + I_2) + RI_1]}{|J|} \tag{2.79}$$

Consider the special case where the elasticity of exports with respect to price is greater than unity, that is at equilibrium $X_1 - I > 0$. Then the first term in parentheses in (2.79), under our usual assumption, is negative. For a given level of output, the tariff causes the domestic price of importables to rise and the substitution effect leads to expenditure switching towards the domestic product. Imports fall. But income rises due to redistributed tariff revenue R and pushes up imports. The (pure) income effect is shown by the second term in (2.79). We have the possibility that tariffs can be expansionary, not only for the domestic (small) economy, but also for the rest of the world. Thus tariffs need not be a begger-my-neighbour policy. This is, of course, diametrically opposite to the case of a quota as we shall see later.

Of the possible combinations of changes in output and the exchange rate that can occur, three are of special interest, namely

$$1 \quad \frac{dV}{dt} > 0, \frac{dr}{dt} > 0$$

$$2 \quad \frac{dV}{dt} > 0, \frac{dr}{dt} < 0$$

$$\tag{2.80}$$

and

$$3 \quad \frac{dV}{dt} < 0, \frac{dr}{dt} < 0$$

Case 3 is the combination that is conventionally stated to be the outcome when a tariff is introduced or an existing tariff increased. We have already commented on this case: attention was drawn to the crucial fact that at the initial level of output the terms of trade could worsen as a consequence of the introduction of a tariff, or increase in the tariff, and yet output could fall when the final equilibrium is established.

Cases 1 and 2 are shown in figures 2.2 and 2.3. In both cases output goes up while the exchange rate may move in either

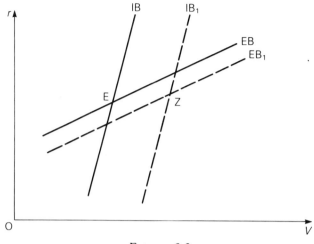

FIGURE 2.2

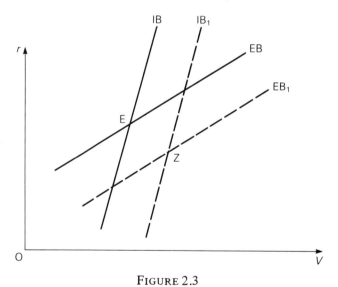

FIGURE 2.3

direction. Both models are (locally) stable and the IB and EB lines slope upwards. These are then the diagrammatic counterpart of the earlier analytical conclusion that the Mundellian results can be overturned and it is possible for domestic output to rise consequent on a tariff.

The Mundellian model can also be utilized to give us some idea of the welfare implications of tariff changes. The problem is to have a suitable representation of the social welfare function. There are obvious candidates; output, disposable income or absorption. Welfare may depend on the behaviour of output in the post-tariff situation, then nothing more need be added to our previous analysis. A more traditional formulation is to make aggregate output *constant* (the assumption of full employment) and investigate the effect of tariffs on real absorption (Tower, 1973). The implicit assumption made is that social welfare is positively related to real absorption, thus $U = U(A^*)$, $U_1 > 0$.

Using equations (2.9), (2.10), (2.11), (2.18), (2.20), we have

$$\bar{V} + trI = PA^* + X(r) - rI \tag{2.11'}$$

$$X(r) = rI \tag{2.18'}$$

$$I = \tilde{I}(PA^*, r(1 + t)) \tag{2.20'}$$

$$P = r^\delta (1 + t)^\delta \tag{2.9'}$$

Remember PA^* is nominal absorption (also the domestic price equals unity). Imports depend on nominal absorption and prices. Output $\bar{V}$ is held constant. There are four endogenous variables in the system: r, I, P and A^*. There is no need to make the assumption that the initial tariff rate is zero.

Taking total differentials, eliminating dP and dI we get

$$P(1 - r\tilde{I}_1)\, dA^* + [X_1 + t\tilde{I} - r(\tilde{I}\tilde{I}_1 + \tilde{I}_2)(1 + t)]\, dr$$

$$= r^2(\tilde{I}\tilde{I}_1 + \tilde{I}_2)\, dt$$

$$(r\tilde{I}_1 P)\, dA^* + [\tilde{I} - X_1 + r(1 + t)(\tilde{I}\tilde{I}_1 + \tilde{I}_2)]\, dr = -r^2(\tilde{I}\tilde{I}_1 + \tilde{I}_2)\, dt$$

Solving for dA^* we have

$$\frac{\partial A^*}{\partial t} = \frac{r^2(\tilde{I}\tilde{I}_1 + \tilde{I}_2)((1 + t)\tilde{I} - X_1 t)}{P(\tilde{I} - X_1 + r(1 + t)\tilde{I}_2)} \tag{2.81}$$

It is clear that if $(\tilde{I}\tilde{I}_1 + \tilde{I}_2) < 0$ (see (2.21)) and the Marshall–Lerner condition holds, $X_1 - \tilde{I} - r(1 + t)\tilde{I}_2 > 0$, a small tariff, starting from zero, *raises* real absorption, thus increasing welfare given a constant level of aggregate output. Tariffs then increase welfare in the full employment case.[4]

We have indicated that even within its own ground rules there are points at which the Mundellian paradigm is not devoid of error. This is largely because the minimum of formal analysis is employed to investigate the macroimpact of a tariff. We have demonstrated analytically that when the model is worked through formally, the outcome is not that the tariff will always reduce output. Expenditure-switching effects that directly or indirectly benefit the economy by increasing output can exist.

The impact effect on the terms of trade, at the original equilibrium level of output, will not always be beneficial; the consequent effect on the level of real disposable income is uncertain. Hence the impact on so-called hoarding is not determinate uniquely. The analytical results we have obtained have been devised by our keeping close to the Mundellian model in that we have specified the behavioural equations in the same way and we have seen that positively-sloped internal and external balance lines have been maintained after the tariff is imposed or is adjusted upwards.[5]

2.6 Permanent and Temporary Tariffs

When relative prices change, people adjust their expenditure pattern within an intertemporal framework, and this affects their consumption allocation, aggregate consumption and saving. Terms of trade effects are no different. As we have seen in the discussion of the Laursen–Metzler effect (as well as in the appendix), these issues raise quite subtle questions. One of the points discussed recently has been the distinction between permanent and temporary terms of trade changes and their concomitant effects. A proper treatment of this problem requires a discussion on the nature and role of expectations in the model. This is beyond the scope of this chapter, but will be discussed more fully in chapter 5. Here we give a simple macroeconomic representation.

Essentially the idea is quite simple. If agents are informed that tariffs are temporary (and they believe this), then the income stream accruing from the disbursement of tariff revenue is also temporary. Thus the effect of tariff revenue on hoarding and expenditure will be different from that of the permanent source of income, that is from output. Instead of treating disposable income as one bulky concept, we have to break it up into constituent parts, one emanating from V and the other from R, expecting that expenditure elasticities with respect to these are different.

We therefore have the following model:

$$H = H\left(\frac{V}{P}, \frac{rtI}{P}\right) \qquad (2.82)$$

$$I = I(V, r(1 + t), rtI) \tag{2.83}$$

$$X = X(r) \tag{2.84}$$

$$B = X - rI = 0 \tag{2.85}$$

$$H = \frac{B}{P} \tag{2.86}$$

$$P = r^\delta (1 + t)^\delta \tag{2.87}$$

The tariff revenue is $R = rtI$, and it is now postulated that it has a separate effect on H and I by equations (2.82) and (2.83). This then is the simplified implication of a temporary tariff which gives rise to transitory income. A fuller specification will have to wait for later chapters. The other equations are standard. Note that $I_3 = \partial I / \partial R$, $H_2 = \partial H / \partial (R/P)$.

As before, taking total differentials of H

$$dH = \frac{H_1}{P}\left(dV - \delta V \frac{dr}{r} - \delta V \, dt\right) + \frac{H_2}{P}\left(rI \, dt - \delta R \frac{dr}{r} - \delta R \, dt\right) \tag{2.88}$$

Similarly for the current account

$$d\left(\frac{B}{P}\right) = \frac{1}{P}\left(X_1 \, dr - I \, dr - rI_1 \, dV - rI_2 \, dr - r^2 I_2 \, dt\right.$$

$$\left. - r^2 II_3 - \frac{B}{P} \, dP\right) \tag{2.89}$$

Collecting terms, evaluating them at equilibrium where $B = 0$, we note that $d(B/P) - dH = 0$, for internal balance requires that

$$(-rI_1 - H_1) \, dV + \left(X_1 - I - rI_2 + \frac{\delta V H_1}{r} + \frac{\delta R H_2}{r}\right)$$

$$= (r^2 I_2 + r^2 II_3 - H_1 \delta V - H_2 \delta R + H_2 rI) \tag{2.90}$$

For external balance we make use of (2.83)–(2.85) and get

$$(rI_1) \, dV + (rI_2 + I - X_1) \, dr = -r^2(I_2 + II_3) \, dt \tag{2.91}$$

As previously, assume that the internal balance line has a greater positive slope than the external balance. Then the following determinant is positive as necessary for stability

$$|J| = \begin{vmatrix} -rI_1 - H_1 & X_1 - I - rI_2 + \delta V \dfrac{H_1}{r} + \delta R \dfrac{H_2}{r} \\ -rI_1 & rI_2 + I - X_1 \end{vmatrix} > 0$$

(2.92)

Using (2.90) and (2.91), the effect of tariffs on output becomes

$$\frac{\partial V}{\partial t} = \frac{1}{|J|} \; [(X_1 - I - rI_2)(\delta H_1 V - \delta H_2 V + RH_2)$$

$$+ \, r(I_2 + II_3)(\delta H_1 V + \delta RH_2)]$$

(2.93)

Once again, there are both positive and negative terms in the expression for $\partial V / \partial t$ and without a knowledge of parameter values, it is difficult to sign the expression. Output can go either way, and the final result will depend on the relative strengths of H_1 and H_2. Distinguishing between temporary and permanent tariffs does not change the nature of our overall conclusions.

2.7   Dynamics

The dynamics (or more properly the pseudo-dynamics, since time paths are not analysed explicitly) of the system are based on the simple Keynesian idea that excess demand for aggregate output causes it to rise, the price of domestic product being fixed. Similarly, an excess demand for foreign exchange ($B < 0$) causes the exchange rate to rise. Equations (2.49) and (2.50) rewritten here

$$\dot{V} = \theta_1 \left(\frac{B}{P} - H \right) \qquad (\theta_1, \theta_2) > 0$$

$$\dot{r} = \theta_2 (rI - X)$$

are then the simplest possible representation of the dynamics of the Mundellian model. One can of course make a wide variety of assumptions regarding the time path of V and r, giving different types of result. In what follows we discuss very briefly some of these specifications. The reader is warned that this is only to give a flavour of the rich variety of results possible, rather than a

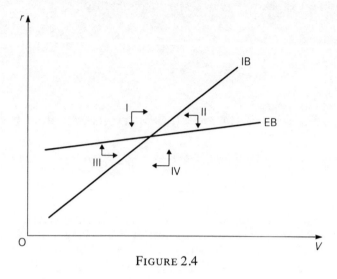

FIGURE 2.4

rigorous analysis of dynamic properties. Proper specification and more formal presentations are left for later analysis; see particularly chapter 5 for various alternatives linked with expectations.

Let us consider figure 2.4 which portrays the phase diagram for the economy on the basis of the standard pseudo-dynamics for this type of model (of the kind, indeed, used by Mundell (1961) in the appendix to his paper). Thus the IB line represents the situation where the first time derivative of output is zero; the supposition would be that that derivative is solely a function of the excess demand for output. Similarly, the EB line denotes the fact that the first time derivative of the exchange rate is zero. We can segment figure 2.4 into the four regions; and the adjustment of the two variables if they differ from their equilibrium values will be indicated by the arrows. Thus, above the IB line there is excess demand; and above the EB line there is a balance of payments surplus. The system, without the tariff, is stable; we have in effect shown earlier that the slope of IB exceeds that of EB.

Consider now an alternative dynamic structure in figure 2.5 which portrays the case where both V and r increase when the tariff is imposed. If we suppose that the exchange rate, in fact, adjusts rapidly after the tariff is imposed to clear internal markets, then the economy's trajectory from E to Z could be described as one which goes from E to N to Z via the arrowed path. Thus, one

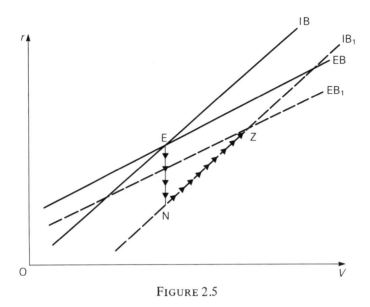

FIGURE 2.5

possibility, depending upon the precise nature of the dynamics (that is, upon the relative strengths of excess demand for domestic output and of the excess demand for foreign currency in determining the change in V and r and the assumed speeds of adjustment of V and r) is that the exchange rate *overshoots* the price equilibrium position. A rapid adjustment of the exchange rate from E to N will result *initially* in there being a balance of payments *deficit*. In order to restore equilibrium in the balance of payments, whilst maintaining internal balance, there will have to be an increase in r (a depreciation of the currency as r is defined here) and an increase in V.

The adjustment path as envisaged on figure 2.5 commences, of course, with a move identical to that used by Mundell to locate the final equilibrium point Z; so that on figure 2.1, the move from point E to point A is the same as that from E to N on figure 2.5. In the latter case, however, the final equilibrium point is to the right of N, with output higher in the tariff-ridden equilibrium. Naturally, in the Mundellian analysis points E and N are taken as reference points; what we are saying in figure 2.5 is that the nature of the adjustment to the tariff could well mean that initially the economy does actually move from E to N. The dynamic analysis, of course, is very *ad hoc*; in later chapters we give a proper specification.

The situation illustrated in figure 2.5 is one that has similar properties to the case of Great Britain after the general tariff imposed in 1932. In the Mundellian analysis, even if output is sluggish and exchange rate appreciates rapidly, it is expected that the transition path will be characterized by a balance of payments surplus. In addition to offering protection and enhancing employment, tariffs are meant to improve the balance of trade position by restricting imports. However, the overshooting of the exchange rate to restore internal balance may mean a very high level of the value of the domestic currency, and this might reduce exports and consequently produce a deficit as the impact effect. The 1932 tariff did actually produce a current account deficit contrary to contemporary expectations.

The 1932 tariff has indeed formed the basis of a detailed, comprehensive, historical study by Eichengreen (1979). His theoretical models (also contained in Eichengreen (1981)) predict generally that with floating exchange rates, the macroeconomic effects of tariffs are adverse, tariffs lower aggregate output and employment. However, he also shows by counter-factual simulations of the case of 1932, that the general tariff did actually *raise* output – when the effects of other variables are removed. The historical analysis of Eichengreen (1979), where the British tariff caused an initial high appreciation of sterling, a balance of payments deficit and finally a rise in output, is mirrored by the analytical models we have presented.

2.8   *Numerical Simulation*

In principle, we have used 'small' changes in tariffs (generally starting from zero) to evaluate the impact effect of commercial policy. In practice, tariffs will change discretely and will probably be large. Clearly, precise analytical results are impossible to derive, so numerical solutions with plausible parameter values are useful to see the general effect of tariffs. The models discussed in the preceding sections have been solved for values of t from 0 per cent to 100 per cent, rising by 1 per cent at each step. We present some sets of results here with tariffs ranging from 0 to 0.1 and also for 0 to 0.2. The sets are differentiated by model specification. In particular we use the previously discussed Krugman-type model based on the concept of real hoarding, with a general import function dependent on disposable income and relative price. This model is specified in 'real' terms, that is in terms of nominal variables deflated by the aggregate price level P. We also give results for an absorption model specified in nominal terms (alternatively in terms of the home good). We assume that the Laursen–Metzler condition holds, thus our analysis is favourable to the underlying assumptions of the Mundellian paradigm. Careful check is done for other side conditions such as Marshall–Lerner.

The numerical solutions have been arrived at by assuming that the behavioural equations are linear. This produces, however, a *non-linear* reduced-form system, as we have indicated in our theoretical discussion (and we also note that the introduction of a tariff, or the increase in a tariff, renders the IB line non-linear; so that, again as intimated previously, the impact of a tariff on output cannot be seen as a straightforward one-off shift of the originally assumed linear IB line parallel to itself). The system of equations has been set up on each occasion to permit solutions to be obtained for all the endogenous variables *including* δ. The approach adopted earlier, and in the literature, has been to assume that the tariff (or its increase) is extremely small. In any simulation results that have been provided to evaluate the macro-economic impact of tariffs the comparison is usually made between a situation where the presence of a tariff is compared with the no-tariff situation; this is usually for a tariff of 10 per cent and δ is assumed fixed, despite what is effectively a discrete jump in the tariff (Krugman, 1982).

The numerical results reported in table 2.1 (and shown graphically in figure 2.6) are based on a linear *real* hoarding function (which incidentally gives a *non-linear* nominal absorption function) as well as a simple linear import demand function. The model therefore is

$$H = H_0 + H_1 \frac{y}{P} \tag{2.94}$$

$$X = X_0 + X_1 r \tag{2.95}$$

$$I = I_0 + I_1 y + I_2 r \tag{2.96}$$

as well as equations (2.39)–(2.44). Output consistently goes up as the tariff rate is increased from 0 to 0.2, the exchange rate falls, but the aggregate price level increases. The deflationary effect of prices pulls down the hoarding function and equilibrium is

TABLE 2.1

t	V	r	I	R	X	P	δ
0.000	3.098	0.112	3.835	0.000	0.431	0.738	0.139
0.010	3.103	0.110	3.842	0.004	0.422	0.740	0.137
0.020	3.104	0.108	3.846	0.008	0.414	0.741	0.136
0.030	3.105	0.106	3.849	0.012	0.407	0.742	0.134
0.040	3.107	0.104	3.853	0.016	0.400	0.743	0.133
0.050	3.108	0.012	3.856	0.020	0.393	0.745	0.132
0.060	3.110	0.100	3.860	0.023	0.386	0.746	0.131
0.070	3.112	0.098	0.864	0.026	0.379	0.747	0.129
0.080	3.114	0.096	0.867	0.030	0.373	0.748	0.128
0.090	3 116	0.095	3.871	0.033	0.367	0.750	0.127
0.100	3.118	0.093	3.875	0.036	0.360	0.751	0.126
0.110	3.120	0.091	3.879	0.039	0.354	0.752	0.124
0.120	3.122	0.090	3.883	0.042	0.348	0.753	0.123
0.130	3.125	0.088	3.887	0.044	0.342	0.755	0.122
0.140	3.127	0.087	3.891	0.047	0.337	0.756	0.121
0.150	3.130	0.085	3.895	0.050	0.331	0.757	0.120
0.160	3.133	0.083	3.900	0.052	0.325	0.758	0.119
0.170	3.135	0.082	3.904	0.054	0.320	0.759	0.117
0.180	3.139	0.080	3.908	0.057	0.315	0.761	0.116
0.190	3.142	0.079	3.913	0.059	0.309	0.762	0.115
0.200	3.145	0.078	3.918	0.061	0.304	0.763	0.114

$H_0 = -1.05$; $H_1 = 0.25$; $X_0 = 0.02$; $X_1 = 3.66$; $I_0 = 2.16$; $I_1 = 0.64$; $I_2 = -2.74$

attained at a higher level of domestic output. In spite of the rise in the price of imports and an adverse terms of trade, the *volume* of imports rises given the impetus from a higher disposable income. Increased imports in such a case reduce the possibility of retaliation from other small open economies. Tariffs are expansionary.

Table 2.2 (figure 2.7) gives essentially the same model but with changed parameter values. In particular, the value of X_1 is reduced, which as we have seen in our previous analysis, is expected to increase the output dampening effect of tariffs. Domestic terms of trade still increase while the exchange rate appreciates. The overall impact on output is negative. Tariffs from 0 to 0.1 will reduce output for the case studied here.

The foregoing figures and tables analysed the impact of tariffs with a real hoarding function. The next model takes a nominal

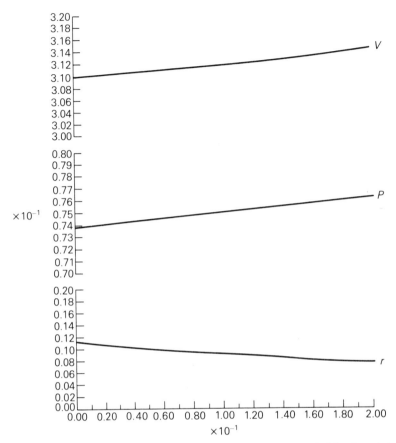

FIGURE 2.6 $H_0 = -1.05$; $H_1 = 0.25$; $X_0 = 0.02$; $X_1 = 3.66$; $I_0 = 2.16$; $I_1 = 0.64; I_2 = -2.74$

absorption function which is non-linear in disposable income but linear in prices. The import demand function has the volume of imports depending only on output and not on disposable income. This would be so (as discussed previously) if imports are predominantly for production and the propensity to imports is similar to an input–output coefficient. The model then is

$$A = A_0 + A_1 y^2 + A_2 p \tag{2.97}$$

$$I = I_0 + I_1 V + I_2 R + I_3 p \tag{2.98}$$

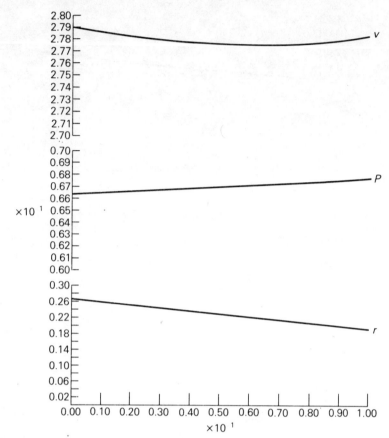

FIGURE 2.7 $H_0 = -1.05$; $H_1 = 0.25$; $X_0 = 0.09$; $X_1 = 2.90$; $I_0 = 2.20$;
$I_1 = 0.61$; $I_2 = -2.50$

$$X = X_0 + X_1 r \tag{2.99}$$

$$y = V + R \tag{2.100}$$

$$y = A + X - rI \tag{2.101}$$

$$B = X - rI = 0 \tag{2.102}$$

$$I_2 = 0, \qquad A_2 = (1 - 2A_1 y) I \tag{2.103}$$

Once again, y is nominal (or in home good units) disposable income, A is absorption and B the balance of trade.

Table 2.3 (and figure 2.8) shows that the exchange rate now *rises* so that there is an additional positive impetus to output. The

TABLE 2.2

t	V	r	I	R	X	P	δ
0.000	2.790	0.266	3.236	0.000	0.862	0.664	0.309
0.010	2.787	0.258	3.249	0.008	0.837	0.665	0.303
0.020	2.783	0.250	3.260	0.016	0.815	0.666	0.297
0.030	2.780	0.243	3.271	0.024	0.793	0.667	0.291
0.040	2.777	0.235	3.283	0.031	0.772	0.669	0.286
0.050	2.776	0.228	3.295	0.037	0.751	0.670	0.280
0.060	2.775	0.221	3.308	0.044	0.730	0.671	0.275
0.070	2.775	0.214	3.321	0.050	0.710	0.673	0.269
0.080	2.776	0.207	3.335	0.055	0.690	0.674	0.263
0.090	2.778	0.200	3.350	0.060	0.669	0.676	0.257
0.100	2.782	0.193	3.367	0.065	0.649	0.678	0.251

$H_0 = -1.05; H_1 = 0.25; X_0 = 0.09; X_1 = 2.90; I_0 = 2.20; I_1 = 0.61; I_2 = -2.50$

TABLE 2.3

t	V	r	I	R	X	P	δ
0.000	17.865	2.343	3.543	0.000	8.302	1.419	0.411
0.010	18.020	2.354	3.543	0.083	8.338	1.430	0.413
0.020	18.177	2.364	3.542	0.167	8.374	1.442	0.416
0.030	18.335	2.374	3.542	0.252	8.411	1.454	0.418
0.040	18.494	2.385	3.542	0.338	8.448	1.466	0.421
0.050	18.655	2.396	3.542	0.424	8.485	1.478	0.423
0.060	18.817	2.406	3.542	0.511	8.523	1.490	0.426
0.070	18.981	2.417	3.541	0.599	8.561	1.502	0.428
0.080	19.146	2.428	3.541	0.688	8.599	1.514	0.430
0.090	19.313	2.429	3.541	0.777	8.638	1.527	0.433
0.100	19.481	2.451	3.541	0.868	8.677	1.540	0.435
0.110	19.651	2.462	3.541	0.959	8.716	1.552	0.438
0.120	19.823	2.473	3.540	1.051	8.756	1.565	0.440
0.130	19.996	2.485	3.540	1.144	8.797	1.579	0.442
0.140	20.171	2.496	3.540	1.237	8.837	1.592	0.444
0.150	20.347	2.508	3.540	1.332	8.878	1.605	0.447
0.160	20.526	2.520	3.540	1.427	8.920	1.619	0.449
0.170	20.706	2.542	3.539	1.523	8.962	1.632	0.451
0.180	20.887	2.544	3.539	1.621	9.004	1.646	0.453
0.190	21.071	2.556	3.539	1.719	9.047	1.660	0.456
0.200	21.256	2.568	3.539	1.818	9.090	1.674	0.458

$A_0 = 0.55; A_1 = 0.40; I_1 = 0.50; I_2 = 0.00; I_3 = -2.30; X_0 = 0.10; X_1 = 3.50$

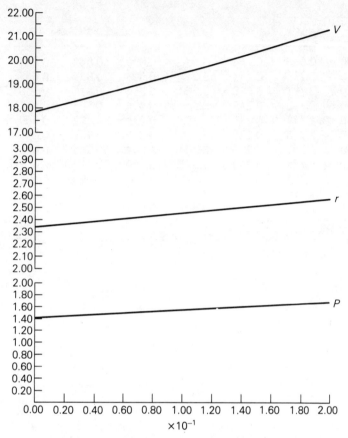

FIGURE 2.8   Model with non-linear absorption function. $A_0 = 0.55$; $A_1 = 0.40$; $I_1 = 0.50$; $I_2 = 0.00$; $I_3 = -2.30$; $X_0 = 0.10$; $X_1 = 3.50$

export multiplier boosts production as the exchange rate depreciates. The price level behaves as before. Given all this positive stimulus, it is not surprising that output rises substantially.

The three sets of numerical results confirm our previous analytical insights, that unlike the emphasis and near certainty of contractionary tariffs postulated in the literature, we should be agnostic about the final macroeconomic effects of a general tariff. The simulation models using discrete changes in tariffs show that three alternatives are possible: (a) both output and the exchange rate fall; (b) output rises but the exchange rate falls; (c) output and the exchange rate both rise.

2.9 Conclusion

Let us conclude briefly. A larger critical survey can be found in Ford and Sen (1984). The thrust of our analysis of the Mundellian, now apodictic, conclusion on the macroeffects of a general tariff (and hence by implication in this Mundellian framework, of a general quota on imports) can be encapsulated in two observations. The first is that a non-retaliatory tariff can have expansionary macroeconomic effects on aggregate domestic output and thus employment. It can even *raise* imports since the income effects from higher production outweigh the expenditure switching that occurs from terms of trade changes. Thus, the spectre of retaliation is minimized, since a virtuous cycle may be set up. The second observation is that parameter values are crucial in the determination of the new outcome, and these need to be clearly specified before judgement is to be passed.

Consider a set of *sufficient* conditions for a contractionary tariff: (a) the Laursen–Metzler condition must hold, thus a rise in the relative price of importables would increase absorption measured in terms of home goods; (b) imports are only for consumer goods, hence the pure substitution effect must be negative given Slutsky; (c) the Metzler paradox should be satisfied, thus an increase in tariffs and a concomitant reduction in the exchange rate will decrease the aggregate price level. We can easily see that a clear-cut contraction in output in the post-tariff economy needs some quite strong and restrictive conditions. Therefore the insistence that tariffs *must* reduce national output and employrent seems misplaced.

We have kept deliberately to the Mundellian framework in this chapter. This was for two reasons. The first of these is implied in the earlier sections of the preceding text, namely the Mundellian 'analysis' and its conclusion have a stranglehold on the literature and constitute the basis of most of the work in the area. The second is that despite the fact that recent work (Eichengreen, 1981; Krugman, 1982) has extended the Mundellian paradigm by, for example, the introduction (separately) of flexible prices and wages, and incorporating the money stock, the findings are almost without exception merely ones which confirm the Mundellian predictions. But those, and other, extensions will occupy our attention in ensuing chapters.

APPENDIX

THE LAURSEN–METZLER EFFECT IN AN OPTIMIZING MODEL

The purpose of this appendix is to construct a simple intertemporal optimizing model which analyses the Laursen–Metzler effect. The representative household consumes two goods, home H and imported I. Any excess of income over expenditure E is used to buy a foreign bond B, which gives an interest rate i fixed by international money markets. The household receives a fixed endowment V of the home good every period, so V can be thought of as the gross domestic product.

The household's instantaneous utility function is given by

$$U = U(H, I, B) \tag{2A.1}$$

with the usual properties

$$U_i > 0, \quad U_{ii} < 0 \quad i = 1, 2, 3, \text{ or } H, I, B \tag{2A.2}$$

We also assume (to avoid non-interior solutions) that

$$\left.\begin{array}{l} \lim_{H \to 0} U_1 = \infty \\[2mm] \lim_{I \to 0} U_2 = \infty \\[2mm] \lim_{B \to 0} U_3 = \infty \end{array}\right\} \tag{2A.2$'$}$$

U has the usual properties, non-negative, strictly increasing in all arguments, concave and (at least) twice continuously differentiable.

In addition we assume for tractability[6] that U is additively separable in B such that

$$U_{13} = U_{23} = U_{31} = U_{32} = 0 \tag{2A.3}$$

The use of B in the utility function can be justified in the same way as that of real money balances affecting utility in macro-models, for which there is a long pedigree (Patinkin, 1965, and in monetary growth models (Levari and Patinkin, 1968). Specifically, owning bonds facilitates transactions in the world market, reduces transactions costs, and probably gives more 'prestige' and financial security to the economy under consideration.

The relative price $p = P_I/P_H$ of foreign to home goods is exogenously fixed for the small open economy. An imposition of tariffs will raise the domestic terms of trade and we shall be considering the dynamic effects of a once and for all rise in p. The implicit assumption is, therefore, of fixed exchange rates but this is not important in an analysis of the L–M effect. Essentially, the L–M condition tries to predict the behaviour of expenditure, for a terms of trade change, and this is precisely what we shall be doing here in the appendix. Furthermore, even if tariffs reduce the exchange rate and make the foreign goods less expensive, ruling out the Metzler paradox, we will still end up with a terms of trade deterioration (higher p).

To reduce the dimensionality of the problem, we shall be working with the indirect utility function

$$W = W(E, p, B) \tag{2A.4}$$

where

$$W(E, p, B) = \max U(H, I, B) \quad \text{s.t. } H + pI = E$$

The function W then gives the maximum utility achievable at given price p and expenditure E.[7] Note that expenditure E is being measured in units of the home good, thus it corresponds to nominal absorption A in the main text (with $P_H = 1$).

The consumer's problem is to maximize the discounted sum of future instantaneous (indirect) utilities, thus maximizing

$$J = \int_0^\infty \exp(-\rho t)\, W(E, p, B)\, dt \tag{2A.5}$$

where t stands for time here, and ρ is the constant rate of time preference. The flow budget constraint relates the consumer's addition to bond holding when income exceeds expenditure. In discrete time, for any period t, we have

$$P_I(B_{t+1} - B_t) = P_H V - P_H H - P_I I + i P_I B_t \tag{2A.6}$$

or dividing by P_H

$$p(B_{t+1} - B_t) = V - H - pI + ipB_t$$

which becomes, using the definition of expenditure E

$$(B_{t+1} - B_t) = \frac{V}{p} - \frac{E}{p} + iB_t \tag{2A.7}$$

In continuous time this can be written as

$$\dot{B} = \frac{V}{p} - \frac{E}{p} + iB \qquad (2A.8)$$

The household then maximizes J given by (2A.5) subject to the budget constraint (2A.8).

However, a major problem remains. B can, in principle, be either positive or negative, in the latter case, of course, the economy is a net borrower from the rest of the world. Thus the possibility remains that the representative consumer can borrow *ad infinitum* and pay interest $(-iB_t)$ which is itself financed by more borrowing. This 'paradox of borrowing' allows the household to increase expenditure and borrowing continuously, thus the integral J may be unbounded and without reasonable solution (Arrow and Kurz, 1970). One way of avoiding this paradox is to impose a further constraint which states that the initial value of bond holding plus capitalized value of lifetime output (income) must be greater or equal to the discounted sum of lifetime expenditure (the interest rate being used as the appropriate discounting factor). This, naturally, will prevent unlimited borrowing. On the other hand, the problem is not acute in our model, since the holding of bonds gives utility to the consumer. Thus it is lending (positive B) which is desirable, though an implicit trade-off exists since more bond holding reduces expenditure for the same level of income. We have less need, therefore, for the second constraint than do standard models with perfect capital markets (Obstfeld, 1982). However, to avoid possible problems with second-order and sufficiency conditions,[8] we shall assume that the household under consideration is always a net lender, thus $B_t \geqslant 0$ (for all t). The case $B = 0$ (together with $\dot{B} = 0$ in the steady state) is the basic Keynesian one with no capital flows.

The household then maximizes

$$J = \int_0^\infty \exp(-\rho t)\, W(E, p, B)\, \mathrm{d}t \qquad (2A.9)$$

subject to

$$\dot{B} = \frac{V}{p} - \frac{E}{p} + iB \qquad (2A.10)$$

and all variables E, p, B, V, H, I being non-negative.

The control is the choice of expenditure E and the state variable is B. Thus at any point of time, B is predetermined (evolving out of the equation of motion (2A.10)), while E has to be chosen within the optimizing framework. The values of E, B and p (generally fixed) then determine the indirect utility function. Roy's identity[9] can be used then to derive the demand for H and I, home and imported goods.

The current value Hamiltonian using (2A.9), (2A.10) is

$$\exp{(\rho t)} \, \bar{H} = W(E, p, B) + \Omega \left(\frac{V}{p} - \frac{E}{p} + iB \right) \qquad (2A.11)$$

where Ω is the relevant shadow price (of bonds). The necessary condition for optimality gives

$$W_1 - \frac{\Omega}{p} = 0 \qquad (2A.12)$$

whence

$$\Omega = pW_1 \qquad (2A.13)$$

where $W_1 = \partial W / \partial E$ as usual. It can also be shown that (2A.12) or (2A.13) does indeed give a maximum for the Hamiltonian.[10] We also have

$$\dot{\Omega} = \Omega(\rho - i) - W_3 \qquad (2A.14)$$

where $W_3 = \partial W / \partial B$.

Taking the time derivative of Ω from (2A.13)

$$\dot{\Omega} = pW_{11}\dot{E} \qquad (2A.15)$$

Note that due to the assumption of separability of the original utility function U, W_1 does not depend on B, thus $W_{13} = 0 = W_{31}$. Equation (2A.14) and (2A.15)

$$pW_{11}\dot{E} = \Omega(\rho - i) - W_3 \qquad (2A.16)$$

Using (2A.13)

$$W_{11}\dot{E} = W_1(\rho - i) - \frac{W_3}{p} \qquad (2A.17)$$

or

$$\dot{E} = \frac{W_1}{W_{11}}(\rho - i) - \frac{W_3}{pW_{11}} \qquad (2A.18)$$

Finally, the law of motion of the state variable is given by

$$\dot{B} = \frac{V}{p} - \frac{E}{p} + iB \tag{2A.19}$$

Equations (2A.18) and (2A.19) then give the dynamics of the system.

The phase diagram for the system (2A.18), (2A.19) can be derived by considering (in the neighbourhood of the stationary state $\dot{E} = \dot{B} = 0$) the following:

$$\left.\frac{dE}{dB}\right|_{\dot{E}=0} = -\left(\frac{\partial\dot{E}/\partial B}{\partial\dot{E}/\partial E}\right)$$

$$= -\left(\frac{-W_{33}/pW_{11}}{(\rho-i)}\right)$$

(Remember the implicit assumption $W_{31} = 0$ and also that W_{11} is a constant.) Then

$$\left.\frac{dE}{dB}\right|_{\dot{E}=0} = \frac{W_{33}}{pW_{11}(\rho-i)} \tag{2A.20}$$

The sign of the expression is positive since W_{33} and W_{11} are negative and $\rho - i = W_3/pW_1$ from (2A.18) with $\dot{E} = 0$. Thus the stationary E line slopes upwards. Consider now the equation for $\dot{B}$ in the same way

$$\left.\frac{dE}{dB}\right|_{\dot{B}=0} = ip > 0 \tag{2A.21}$$

Thus $\dot{B} = 0$ also slopes upwards.

We note for future use that

$$\left.\begin{aligned}
\frac{\partial\dot{E}}{\partial E} &= (\rho-i) > 0 \\[6pt]
\frac{\partial\dot{E}}{\partial B} &= -\frac{W_{33}}{pW_{11}} < 0 \\[6pt]
\frac{\partial\dot{B}}{\partial E} &= -\frac{1}{p} < 0 \\[6pt]
\frac{\partial\dot{B}}{\partial B} &= i > 0
\end{aligned}\right\} \tag{2A.22}$$

Using all this information we find that depending on the relative slopes of $\dot{E} = 0$ and $\dot{B} = 0$ there are two alternative possibilities given in figures 2A.1 and 2A.2. Figure 2A.2 shows the case where the model is totally unstable, which we ignore as uninteresting from an economic point of view.

Considering figure 2A.1, we find, as is usual in these models, that equilibrium Q depicts saddle point stability, so that the only convergent path is SS. For a given level of B, the optimizing household chooses the appropriate level of E on the saddle path SS and moves towards the stationary equilibrium. As the Mangasarian theorem (1966) shows, this is also the grand optimum path.[11]

The Jacobian or matrix of first partial derivatives for (2A.18), (2A.19) is

$$
J = \begin{bmatrix} \dfrac{\partial \dot{E}}{\partial E} & \dfrac{\partial \dot{E}}{\partial B} \\[2ex] \dfrac{\partial \dot{B}}{\partial E} & \dfrac{\partial \dot{B}}{\partial B} \end{bmatrix} = \begin{bmatrix} (\rho - i) & -\dfrac{W_{33}}{p W_{11}} \\[2ex] -\dfrac{1}{p} & i \end{bmatrix}
$$

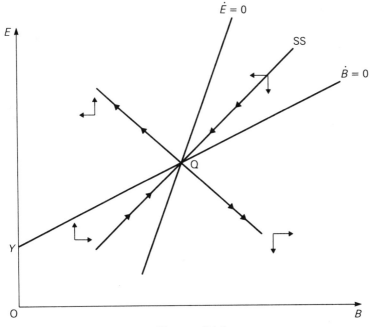

FIGURE 2A.1

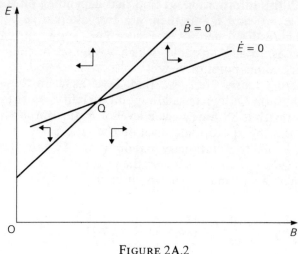

FIGURE 2A.2

Since the trace is positive, one of the characteristic roots must be positive. Thus the determinant $|J|$ must be negative for saddle point stability. Negativity of $|J|$ gives the shape of the E and B stationary lines in figure 2A.1.

Now consider a change in p and the consequent Laursen-Metzler effect, that is the effect of a rise in p on E, expenditure measured in terms of the home good. We are concerned here with *both* the effect in long run equilibrium as well as that on the transition path. Essentially the change in p will cause both $\dot{E}=0$ and $\dot{B}=0$ lines to shift, thus changing the stationary state Q and the long run levels of expenditure E. The short run response of the control variable E will also be different. In general the outcome is not clear and it is this that causes the ambiguity in the Laursen-Metzler effect.

Let the terms of trade p rise (say by an imposition of tariffs). The line depicting $\dot{B}=0$ will swivel anticlockwise around the point $(V, 0)$ in the (E, B) plane. This is because for $\dot{B}=0=B$, $E=V$ always (see equation (2A.19)). This is simple. The change in $\dot{E}=0$ is, however, not at all clear cut and different possibilities remain. To consider the behaviour of the E stationary line, take from (2A.18)

$$\dot{E} = 0 = \frac{W_1}{W_{11}}(\rho - i) - \frac{W_3}{pW_{11}} \tag{2A.23}$$

and totally differentiate with respect to all arguments. Remember the simplifying assumptions already made. Then we have

$$(\rho - i)\, dE - \frac{W_{33}}{pW_{11}}\, dB = -\frac{1}{W_{11}}\left((\rho - i)\, W_{12} + \frac{W_3}{p^2}\right) dp \quad (2A.24)$$

Since the coefficient of dp on the right-hand side of equation (2A.24) cannot be unambiguously signed (due to the presence of W_{12}), we do not know whether $\dot{E} = 0$ will shift upwards or downwards.

Consider a very special case with the Cobb–Douglas utility function in log linear form (Varian, 1984). Then the indirect utility function is

$$W = \log E - \alpha_1 \log p + \alpha_2 \log B \qquad (2A.25)$$

Then $W_{12} = 0$, and (2A.24) becomes

$$(\rho - i)\, dE - \frac{W_{33}}{W_{11}}\, dB = -\frac{W_3}{W_{11}}\, dp \qquad (2A.26)$$

It is clear that a rise in p will cause E to increase *for any given B* to maintain $\dot{E} = 0$. The $\dot{E} = 0$ line will therefore shift upwards.

One possibility is shown in figure 2A.3 where the initial equilibrium is Q_1 and the post terms of trade deterioration equilibrium is Q_2. With a rise in p, the stationary lines $\dot{E} = 0 = \dot{B}$ shift as shown, so does the stationary state Q_1 to Q_2. However, since B is predetermined at B_1, the control is adjusted to attain the new saddle path $S_2 S_2$. Initially, therefore the household moves from Q_1 to F, this entails a *rise* in E, expenditure measured in home goods.

The Laursen–Metzler effect is vindicated, since E rises with p. However, the saddle path is negatively sloped, so along it E *falls*. Thus we have an initial rise in E followed by a continuous decline on the transition path. Comparing long run equilibria Q_1 and Q_2 it is also clear that expenditure falls in the long run. (This of course may not be necessarily so.)

Alternatively, we may have $W_{12} < 0$ and sufficiently strong to make

$$\partial E / \partial p \,|_{\dot{E} = 0} < 0 \quad \text{for given } B$$

(see (2A.24)). Then $\dot{E} = 0$ shifts downwards (rightwards) and we may get the case of figure 2A.4.[12] Here the long run values of E and B are higher after the terms of trade deterioration so that E rises with p in the *very long run*. However, the transitional phase

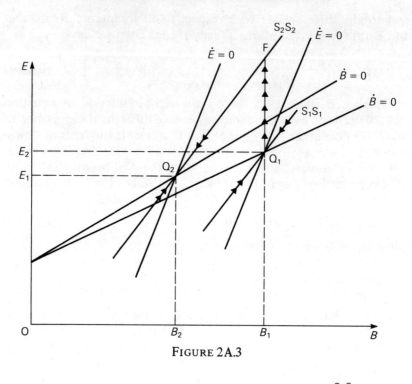

FIGURE 2A.3

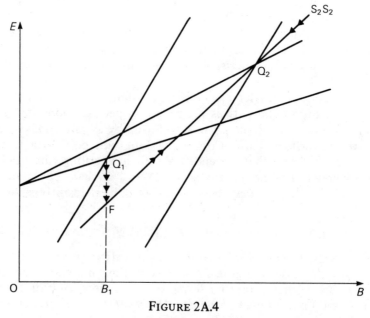

FIGURE 2A.4

shows E *falling* at the time of the rise in relative price. The representative household first reduces expenditure (measured in home goods) from Q_1 to F and then raises it from F to Q_2.

Note that both cases consider an unanticipated rise in p which is also expected to be permanent. An announced or anticipated change in p that is expected to occur τ periods hence will essentially have similar effects, except that the household will start moving towards the saddle path even before the change in p has actually taken place, so that it will reach S_2S_2 τ periods hence, that is when the change occurs. Again this may entail either a fall or rise in E consequent on a terms of trade deterioration.

Finally, we must remember that the analysis has been conducted (as the diagrams clearly show) on the basis of a positive bond holding $B > 0$. The original Laursen–Metzler world was strictly Keynesian in the sense that B was zero. It is quite simple to reorient the analysis in terms of initial $B = B_1 = 0$ and the conclusions are very similar.

It is clear, therefore, that the Laursen–Metzler effect has to be used with caution. It is not unambiguous at all, rather both the short-run and the long-run effect of p on E can go either way. This appendix is a formal justification of the fact that $\partial E / \partial p$ cannot be signed unequivocally, unless much more information is available regarding the parameters of the model.

Notes

1 This is also the method used by Krugman (1982).
2 The model has been set up in excess demand form so that the pseudo-dynamic structure we would postulate for it would be one wherein output and the exchange rate rise when there is an excess demand for them. Therefore, the (time) differential equations for output and the exchange rate would have positive speed-of-adjustment coefficients on the respective excess demands. Assuming that the latter were linear or could be linearized around the equilibrium values of output and the exchange rate, then we could write

$$\frac{dV}{d\tau} = \theta_1(C_1 + a_{11}V + a_{12}r) \tag{1}$$

$$\frac{dr}{d\tau} = \theta_2(C_2 + a_{21}V + a_{22}r) \tag{2}$$

Here the parameters C_1 and C_2 denote constants, $a_i \gtrless 0$ and θ_1, θ_2 are positive by construction. The general solution to this second-order differential equation system will be of this nature

$$V(\tau) = \bar{V} + \alpha_1 \exp(\lambda_1 t) + \beta_1 \exp(\lambda_2 t) \tag{3}$$

$$r(\tau) = \bar{r} + \alpha_2 \exp(\lambda_1 t) + \beta_2 \exp(\lambda_2 t) \tag{4}$$

Here: $\bar{V}$ and $\bar{r}$ denote the equilibrium values of output and the rate of exchange; α_i, β_i are constants dependent upon, *inter alia*, the initial conditions in the model (the starting values at some arbitrary $t = 0$, of output and of the rate of exchange); and λ_1, λ_2 are the roots of the characteristic equation of the system described by equations (3) and (4) which is

$$|A - \lambda I| = 0 \tag{5}$$

where

$$A = \begin{bmatrix} \theta_1 a_{11} & \theta_1 a_{12} \\ \theta_2 a_{21} & \theta_2 a_{22} \end{bmatrix} \tag{6}$$

and I is the (2×2) identity matrix. In the current example, this equation will be a second degree polynomial in λ, producing the two values of λ_1 and λ_2 required in the solutions to this second-order system, epitomized in (3) and (4). From those equations it is apparent that any difference that does occur between $V(t)$ and $\bar{V}$ will gradually disappear as time elapses if λ_1 and λ_2 are negative; since the two exponential terms converge on zero as time τ approaches infinity. If equation (5) yields complex roots the requirement for

$$V(\tau) \underset{\tau \to \infty}{\to} \bar{V}$$

is that the *real* parts of those roots be negative. In that eventuality the equations describing the path of V and of r will exhibit fluctuations but those fluctuations will be damped. The conditions that engender negative real roots, or negative real parts to complex roots, are conditions appertaining to the properties of the matrix A, and hence to the Jacobian of the comparative statics system. Thus, in full, we have that equation (5) is

$$\lambda^2 - (\theta_1 a_{11} + \theta_2 a_{22})\lambda + \theta_1 \theta_2 (a_{11} a_{22} - a_{12} a_{21}) = 0 \tag{7}$$

The term in λ in equation (7) is the sum of the elements on the leading diagonal of the matrix A, namely its trace. If $\theta_1 = \theta_2$ that is identical with the trace of the Jacobian of the comparative statics system. The constant term in equation (3) is the determinant of that Jacobian multiplied by the product of the two adjustment coefficients. The standard formula for solving a quadratic equation reveals that λ_1 and λ_2 will be real (or have negative real parts) iff trace $A < 0$ and det $A > 0$. Therefore, as Samuelson's (1947) correspondence principle informs us, the stability requirements of any model have implications for the sign of the determinant of its comparative statics formulation. In the above we have referred to stability conditions for a second-order system. Later on in the book we shall need to employ stability conditions from at least a third-order system. The Routh theorem (Routh, 1955; Samuelson, 1947) permits us to generalize the results to an nth order system, composed of n first-order differential equations. We define A to be the Jacobian matrix of the appropriate comparative statics system

$$dy = A^{-1} \, dx \tag{8}$$

Here dy is a vector of changes in the n endogenous variables; and dx is the vector of changes in the exogenous variables. Therefore

$$\dot{y} = Ay \tag{9}$$

where $\dot{y} = dy/d\tau$, speeds of adjustment are assumed to be unity for simplicity and the excess demand/supply functions are linear either *per se*, or at the equilibrium configurations of the economic system. The characteristic equation from (9) will be an nth degree polynomial

$$a_0 \lambda^n + a_1 \lambda^{n-1} + \ldots + a_{n-1} \lambda + a_n = 0 \tag{10}$$

The Routh theorem provides us with the conditions under which the real parts of all of the n roots will be negative. In essence they will be negative if and only if the first n determinants in this sequence are positive

$$|a_1|, \quad \begin{vmatrix} a_1 & a_3 \\ a_0 & a_2 \end{vmatrix}, \quad \begin{vmatrix} a_1 & a_3 & a_5 \\ a_0 & a_2 & a_4 \\ 0 & a_1 & a_3 \end{vmatrix}, \quad \begin{vmatrix} a_1 & a_3 & a_5 & a_7 \\ a_0 & a_2 & a_4 & a_6 \\ 0 & a_1 & a_3 & a_5 \\ 0 & a_0 & a_2 & a_4 \end{vmatrix}, \ldots \tag{11}$$

with $a_m = 0$, for $m > n$, and a_0 is always taken to be positive. We deduce that for the second-order system described above these requirements amount to trace $A < 0$, det $A > 0$. For the case of a third-order system the Routhian conditions state that for stability: trace $A < 0$ *but* det $A < 0$ and additionally

$$[(a_{11}a_{22} - a_{21}a_{12}) + (a_{11}a_{33} - a_{31}a_{13}) + (a_{22}a_{33} - a_{32}a_{23})] > 0$$

In general, the Routhian conditions stipulate that the sign of det A should be the sign of $(-1)^n$, where n is the order of the system. Strictly speaking, when we have to resort to a pseudo-dynamic specification of a model and linearize it around its equilibrium, the stability conditions relate only to local stability.

3 Taking total differentials of the hoarding function $H(.)$ and assuming the initial tariff rate is zero

$$dH = \frac{H_1}{P}(dV + rI \, dt) - \frac{H_1}{P} y \frac{dP}{P} \tag{12}$$

Tariff revenues are redistributed to households and $R > 0$. Since

$$\frac{dP}{P} = \delta\,\frac{dr}{r} + \delta\,dt \tag{13}$$

We can substitute this into (12) to get

$$dH = \frac{H_1}{P}\left[dV + \left(-\frac{\delta y}{r}\right) dr + (rI - \delta y)\,dt \right] \tag{14}$$

Now take total differentials of B/P where B is value of exports minus imports

$$d\frac{B}{P} = \frac{1}{P}\left[(X_1\,dr - r\,dI - I\,dr) - \frac{B}{P}\,dP \right] \tag{15}$$

From (2.69)

$$dI = I_1\,dV + I_1 rI\,dt + I_2\,dr + I_2 r\,dt \tag{16}$$

Substituting (16) into (15) we get

$$d\frac{B}{P} = \frac{1}{P}\left\{ (-rI_1)\,dV + \left(X_1 - I - rI_2 - \frac{\delta B}{r}\right) dr \right.$$

$$\left. + \,[-r^2(I_1 I + I_2) - \delta B]\,dt \right\} \tag{17}$$

Substituting (17) and (14) into equation (2.70) and rearranging terms produces equation (2.72). Given $dX = X_1\,dr$ and equation (16), it can be seen that equation (2.73) is immediate.

4   Strictly, this is true for all tariff rates below the optimum tariff t^*. The latter is given when $dA^*/dt = 0$, $dA^{*2}/d^2 t < 0$. For this to hold we need

$$t^* = \frac{I}{X_1 - \tilde{I}}$$

which using the equilibrium condition $X = r\tilde{I}$ comes out to be

$$t^* = \frac{1}{x - 1} \tag{18}$$

where x is the price elasticity of exports of the home country, alternatively the price elasticity of import demand of the rest of the world. Assuming $x - 1 > 0$, we get $t^* > 0$. Thus if the initial tariff is *zero* and $x > 1$, then welfare *must* increase after the imposition of tariffs in the full employment case.

5   We have also retained the assumption that the government does not claim any of the tariff revenue for itself; should it do that, together with how it apportions its expenditure on imported and domestically pro-

duced goods, it can produce different effects on the real macroeconomy. The only paper that has analysed the question of the disbursement of the revenues is by Tower (1973); he considered several possibilities: the one that gives a definite boost to output is if the government hands the tariff revenue to foreigners.

6 This does not change any essential conclusion.

7 This follows Obstfeld (1982). See also Varian (1984) for the properties of W which is assumed to be well defined.

8 These formal problems arise in the case of the 'paradox of borrowing'.

9 The indirect utility function is actually

$$W = W(P_H E, P_H, P_I, P_I B)$$

which by its homogeneity property (of degree zero) is written as

$$W = W(E, p, B)$$

Roy's identity states that

$$H = \frac{-\partial W/\partial P_H}{\partial W/\partial P_H E}$$

$$I = \frac{-\partial W/\partial P_I}{\partial W/\partial P_H E}$$

10 Ignoring the exponential term we have

$$\hat{H} = W(E, p, B) + \Omega \left(\frac{V}{p} - \frac{E}{p} + iB \right)$$

$$\left[\frac{\partial \hat{H}}{\partial E} = W_1 - \frac{\Omega}{p} \right]\left[\frac{\partial^2 \hat{H}}{\partial E^2} = W_{11} < 0 \right]$$

thus $\hat{H}$ is strictly concave in E and satisfies the second-order condition for a maximand. Also the maximum value of $\hat{H}$ corresponds to a unique value of E.

11 The path which converges to the stationary state SS is indeed optimal given the sufficiency conditions for optimal controls. These are

$$B \geqslant 0$$

$$\lim_{t \to \infty} \exp (-\rho t) B = 0$$

12 This result is similar to that of Obstfeld (1982), except that his model has a different specification.

3

Output, the Exchange Rate
and Quotas

The attempted protection of domestic industry, in the hope that short- and long-run economic activity can thereby be stimulated by seeking to reduce imports (at least initially, since that might be all that is required, as we have already proved in chapter 2), through the levying of a general tariff is not the only restrictive device, of course, that can be used by the government. Rather than work through the mechanism of price adjustment, the government can adopt a policy of imposing quantity limits on the importables that it will permit to cross its frontier.

The choice of either controlling price or quantity is a familiar one in all the theoretical analysis of economic policy, whether it be of a micro- or a macronature. In a world of *certainty* for one simple market then there is no need for the government to make an effective choice between these because they can be shown to be equivalent. The definition of equivalence that is used is something like this: if the government should intervene in the market for a particular commodity to raise its price to a pre-assigned level with the aim of increasing the share of sales obtained by domestic suppliers, they can impose a certain level of tariff t^*, but to that t^* there will correspond a limit on the quantity of imports I^* that could be imposed instead, and the outcome would be the same, in respect of all of the characteristics of the market, as the imposition of t^* would be.

Let us consider a simple illustrative example of a market for one commodity, say fountain pens. If this market is a perfectly competitive one (in the domestic economy) and is small in relationship to the total level of production in the economy, then we can characterize the market situation by elementary demand and supply equations. The demand for fountain pens, in aggregate, will be dependent upon their own price, *ceteris paribus*, where

64

the latter will consist of the inevitable set of variables, income and the prices of other competing and complementary goods. By construction we can ignore that set whilst examining the 'price versus quantity' issue of controlling the fountain pen market. Again, under the assumptions made concerning domestic production, if firms in the industry maximize their profits, we can invoke the elementary textbook representation of supply, by relating supply positively to price.

Hence, the situation will be the familiar one depicted on figure 3.1, where P denotes the price of a fountain pen and Q stands for quantity (bought and/or sold). The demand by domestic residents for fountain pens is epitomized in DD, and the willingness of home manufacturers to place quantities of pens on the home market is encapsulated in SS. Naturally, on the *ceteris paribus* assumption, equilibrium will be established at a point such as E, with price equal to P_0 and quantity traded equal to Q_0.

Suppose now that the domestic market has been infiltrated by manufacturers of pens in the rest of the world. Further, let us imagine that the supply schedule of those manufacturers is perfectly elastic at the world price of P_w; hence the schedule $P_w P_w$ on figure 3.1. The consequence of the government's permitting free entry of overseas supplies of pens onto the domestic

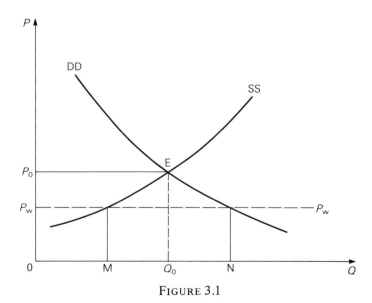

FIGURE 3.1

market will be that the price falls to P_w and the amount supplied by domestic producers is reduced to M from Q_0; imports of MN make up the difference between home demand and home supply at the prevailing price.

Should the government wish to redress the balance and protect domestic industry to the full by restraining foreign competition it can do so without any difficulty. It is at once apparent that it could impose one kind of tariff or another on importables to restore output to the level Q_0. Either a specific tariff (i.e. tariff/tax per unit) of $P_0 P_w$ or an *ad valorem* tariff of $P_0 P_w / P_w$ per cent would accomplish the government's objective. A complete brake has been imposed on imports without any difficulty; the only costs (in reality) would be of an administrative nature, arising out of the need to supervise the payment and collection of the import tax.

A figure such as figure 3.1 enables us to construct the domestic economy's import demand schedule (I) for pens, which is drawn on figure 3.2. At $P = P_0$, imports fall to zero, and they approach their maximum as P approaches zero.

As the world price fluctuates between zero and P_0, *ceteris paribus*, imports also fluctuate between Q_{max} and zero respectively. Strictly, for given income, the 'import demand' function drawn is the inverse of the import demand function, $I = I(P, Y)$, of the

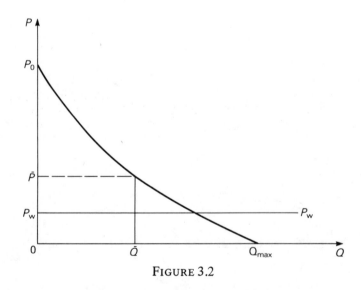

FIGURE 3.2

kind we have used in chapters 1 and 2. Suppose the government wishes to adopt a strategy to contain imports to the quantity $\bar{Q}$ on figure 3.2. It can achieve that outcome by 'choosing' the domestic price of fountain pens. It is able to accomplish that task by imposing a tariff on the world price P_w.

Alternatively, since the presumption is that the government is all-omniscient, as it knows the exact specification of $I(.)$ and P_w, the government can fix the quantity of imports at the level $\bar{Q}$. Such a quota policy must produce the same outcome as the imposition of a tariff to lever up P_w to $\bar{P}$: this outcome is guaranteed *ex hypothesi*. The quota $\bar{Q}$ will be equivalent to the specific tariff $\bar{P}P_w$; both will produce the same level of imports, of domestic output, of price (and by implication, of domestic demand). In sum, the two policies will generate an identical vector of market characteristics at the new, trade-restricting, equilibrium.

That equivalence theorem was first demonstrated by Bhagwati (1965) and is, with hindsight, quite transparent. The particular assumptions that enable this equivalence to emerge are that the government has full information about the market for pens; and it can exploit that information because of the *ceteris paribus* assumption. There is no necessity to consider the repercussions of the tariff/quota on the level of *income*. Effectively, the government can exploit the one-to-one relationship between price and quantity, by controlling either variable and letting the other be determined in a known way by the market participants.

A world of uncertainty can cause the equivalence of price and quantity control to be broken. There is an extensive literature on this topic, for individual markets both in terms of planning models for Soviet-type economies (Weitzman, 1974; Yohe, 1977) and especially in the context of international trade (Young, 1980, Dickinson, Driscoll and Ford, 1982); but the non-equivalence that has been the overwhelming conclusion of the literature on the comparison of tariffs and quotas under uncertainty, is not without objection. We have shown elsewhere, for example, that for some stated objectives, such as protection (of domestic industry), tariffs and quotas can be equivalent if a Kalman filter policy (a maximum information policy) is followed by government in setting the optimal tariff or quota. Uncertainty about the location of the domestic economy's import demand function and/or about the foreign price, need not overly concern the government. It does not need to choose a tariff level or a quota, it changes the price of fountain pens according to the (current period) quantity imported, or it changes the quota imported given the (current period) price of pens. The 'filtering' of information by observation of the market and the consequent adaptation of policy is the optimal strategy to adopt. However, we cannot pursue an exposition of that proposition here (Driscoll and Ford, 1983).

Our concern, essentially, is with a world of 'certainty', but with one which can be buffeted this way and that by random forces on a one-off basis. This is the type of scenario that obtains implicitly when the pseudo-dynamic or true dynamic path of the variables in the macroeconomy are studied in later chapters. However, we are not concerned with what we might call true uncertainty, or risk (depending upon preference), whereby the behavioural functions in the model are subject to random disturbances (i.e. have additive errors attached to them à la econometrics) or have random parameters (i.e. there exist multiplicative, random disturbances).

There are two issues that are germane to the idea of the equivalence of tariffs and quotas in our macromodel. The first stems from the fact that the one market model is able, quite legitimately and with little sacrifice of generality, to ignore any spill-over effects from the fountain pen market to the rest of the markets in the economy. Here we are evaluating the role of price quantity controls on the whole of the demand for imported goods and thence on the whole economy. The other issue relates to the fact that equivalence is defined with reference to some policy objective. The tariff and the quota are only equivalent because for any tariff t^* that will generate a (P, Q) in the fountain pen market there is a quota $\bar{Q}$ that will achieve the same result. That does *not* permit us to draw the implication that a change in a tariff will produce identical effects on the market as will a change in a quota. The multiplier effects may be dissimilar in general. The government must solve the economic model first before it imposes a t^*; and likewise if it operates a quota $\bar{Q}$ that is designed to be as effective as t^*.

The literature on quotas as an instrument of macroeconomic policy under floating exchange rates has tended to the view that they are equivalent to tariffs. Indeed, in certain conditions tariffs and quotas will be fully equivalent to each other, but the conditions that must hold for stability will be different for the two types of policy and their multiplier effects will diverge. Nevertheless, for expositional purposes, the models used to analyse quotas have to be set out in such a format that their construction assumes the existence of a tariff-equivalent quota, under certain conditions.

There are four different ways in which we can view the equivalence/non-equivalence problem. In terms of policy objectives, for a given target, there exists a set of equivalent tariff and quota in the Bhagwati (1965) sense. For a single market, if the government wishes to curtail imports to a certain level it can do so by means of a quota or alternatively by a tariff. In our macroeconomic model, if the authorities desire to change output by a specified level through commercial policies it can impose a tariff, causing expenditure switching, which may achieve the target; alternatively, it can impose a quota.

The second concept deals with market structure. A quota is a quantitative restriction, buyers are rationed, and this drives prices upwards. To compare the tariff/quota effects it is desirable to have a similar model formulation. Thus, we assume that the quotas are auctioned off to bidders who, given a lower domestic supply of importables, will bid up prices. The government thus collects a revenue from the quota, similar to tariff revenues, and the implicit quota rate (or factor) is the amount by which prices have increased. However, unlike the case for tariffs, there is no price arbitrage at the margin and the domestic price of importables is completely divorced from world prices.

It is possible that if there is competition all round, the effects of both policies on other macroeconomic variables, in addition to the target, might be the same. But quotas, by their very nature, impose physical controls on imports and may lead to a reduction in the degree of competition. The growth of oligopolistic structures sheltered under quantitative restrictions will have more basic effects than can be analysed in traditional macromodels.

It is often argued that restrictive commercial policies, by reducing competition, would lead to a fall in productivity. If this were to be so, it would have important implications for the form of the functions that we use in our models. For example, if decisions regarding investment strategy are altered as a result of policy, the investment schedule might alter and so will the hoarding function. The policy might also affect (should there be one) the aggregate supply function. In so far as alternative commercial policies, tariffs and quotas, have different effects on market structures there may be non-equivalence.

However, we should be especially careful about the foregoing point of view. Conventional theories of the firm imply that the degree of 'competitiveness' in the product market does not affect the cost minimization/profit maximization decisions of the firm. Therefore, a reduction in competition *per se* should not alter the input–output mix that the firm chooses optimally. Thus, productivity should not be affected by commercial policy-induced changes in competition. However, the *scale* of the firm might be affected, and this in turn might lead to productivity shifts.

The third way in which the equivalence issue can be looked at is in terms of the formal apparatus needed to handle the problem, and the concomitant economic intuition. As we shall see in the next section, even though there are a number of similarities between the quota and tariff models, they operate in different ways, particularly out of equilibrium. This will become clear as we proceed.

Finally, even under competition, the effects of a quota and tariff, which achieve the same level of targeted national output, may be different on other variables of the model. For example, a quota which raises prices of importables by 1 per cent will not normally have the same import effect as a tariff of 1 per cent. This will be proved formally later. In this sense there may be non-equivalence. But a more important difference remains.

In the ensuing section we shall state the conceptual changes that have to be effected to the MM (Mundellian model) to render it amenable to the analysis of a quota. We shall also demonstrate the equivalence of the quota and the tariff in the first sense mentioned earlier, despite the fact that the government now has to take cognizance of the interdependence between the quota and national output and, in the reverse direction, of the link between national output and the domestic price of importables, completely separated now from the rest of the world due to rationing at home. We draw attention to the fact that the analysis of commercial policy as applied to one market is concerned exclusively with protectionism. The aim of the government is to reduce the level of imports; and, thereby, to increase the share that domestic producers can claim of the market for the given commodity. At the macrolevel the initial objective of the government in implementing commercial policies is to cause expenditure switching of that kind; which, initially, at the least, will raise domestic output, as in the case of the 'particular equilibrium' of the one-commodity framework. But because of its income effects in a macrosetting, the eventual outcome can be that imports rise with a general tariff. A general quota set below the free-trade equilibrium must, *ex hypothesi*, in the context of a macromodel, reduce the level of imports, no matter what its impact on output happens to be. It is possible to have an expansionary tariff in the more general sense that the sale of foreign goods can also rise. A quota is essentially a beggar-my-neighbour policy.

3.1   *Quotas and the Mundellian (Keynesian) Model*

For our purposes, since we need only to pay limited attention to quotas, we shall utilize the basic Mundellian model (MM) portrayed in chapter 2. The MM constructed to handle a general quota on importables can be characterized by the equations

$$H = \frac{X(r) - r\bar{I}}{P} \tag{3.1}$$

$$X(r) = r\bar{I} \tag{3.2}$$

$$H = H\left(\frac{y}{P}\right) \tag{3.3}$$

$$y = V + R \tag{3.4}$$

$$R = \tau r \bar{I} \tag{3.5}$$

$$P = P_m^\delta \tag{3.6}$$

$$P_m = F(V + \tau r \bar{I}, \bar{I}), \quad \text{given } I = I(V + \tau r I, P_m)$$
$$\text{and } I = \bar{I} \tag{3.7}$$

$$P_m = r(1 + \tau) \tag{3.8}$$

Most of these relationships and definitions are familiar enough at this stage, but we should perhaps pass a comment or two about them. Equations (3.1) and (3.2) represent the conditions required for the attainment of internal and external balance respectively. In using equation (3.2) specified in this way we are implying that the quota is binding in the new equilibrium. $H(.)$ is the hoarding function. $\bar{I}$ is the quota level of imports. The revenue generated by the quota is defined in equation (3.5) where τ is the implicit quota rate associated with the quota. P_m is the domestic price of importables (recall our definition of the exchange rate and the fact that the rest of the world's price at which it will supply importables is set at unity in world currency units). $F(.)$ is the inverse of the import demand function $I(.)$; and it is $F(.)$ which, *ceteris paribus*, determines for a specified quota $\bar{I}$ the level of τ. Equation (3.7) states that the supply and demand for I is equal so there is equilibrium in the market for importables.

How, in effect, does the quota system operate? In essence we assume that licences to import are auctioned off to competitive bidders; these may be the overseas producers themselves or some agent acting on their behalf in the domestic economy. We assume that the licences have to be purchased. The revenue so generated is retained by the government (which issues the licences, of course) and given as a transfer payment to the domestic non-government sector. We do not, therefore, become entangled in considering alternative disbursement of the revenue, along the lines indicated in chapter 2: some variations on this theme have been discussed by Tower (1973). The price that importers are prepared to pay for the licences depends upon their view of the equilibrium price that will be made on the domestic market after the quota has been imposed and revenues disbursed and spent. In effect, it is assumed that importers solve the model of the economy given by equations (3.1)–(3.8) to determine that equilibrium price; they therefore are willing to incur a cost at the margin equal to the marginal revenue from the licence. Given the 'certainty' implicit in these kinds of macromodel, economic agents can be endowed with rational expectations. The difference between the market clearing prices before and after the imposition of the quota provides us with the *implicit* quota rate of the sort portrayed, therefore, on figure 3.1.

There were two endogenous variables in the tariff model, output and the exchange rate. Given a parametrically fixed tariff rate, V and r were determined by the model, imports emerged as a residual. In the quota model, however, there are three endogenous variables, since V, r and τ have to be determined simultaneously. Thus, there are three implicit dynamic (or pseudo-dynamic) equations, to describe the behaviour of these variables, out of equilibrium. These are

$$\dot{V} = \alpha \left(\frac{X(r) - r\bar{I}}{P} - H \right) \tag{3.9}$$

$$\dot{r} = \beta [r\bar{I} - X(r)] \tag{3.10}$$

$$\dot{\tau} = \gamma [F(V + \tau r\bar{I}, \bar{I}) - r(1 + \tau)] \tag{3.11}$$

where α, β, $\gamma > 0$. Equations (3.9) and (3.10) are standard; excess demand for output increases supply; a trade deficit causes the exchange rate to depreciate. Equation (3.11) considers the domestic market for importables, whose price is now $r(1 + \tau)$. The $F(.)$ function gives the demand price of importables when the quota is binding. Thus if the actual price is below the level given by $F(.)$, there is excess demand for I and τ will rise. This will increase P_m, hence equilibrating the importables market.

The partial derivatives of $F(.)$ and $I(.)$, of course, are related. It can be shown easily that

$$F_1 = -\frac{I_1}{I_2}, \quad F_2 = \frac{1}{I_2} \tag{3.12}$$

If we make the usual single-market stability assumption, then an excess demand for importables, within the economy, will drive the implicit quota rate τ upwards. So we need

$$\frac{\partial \dot{\tau}}{\partial \tau} = r(F_1 \bar{I} - 1) < 0 \tag{3.13}$$

This is equivalent to assuming that $(II_1 + I_2) < 0$. In view of our earlier discussion, condition (3.13) may not hold. The overall dynamic model (3.9)–(3.11) can still be stable depending on other assumptions necessary to satisfy the Routhian stability conditions. Let us, however, assume for simplicity that (3.13) holds, this will not change our final conclusions.

On the supposition that to each $\bar{I}$ there must be a τ, in the way outlined, and that the revenue is transferred to the non-government sector, we can see quite transparently from equations (3.1)–(3.8), considered in conjunction with their counterparts for the general tariff, that the government *can* establish a value for $\bar{I}$ that will produce a Bhagwati equivalence between that quota and a specified level of the general tariff t. Thus, for a value of the latter of t^* there must be a level of imports I^*. If the government sets $\bar{I} = I^*$, the two commercial policies must be equivalent in terms of their impact on the importables market in the domestic economy (that is, we do have Bhagwati equivalence). But it follows, *mutatis mutandis*, that we have macroeconomic, or economy-wide, equivalence of the two forms of commercial policy in this MM. This is because I^*, t^*, *ex definitione*, must generate the same (V, r) in the economy as each other. The solution of $\bar{I} = I^*$ does not only mean that the quantity traded, and the domestic price, of importables are identical with the outcome for t^*; the intervening scalar variable in the import demand function must, by implication, be the same for I^* as for t^*. The economy-wide dimension to the model does not prevent Bhagwati equivalence from bringing about macroeconomic equivalence: but in essence this notion of equivalence is a tautology. It is true *ex definitione*. However, in a more general sense, as mentioned earlier, there will be major differences between quotas and tariffs and it is these that we shall stress.

Let us now turn, briefly, to consider the multiplier effects of a general quota. Import levels will now be restricted to be below their free trade quantities, and we shall investigate the effect on V, r and τ for a given $d\bar{I} < 0$. From equations (3.1)–(3.8) we deduce that (at trade balance equal to zero, $X(r) = r\bar{I}$)

$$\begin{bmatrix} a_{11} & a_{12} & a_{13} \\ a_{21} & a_{22} & a_{23} \\ a_{31} & a_{32} & a_{33} \end{bmatrix} \begin{bmatrix} dV \\ dr \\ d\tau \end{bmatrix} = \begin{bmatrix} K_1 \\ K_2 \\ K_3 \end{bmatrix} \qquad (3.14)$$

where

$$a_{11} = -H_1 \qquad (3.14a)$$

$$a_{12} = \frac{X_1 - \bar{I} + H_1\bar{I} + H_1R}{r} \qquad (3.14b)$$

$$a_{13} = H_1R \qquad (3.14c)$$

$$a_{21} = a_{23} = 0 \qquad (3.14d)$$

$$a_{22} = (\bar{I} - X_1) \qquad (3.14e)$$

$$a_{31} = F_1 \qquad (3.14f)$$

$$a_{32} = -1 \qquad (3.14g)$$

$$a_{33} = r(F_1\bar{I} - 1) \qquad (3.14h)$$

$$K_1 = r\,d\bar{I} \qquad (3.14i)$$

$$K_2 = -r\,d\bar{I} \qquad (3.14j)$$

$$K_3 = -F_2\,d\bar{I} \qquad (3.14k)$$

We have used the following conditions in the derivation of (3.14); $\delta = (rI + R/V + \tau r\bar{I})$, initial $\tau = 0$, $dP_m/P_m = [(dr/r) + d\tau]$. Let us stress once again that all variables are evaluated at the new equilibrium, while partial derivatives of functions are evaluated at the initial equilibrium. Given infinitesimal changes, the latter is a standard assumption. The former is required if we wish to preserve the effect of quotas in the model, otherwise there is a danger of removing the effects of policy. Thus, for example, the revenue R is not put equal to zero.

The determinant of the Jacobian is

$$|J| = H_1(X_1 - I)(-r + F_1 r\bar{I} + RF_1) < 0 \qquad (3.15)$$

which is assumed negative for stability. Note that it is not *necessary* to assume that $(X_1 - I) > 0$ for stability of the whole system. But since it is a reasonable assumption, given the Marshall–Lerner conditions for the quota model as well as some empirical support that export price elasticity x is greater than unity (in equilibrium $X_1 - I = I(x - 1)$), we maintain it. The Laursen–Metzler condition requires that $H_1 > 0$. Then $(-r + F_1 r\bar{I} + RF_1)$ < 0. Further, note that $|J|$ is negative, since the total differentials are taken by setting up the original system in excess demand form.

The output multiplier is

$$\frac{\partial V}{\partial I} = \frac{H_1\bar{I}}{|J|} [r^2(F_1\bar{I} - 1) + \frac{H_1 R}{|J|} [F_1 r\bar{I} + F_2(I - X_1)] \qquad (3.16)$$

From (3.16) we observe that $\partial V/\partial\bar{I}$ has two terms, one of which is positive, given $(F_1\bar{I} - 1) < 0$, but the other is negative, given $(X_1 - I) > 0$, $F_2 < 0$, $F_1 > 0$. Thus the final effect on V for a change in $\bar{I}$ is unclear. If the second term dominates then it is possible for $\partial V/\partial\bar{I} < 0$. Therefore the more stringent is the quota the higher can output be.

We can understand what is happening more clearly by using (3.12) in the second expression for (3.16). This now becomes

$$\left(\frac{-H_1 R\bar{I}}{|J| I_2}\right) (rI_1 + x - 1)$$

Again the Metzler non-paradox (recall the discussion in chapter 2) requires $(rI_1 + x - 1) > 0$. In any case we have assumed that $x > 1$, where $x = rX_1/X$ is the export elasticity, thus the Metzler paradox cannot hold. The similarity with the tariff case is obvious.

The effect on the exchange rate is clear since it *must* come down to preserve external balance, given a binding quota set at a lower level than the free-trade situation. Formally

$$\frac{\partial r}{\partial\bar{I}} = \frac{r}{X_1 - \bar{I}} \qquad (3.17)$$

Finally, consider the change in the price of importables. We have first

$$\frac{\partial \tau}{\partial \bar{I}} = -\left(\frac{F_2}{-r + F_1 r \bar{I} + RF_1} + \frac{1}{X_1 - \bar{I}}\right) \tag{3.18}$$

which is negative given (3.15). Thus as $\bar{I}$ falls with a stricter quota, τ rises as expected. Since the exchange rate appreciates and the implicit quota rate increases, it is important to observe the effect on the price of importables P_m. Noting $P_m = r(1 + \tau)$

$$\frac{\partial P_m}{\partial \bar{I}} = \left(\frac{F_2 P_m}{r - F_1 r \bar{I} - RF_1}\right) \tag{3.19}$$

Equation (3.19) shows that $\partial P_m / \partial \bar{I}$ is positive, thus a reduction in the quota increases the domestic price of importables, again as expected.

Let us now return to the equivalence concepts mentioned earlier. Consider a change in the quota which raises the domestic price of the import good by 1 per cent. Thus $dP_m/P_m = 1$. From (3.19), the corresponding quota change is given by

$$d\bar{I}|_{dP_m/P_m} = \frac{r - F_1 r \bar{I} - RF_1}{F_2} \tag{3.20}$$

which using (3.12) becomes

$$d\bar{I}|_{dP_m/P_m} = r(II_1 + I_2) + RI_1 \tag{3.21}$$

But from chapter 2, equation (2.79), we note, after making suitable substitutions, that

$$\frac{dI}{dt} = \frac{(X_1 - I)[r(II_1 + I_2) + RI_1]}{X_1 - I - rI_2 + rII_1}$$

If the initial tariff rate is zero, then a 1 per cent change in tariffs can be written as $dt = 1$. Thus, the change in imports becomes

$$d I|_{dt=1\%} = \frac{r(II_1 + I_2) + RI_1}{1 + [(rII_1 - rI_2)/(X_1 - I)]} \tag{3.22}$$

Comparing (3.21) and (3.22) we see that there may be dissimilar effects of tariffs and quotas. Specifically, a 1 per cent tariff rise will change imports by a different amount relative to a change in quota required to raise domestic (import) price by 1 per cent.

A glance back at chapter 2 will also reveal two things: the one is that $\partial V/\partial \bar{I}$ and $\partial V/\partial t$ will not necessarily be equal, except fortuitously; and the other is that the stability conditions for the quota and the general tariff are in principle different; we do not need to impose the condition $X_1 > I$, for example, for the general tariff, we need only the weaker condition that $X_1 > I + rI_2$.

It is also transparent that there will always be changes in $\bar{I}$ that will generate the same impact on the economy as changes in t (for any given base, of zero tariff or otherwise); since those total impacts depend upon $(d\bar{I}, dt)$ as well as $(\partial V/\partial\bar{I}, \partial V/\partial t)$. But, it can happen that the quota needs to be set above the initial, free-trade, level of imports. An import quota is thought of conventionally as a restrictionist policy, to the effect that it imposes a control on imports: in that event, *ex hypothesi*, $\bar{I}$ must be lower than the free-trade level of I. As a consequence, a general tariff and a general quota need not be equivalent. Why? The answer is immediate: we have demonstrated in chapter 2 that even within the framework of the basic MM used here, an increase in a general tariff (from zero or a range of initial levels) can increase output to such an extent, even though it simultaneously raises P_m, that it increases the *quantity* of imports (which equals the value, in foreign currency, of imports since the foreign price is unity). An equivalent quota, therefore, can mean permitting imports to exceed their original level. Again we may note that agents who import will still be prepared to pay a licence fee to import because they will be able to deduce that it is beneficial for them to do so, since the quantity they supply will be purchased and at a high domestic price (so that their potential profit, in domestic currency terms, is not creamed off by the licence fees they have to pay). The possible dominance of a general tariff over a quota in respect of its stimulating effect on imports reinforces the fact that the two forms of commercial policy will only be equivalent if they are derived so that they are, in fact, equivalent. The impact on imports of a general tariff in a model of real wage rigidity in contrast to the quota will be noted again in chapter 7 though we shall provide an analysis of the case for a general quota.

The economic impact of quotas on other macrovariables can be explained by a diagrammatic exposition which will help to clarify matters. There is a major difference, from the case of tariffs, since the external balance (EB) line is now horizontal rather than upward sloping. This is because, for fixed $\bar{I}$, trade balance only depends on the exchange rate. If we now wish to compare the situation of no quotas with that of a binding and effective quota, then the positively sloped EB line will pivot downwards and become horizontal. But its precise position is unclear without numerical simulation. To get rid of this intractable difficulty, at a theoretical level, we assume that the initial EB line is also horizontal. This creates a problem for the formal analysis since we cannot, strictly, use the condition that initial $\tau = 0$. So let us assume that the initial situation is in the close neighbourhood of the free-trade position. In figure 3.3, IB_1 and EB represent free-trade internal and external balance. EB_1 gives the case where there is a binding quota which is very 'near' the free-trade demand for I. Thus, in effect, initial $\tau \cong 0$. IB_1 and EB_1 are shown again in figure 3.4 where the rest of the analysis will be conducted henceforth.

The Q_1Q_1 line represents market clearing conditions for importables. For a given $\bar{I}$ and τ, and provided the quota is binding, Q_1Q_1 slopes upwards. A rise in r causes an excess supply of importables, thus V must rise to increase demand and clear the market for I. Using equations (3.7) and (3.8), we have (initial $\tau = 0$)

$$\mathrm{d}r - F_1\,\mathrm{d}V = (F_1 r\bar{I} - r)\,\mathrm{d}\tau + F_2\,\mathrm{d}\bar{I} \tag{3.23}$$

Remember $(F_1 r\bar{I} - r) < 0$ by stability of the importables market. Thus an increase in τ shifts Q_1Q_1 downwards, while a decrease in $\bar{I}$ shifts Q_1Q_1 upwards (F_2 is negative). Initial equilibrium is at K_1. In what follows we always assume that the quota is binding.

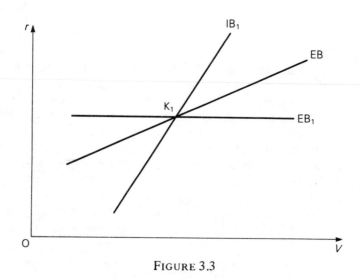

FIGURE 3.3

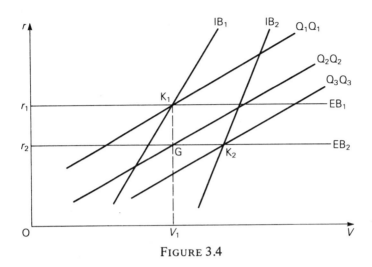

FIGURE 3.4

Now, consider a more stringent quota, that is $\bar{I}$ is reduced. The external balance line shifts to EB_2 as the exchange rate appreciates to preserve external balance. The new r equals r_2. Consider the point (r_2, V_1). Output is held parametrically constant at the same level as that at the point K_1. The decrease in r causes an excess demand for I, given the *new* effective quota, and the implicit quota rate τ must rise. This causes Q_1Q_1 to shift downwards to the line Q_2Q_2 passing through the point G. The change in τ is given from (3.23) as

$$d\tau|_{r_2V_1} = \left[\frac{1}{F_1 r\bar{I} - r}\right]\left[\frac{r}{X_1 - \bar{I}} - F_2\right]d\bar{I} \qquad (3.24)$$

Note $dr/d\bar{I} = (r/X_1 - \bar{I})$.

Now look at internal balance. A rise in the quota induced τ, just as in the case of tariffs, will shift IB rightwards. At G, trade balance is equal to zero and hoarding is

$$H = H\left[\frac{V + \tau r\bar{I}}{r^\delta(1 + \tau)^\delta}\right] \qquad (3.25)$$

The proportionate change in the numerator of the term within $H(.)$ is (R/V), where $R = \tau r\bar{I}$. The proportionate change in the

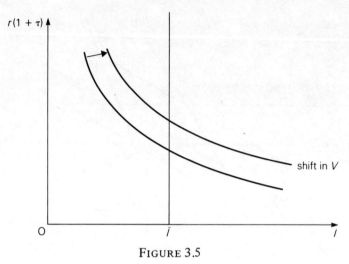

FIGURE 3.5

denominator for a unit change in $\bar{I}$ is

$$\delta \frac{dr}{r} + \delta \, d\tau = \delta \left[\frac{1}{X_1 - \bar{I}} + \frac{r}{(X_1 - \bar{I})(F_1 r\bar{I} - r)} - \frac{F_2}{F_1 r\bar{I} - r} \right]$$

which can be simplified to

$$\delta \frac{dr}{r} + \delta \, d\tau = \delta \left[\frac{F_1 r\bar{I} - F_2(X_1 - I)}{(X_1 - I)(F_1 r\bar{I} - r)} \right] \tag{3.26}$$

Noting that $F_1 = -I_1/I_2$ and $F_2 = 1/I_2$ we can further reduce (3.26), in terms of our previous analysis, to

$$\delta \frac{dr}{r} + \delta \, d\tau = \delta \left[\frac{rII_1 + X_1 - I}{(X_1 - I)(II_1 + I_2)} \right] \tag{3.27}$$

Consider the first of these two equivalent conditions. Equation (3.26) tells us that the change in the denominator of H is positive, given $d\bar{I} < 0$. Thus both denominator and numerator of H rise and we cannot be sure of the final effect on H. Economic intuition is revealed more cleanly by (3.27). Given the traditional assumptions that $(X_1 - I) > 0$, $(II_1 + I_2) < 0$, we need to stress the importance of the non-occurrence of the Metzler paradox. If the paradox does *not* hold then $(rII_1 + X_1 - I) > 0$ and the denominator of the H function rises.

If H, therefore, can both rise or fall, depending on parameter values, output can correspondingly decrease or increase. Consider now the case of an expansionary quota. At G in figure 3.4, the denominator from (3.3) has risen proportionately more than the numerator and H has fallen from its initial level of zero. Thus hoarding becomes negative and there is excess demand for output, V increases. The final shift in IB will take it to IB_2; the new general equilibrium will be at K_2, characterized by an increase in output and a fall in the exchange rate.

For consistency we also require Q_1Q_1 to shift downwards to Q_3Q_3 in order to pass through K_2. But remember at point K_2, output rose. This will shift the import demand function rightwards in the $(r(1 + \tau), I)$ space as in figure 3.5. The excess demand for importables, consequent on a rise in output and income, will increase the implicit quota rate τ. As τ rises, the Q_1Q_1 line shifts downwards to Q_3Q_3 to preserve equilibrium in the importables market.

The effect of a quota on output is ambiguous as in the case of tariffs. It is possible to have an increase in V depending on parameter values and the size of the quota revenue. This is similar to the case of tariffs. On the other hand, the exchange rate must appreciate (given $X_1 - \bar{I} > 0$) and imports fall if the quota is binding and effective. In terms of targeted output stimulation, tariffs and quotas are equivalent because they can both lead to domestic expansionary policies. In terms of the effect on imports the two policies might be dissimilar; a quota always reduces imports, if binding, and sets a lower than free-trade level, while tariffs may increase imports if its impact on income is sufficiently expansionary.

4
Commercial Policy, Capital Mobility in the Fix-price Model with a Money Sector

The discussions and analyses of the previous chapters have been conducted without reference to a money sector; this was in accordance with the early, seminal, literature in the field and also with much of the research that followed. Essentially, of course, as we noted *en passant*, the implication in the models utilized so far is that there is a demand for money exclusively for transaction purposes, and this demand is accommodated perfectly by some form of monetary authority, so that the money stock becomes demand determined.

In this chapter we shall incorporate a money sector explicitly into our preceding models. We shall do so in the simple way adopted in almost all macromodels by means of the assumption that the money/financial sector consists of only two assets for the non-Government sector, namely money and bonds. The latter bear a rate of interest denoted by i. The demand for money and for bonds are aggregate demands; again following standard practice in macroeconomics so that the aggregation requirements are stringent.

The supposition is made normally that there is only one type of bond and that, because of Walras's law, in handling equilibrium configurations of the endogenous variables in the economy, 'the' bond market can be eliminated from having an explicit role in the model. Strictly speaking, that can only be done if we include wealth as an *explicit*, independent, variable in the money demand function. Most of the 'money market variants' of the Mundellian model, in fact, omit wealth (Krugman, 1982), and only include it in the model if they are, as they say, adopting 'a portfolio approach' to the money sector (Kouri, 1978; Calvo and Rodriguez, 1977; Dornbusch and Fischer, 1980; Eichengreen,

1981; Kimbrough, 1982). In the Mundellian models that have been based on that portfolio approach, (which is rather a grandiose name assigned to a procedure which permits foreign assets to compete for a place in private investors' portfolios; the models used, as we shall see, being extremely aggregative in terms of existing portfolio theory), it is concluded that the imposition of a *tariff* might just occasionally have a *positive* impact on output and employment. But we defer discussion of the 'portfolio approach' until chapter 6.

In all of the Mundellian models, however, that have been extended to encompass a 'money sector', the findings have been invariably that tariffs can only have a negative impact on the key real variables in the economy, in both the long and the short run. Those extensions also, to reiterate the point, omit wealth from the explicit structure of the model. In examining commercial policy in these genre of models, and in effect in analysing them rigorously, we shall largely retain that assumption for ease of comparability; but we shall include a footnote analysis of one model that embodies wealth. We shall consider two broad specifications of the model: the one is where there is no capital mobility between countries, the other being where perfect capital mobility is present.

4.1   No Capital Mobility: A Mundell–Krugman Framework

The inclusion of a money sector and a rate of interest, naturally, implies that the rate of interest impinges on real markets somewhere and, as we have already observed, it means that a financial claim besides money ('a' bond) must exist. If the rate of interest is to have an effect on real markets in the Mundellian models it can obviously only do so through one of the expenditure functions, $A(.)$, $X(.)$ or $I(.)$. The Krugman (1982) type extensions of the Mundellian model incorporate the real effects of i on the economy via the absorption function $A(.)$. Since $I(.)$ is assumed not to include i this again leads to a possible specification error; or to the supposition that imported commodities are only consumables. Despite that fact, in this section we shall keep to the Krugman model so that we may describe the results that are claimed to occur in a Mundellian framework when explicit recognition is given to the money sector, and illustrate why it is possible to question their verity.

Krugman's exposition of the role of money in the Mundellian model is predicated on the view that it might be possible in a monetary world to challenge the contractionary terms-of-trade effect on output when a Government resorts to commercial policy to increase output and employment. However, his general presumption is that it will not be possible to argue against the output-reducing effects of such policy generated through the money sector. Thus the summary of his position presented in the preamble to his analysis of the Mundellian monetary model is this:

> A tariff raises the price which consumers must pay for goods while providing an offsetting increase in nominal income through the revenue it generates. In effect, [a] tariff adds another channel to the circular flow of spending. This extra channel will require money balances for transaction purposes. If the money supply is held fixed when a tariff is imposed, the extra demand for money will drive up interest rates and lead to a contraction of income. (Krugman, 1982, pp. 146–8)

The inclusion of the interest rate in the absorption function, with a demand for money dependent upon disposable income and the rate of interest, together with a fixed nominal stock of money, are regarded as being sufficient to generate the alleged output contraction.

We recall that the Mundellian models specify internal balance (the 'IS' schedule) by means of real hoarding H, where H is measured in terms of the price of absorption P, the consumer price index. Equilibrium in the no-tariff world is where real hoarding is equal to the real balance of payments B/P

$$H = \frac{V - A}{P} = \frac{B}{P} \tag{4.1}$$

Real hoarding is defined with respect to real disposable income Y where

$$Y = \frac{V + R}{P} = \frac{V + trI}{P} \tag{4.2}$$

The equilibrium condition, with tariffs, in the domestic output market becomes

$$\frac{(V + R) - A}{P} = H = \frac{B}{P} \tag{4.1'}$$

With an interest rate present, H is defined as

$$H = H(Y, i), \quad H_2 > 0 \tag{4.3}$$

P, as hitherto, is the 'consumer' price index in the home country or the cost of living index, with again

$$P = r^\delta (1 + t)^\delta \tag{4.4}$$

on the basis of fixed normalization (at unity) of domestic and foreign commodity prices. The current account is given by

$$B = X(r) - rI[V, r(1 + t)] \tag{4.5}$$

so that, again, the demand for imported goods is seen to have output V as its scalar variable, also, as before, $r(1 + t)$ is the 'terms of trade' when the tariff is present, since we have normalized domestic and foreign commodity prices at unity (the net barter terms of trade still being r). External balance, naturally, occurs when equation (4.5) becomes zero.

The rate of interest i is solved for, within the domestic economy (since we have excluded capital movements between countries), by the domestic money market. In the latter the demand function for nominal money balances is posited to be

$$M = yL(i), \quad L_1 < 0 \tag{4.6}$$

y is $V + trI$, namely nominal income. Therefore, equation (4.6) informs us that the demand for nominal money balances is independent of the cost of living index: velocity depends solely upon the rate of interest. The nominal money stock M^S is assumed to be determined exogenously by the government.

Letting M^S equal the left-hand side of equation (4.6) provides us with the LM schedule. This together with equation (4.1′), the IS schedule, is assumed to produce the kind of situation depicted on figure 4.1 for a given exchange rate r. Thus we have a commonplace diagrammatical representation of equilibrium in the money and goods markets.

Krugman (1982) then argues in this fashion:

> Devaluation shifts IS right, raising output and the interest rate; thus in Figure 4 [figure 4.3] we show the internal-balance schedule as upward sloping. A tariff, however, raises the demand for domestic money as well as the demand for domestic output through its revenue effect. Both IS and LM shift up, and the effect on output is ambiguous.

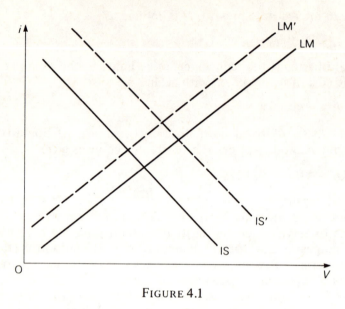

FIGURE 4.1

As Figure 3 [figure 4.2] shows, however, once we allow the exchange rate to adjust, the effect of a tariff on output becomes unambiguously negative. The tariff improves the trade balance at the initial exchange rate, so the external balance schedule shifts down. It may actually reduce output at the initial exchange rate, shifting the internal-balance schedule left; in this case the effect is clearly contractionary. Even if the internal balance line shifts down, it does so by less than the external balance line. Again, consider point A [figure 4.2], where output and the trade balance are unchanged. Here both real income and the interest rate have risen, so there is excess supply of domestic output. Thus, output must fall in this case as well. (Krugman, 1982, pp. 148, 152)

The two diagrams referred to by Krugman in this explanation of the output effects of the tariff are shown here as figures 4.2 and 4.3.

Let us now consider the steps in Krugman's argument. Obviously we have no dispute with the portrayal of the LM and IS schedules on figure 4.1; except we note that, of course, whether they are linear or not depends upon the specific forms assumed for the

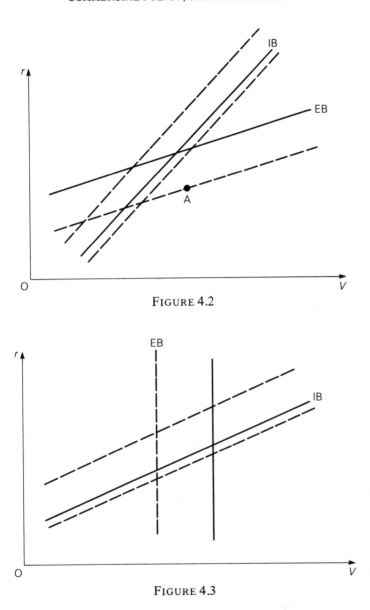

FIGURE 4.2

FIGURE 4.3

relevant behavioural functions. If we examine the LM schedule before and after the imposition of a tariff, then it will follow that for any given V, i must be higher than when there is a zero tariff, since it has been hypothesized that the demand for the (fixed) nominal stock of money depends, positively, upon t via the tariff revenue. Hence, the LM schedule must shift upwards to, say, LM'. For any given exchange rate, when a tariff is imposed it must also shift the IS schedule upwards to, say, IS'. The imposition of a tariff amounts to an increase in the 'effective' rate of exchange at any given value of the actual rate of exchange r. This reduces imports and so leads to an increase in output, with fixed values of the exchange rate and at any given level of the rate of interest. If the Marshall–Lerner condition holds then the IB schedule will be upward sloping in (r, V) space.

The levying of a tariff can shift the IB schedule rightward or leftward of its free-trade position in this monetary model, just as it did in the muliplier models of chapters 2 and 3. Suppose that it does shift rightward. Krugman's argument is that at A on figure 4.2 the same outcome obtains as in the Mundellian multiplier models, thus at the same value of output as was produced at the free-trade equilibrium position and with balanced trade along the new EB line, real income will be higher than in the free-trade situation because of the tariff-revenue term R that has to be added to output and the improvement in the terms of trade. Consequently real hoarding will rise and hence there will be an excess demand for the specific level of output. Additionally, the real demand for home goods will be lower because the rate of interest will be higher at the given V now that *money* income $(V + R)$ is higher than at the original, free-trade equilibrium.

It is certainly true that at the specified value of output, if imports are non-zero, the rate of interest i will be higher than under free trade, with a fixed supply of money. Consequently, since imports have not been assumed to be dependent upon the rate of interest, the implication must be that the increase in $H(.)$ as the rate of interest rises is borne entirely by a fall in domestic residents' demand for domestically produced goods. The specification of $I(.)$ biases the outcome against the tariff, yet the impact on the demand for those goods as a consequence of the change in real income is not as definitive as has been alleged nor, therefore, is the effect on the domestic residents' demand for domestically produced goods coming through the channel, as it were, of 'consumption' goods. In essence, even if real income rises and hoarding $H(.)$ is posited to depend positively on real income, this itself does not mean that the demand for domestic goods by the home economy has fallen: $H(.)$ has been defined in respect of the absorption basket. Additionally, and of central importance, real income could fall at the level of V given by point A.

The arguments here are identical with those we employed in chapter 2 to support our intuition that in the Mundellian model, without an overt money sector, the conventional, comparative statics, conclusions on the output impact of general tariff (or quota) were potentially problematical. Thus, at given V, since exports and imports will be non-zero at point A on figure 4.2, it follows that y, the value of money income, will be higher, by the tariff revenue component. But it does not follow from this fact that real income Y will be higher; this is because the higher y has to be discounted by a differently constructed consumer price index P. Now we have $P = r^\delta (1 + t)^\delta$, rather than $P = r^\delta$. Making the assumption that δ is the same at A as it is at the old equilibrium will not permit us to state unequivocally that P is lower at A (than at the old equilibrium) despite the fact that r (the world, or net barter terms of trade) is lower. The net effect on real income of the tariff revenue raising money income and possibly increasing (worsening) the 'effective' terms of the trade cannot be deduced on intuitive grounds. The Mundellian result relies upon the hypothesis that the terms of trade will always improve (i.e. P will fall) at a point such as A, after a general tariff has been levied. We demonstrated in chapter 2, in effect, that such an outcome is not guaranteed; that finding pertains to the 'money sector' version of the model.

4.2 A Formal Analysis of the No Capital Mobility Mundellian Monetary Model (MMM)

We shall evaluate the impact on the macroeconomy of a general tariff on the standard supposition that the government imposes a tariff in a previously free-trade world: this makes the analytics simple and provides a direct comparison with the conclusions of the MMM. For a newly-levied tariff we know, from our discussion in chapter 2, that

$$dR = Ir\, dt\, (= Irt = R) \tag{4.7}$$

and, assuming δ does not alter

$$\frac{dP}{P} = \delta\, \frac{dr}{r} + \delta\, dt \tag{4.8}$$

But δ has to be evaluated at the new equilibrium, and so dP is not base weighted; otherwise the tariff has been eliminated altogether at the final equilibrium; and we note that, given the bracketed conditions in (4.7) that hold by construction, Ir must be the final equilibrium value of imports, exclusive of the tariff.

At the most general level we can allow δ to vary; which is something that has not been attempted in the literature; as a consequence we have seen this had led to the, possibly, incorrect use of δ as the original, tariff-free, share of imports in absorption. In our simulation studies reported in chapter 2, we let δ vary. If a more comprehensive analysis is developed, with the adjustments to δ embodied in the model, we have, in the MMM with $I = I(V, \ r(1 + t))$ not dependent upon total real disposable income (hence not on R)

$$\frac{dP}{P}\bigg|_{t=0} = \delta\left(\frac{dr}{r} + dt\right) + \log r \, d\delta \tag{4.8'}$$

Hence

$$\frac{dP}{P} = a \, dr + b \, dt + c \, dV + e \, di \tag{4.9}$$

where

$$a = \left(\frac{\delta}{r} + \frac{I_2 r + I}{A} \log r\right)\bigg/(1 + \delta H_1 \log r) \tag{4.9a}$$

$$b = \left[\delta + \frac{I_2 r^2 + Ir - \delta(1 - H_1)Ir}{A} \log r\right]\bigg/(1 + \delta H_1 \log r) \tag{4.9b}$$

$$c = \left[\frac{rI_1}{A} \log r - \frac{(1 - H_1)\delta}{y} \log r\right]\bigg/(1 + \delta H_1 \log r) \tag{4.9c}$$

and

$$e = \frac{PH_2\delta}{y} \log r/(1 + \delta H_1 \log r) \tag{4.9e}$$

We shall present the results obtained from utilizing (4.8') and (4.9) later. Reverting to the simpler case we have

$$\begin{bmatrix} a_{11} & a_{12} & a_{13} \\ a_{21} & a_{22} & a_{23} \\ a_{31} & a_{32} & a_{33} \end{bmatrix} \begin{bmatrix} dV \\ dr \\ di \end{bmatrix} = \begin{bmatrix} K_1 \\ K_2 \\ K_3 \end{bmatrix} \tag{4.10}$$

where

$$a_{11} = -\left(\frac{H_1 + rI_1}{P}\right)$$

$$a_{12} = \left(\frac{H_1 y\delta}{Pr} + \frac{X_1 - I - rI_2}{P}\right)$$

$$a_{13} = -H_2$$

$$K_1 = \left(\frac{r^2 I_2 - H_1 y\delta + H_1 rI}{P}\right) dt$$

$$a_{21} = rI_1$$

$$a_{22} = rI_2 + I - X_1$$

$$a_{23} = 0$$

$$K_2 = -r^2 I_2 \, dt$$

$$a_{31} = L(i)$$

$$a_{32} = 0$$

$$a_{33} = yL_1$$

$$K_3 = dM^S - L(i)rI \, dt$$

The IS, EB and LM schedules have been set out in excess demand form so that, in accorance with the Routhian conditions, the determinant Δ of the Jacobian of equation (4.10) should be negative. In effect

$$\Delta = \left[\frac{H_1 yL_1}{P}(X_1 - I) - r(I_2 + II_1)\right]$$

$$+ [L(i)H_2(I + rI_2 - X_1)] \tag{4.11}$$

The determinant is evaluated at zero tariff, and it is assumed that its sign is invariant to the imposition of any positive tariffs. Otherwise, of course, the model is (locally) unstable. Given $H_2 > 0$, a sufficient condition for Δ to be negative is that $(X_1 - I) > 0$. We assume, as before, that $(I_2 + II_1) < 0$ and $(X_1 - I - rI_2) > 0$ (the Marshall–Lerner condition). Thus if price elasticity of exports is greater than unity, which is equivalent to $(X_1 - 1) > 0$ at equilibrium, Δ will be negative.

The expression for the impact of the tariff on output is

$$\frac{dV}{dt} = \frac{\{[(H_1/P)(rI - y\delta)](I + rI_2 - X_1)yL_1\} + [(rI_2yL_1)(H_1y\delta/P)][-LrIH_2(I + rI_2 - X_1)]}{\Delta}$$

(4.12)

Now $\delta \equiv r(1 + t)I/A$, and $A \equiv y$ in any equilibrium with trade balance, so that (4.12) becomes

$$\frac{dV}{dt} = \frac{[(H_1R/P)(X_1 - I)yL_1] + [(r^2yIH_1I_2L)/P] - [rILH_2(I + rI_2 - X_1)]}{\Delta}$$

(4.13)

If δ is set at rI/A, or equivalently $R = rtI$ is set at zero in equation (4.13), we have reduced the tariff revenue to zero and are analysing the effect on output of a non-existent tariff. In that case we appear to have derived the result that $dV/dt < 0$, since the second and third terms in the numerator of equation (4.13) are positive (given $H_2 > 0$) and $\Delta < 0$.

With $H_2 > 0$, the necessary condition for $dV/dt > 0$ is that $(X_1 - I) > 0$. We have met this elasticity condition often before, and in this particular model it also guarantees stability. It has intimate links with the quota model, and, finally, is empirically validated. Thus we can have a newly-levied tariff creating an increase in output.

An evaluation of the effect of the general tariff on the exchange rate indicates that it could be affected in any direction. Of more particular interest, for this model, is the comparative static behaviour of the interest rate 'i'. We have from (4.10)

$$\frac{di}{dt} = \frac{\{yL_1[X_1 - I - r(I_2 + II_1)]\} - R[I_1 + L(i)(X_1 - I)] - (r^2ILI_2)}{\Delta}$$

(4.14)

If the tariff is small, thus tariff revenue $R = rtI$ is low, then the other two terms being negative, given $\Delta < 0$, $di/dt > 0$. This is, of course, with the proviso that money supply does not change, $dM/dt = 0$.

Consider now the most general variant of the MMM, where equation (4.9) is used to describe the change in the price of absorption or of the consumer price index. The effect is to change the specification of a_{11} to a_{13} and K_1 in equation (4.10). These now become

$$a_{11} = -\left(\frac{rI_1 + H_1}{P} - H_1 \frac{y}{P}\right)c$$

$$a_{12} = \left(H_1\left(\frac{y}{P}\right)a + \frac{X_1 - I - rI_2}{P}\right) \tag{4.15}$$

$$a_{13} = -\left(H_2 - H_1\left(\frac{y}{P}\right)e\right)$$

$$K_1 = \left(\frac{r^2I_2 + H_1Ir - H_1yb}{P}\right) \tag{4.16}$$

where a–e are defined in equations (4.9)–(4.9e) respectively. Now, we find that

$$\frac{dV}{dt} = \frac{(H_1IryL_1/P)(I + rI_2 - X_1)[1 + \delta(1 - H_1)\log r] - IrL(i)(I + rI_2 - X_1)[1 - P(\delta/y)\log r]H_2}{|\Delta|} \tag{4.17}$$

where $|\Delta|$ is the determinant of the Jacobian of the system.[1] We must have $|\Delta| < 0$; if $H_1\delta \log r - 1 < 0$ this is more likely to be attained, since the only positive element remaining in Δ is the second term. Note one important point by way of reiteration of what we said in chapter 2 of the MM model as interpreted especially by Tower (1973): if it is posited that the initial exchange rate is unity, $H_1\delta \log r - 1 = -1$ and the numerator of equation (4.17) becomes positive automatically. In essence, letting $r = 1$, implies from equation (4.9) that consideration of $d\delta$ can be omitted from the model; *and* if δ is measured by its pre-tariff magnitude, we have a world where there is no general tariff.

With $|\Delta| < 0$, we observe that dV/dt can be positive from equation (4.17). That will happen the larger H_1 is, hence the smaller is the first (negative) expression in the numerator, and if $1 < P(\delta/y) \log r$. Now inequality can exist alongside the requirement that $H_1\delta \log r < 1$ for $|\Delta| < 0$. Thus the higher are δ and r, the higher are the chances that $1 < P(\delta/y) \log r$, and that, with H_1 approaching unity, $dV/dt > 0$. Again, the exchange rate changes can be positive, negative or zero; the rate of interest will rise if the money stock is fixed, when output increases.

It follows from elementary intuition that, should the monetary authorities expand the money supply when they impose the tariff, the output effects will be greater than without such an expansion, since the impact of the increased income will provoke less of a break on the final level of expansion by curbing the concomitant rise in the interest rate. That result can easily be confirmed by adding the term in dM^S/dt to the numerator of dV/dt in equations (4.13) and (4.17): it is also apparent that for any desired increase required in output the government can choose a combination of dM and dt.

The MMM omits any reference to wealth. Suppose that we include such a variable in the money demand function so that it is, for example, of the form

$$L = yL(i, W) \tag{4.18}$$

where

$$W = \frac{M^S + B^S}{P} \tag{4.19}$$

with B^S denoting the value of the stock of bonds placed on the market by the monetary authorities. We find, even with fixed stocks of money and bonds (to keep the value of the latter fixed we can assume that they are variable coupon bonds), the impact on the rate of interest of a general tariff will be that much less than under the world epitomized in the textbook Keynesian money demand function, equation (4.6). This lessening of the impact on i can occur because, say, with P rising, even if real income is rising, a positive response of the demand for real money balances to real wealth will mean that, *ceteris paribus*, there is more money available for transactions requirements, the money released from speculative balances via the wealth effect, serving to suppress the interest rate somewhat. That itself will have a beneficial effect on domestic output, since in the MMM it is *implicitly* assumed that only the domestic residents' demand for home-produced goods is affected by a change in the interest rate.

Additionally, following on from that point, it is useful to observe that should $I(\,.\,)$ be defined to include the rate of interest, just as $A(\,.\,)$ does, the impact of any increase in the rate of interest that is engendered in the model (whether the model be founded on $L(.)$ in (4.6) or in (4.18)) being on the demand for both home goods and importables, it will be less detrimental directly to home output than in the MMM; this has to be set against the fact that it will be indirectly unfavourable, because it will produce *ceteris paribus* movements in the rate of exchange which will reduce export demand (via its causing r to fall). In the context of a full model, worked out in comparative statics terms, to assimilate the extra interdependencies between the markets generated by the respecification of $L(.)$ and $I(.)$ can produce any conceivable outcome *in toto*.[2]

The discussion and analysis (as limited at the general level as it had to be) of the preceding sections has ruled out the possibility of mobility of capital, or trading in financial assets, between the home country and the 'rest of the world'. In the next section we shall continue by rescinding the capital immobility assumption. Rather than concern ourselves with 'intermediate' capital mobility we shall move to the other extreme and assume that there is perfect capital mobility, something which is becoming much nearer the case nowadays for the developed nations of the world.

4.3   Perfect Capital Mobility with Static Expectations

If perfect capital mobility exists we know that

$$i = \bar{i} + e \tag{4.20}$$

where $\bar{i}$ is the 'world' interest rate and e is the expected rate of appreciation of the exchange rate $\dot{r}/r$. Several assumptions are possible regarding e. The most manageable is the Hicksian one of static expectations concerning the exchange rate r; which implies that $e = 0$. This is discussed here (the classic Mundell-Fleming model); a rational expectations version is left for the next chapter, (see Mundell, 1962).

We proceed, therefore, on an analytical level with the supposition that $e = 0$. When there is *perfect* mobility of capital the balance of payments equilibrium conditions (now over both trade and capital accounts, naturally) must be explained by the equilibrium condition given by equation (4.20), namely $i = \bar{i}$, given e is zero. With flexible exchange rates and perfect capital mobility, each, and hence both, elements of the balance of payments must always balance in full equilibrium.

To the fix-price Mundellian–Keynesian paradigm we shall add a money sector but we shall not incorporate the influence of wealth. We shall leave the MMM as it stood in section 4.2. However, because we do not, as it were, need any longer to question the traditional view on its own ground, we shall operate in terms of absorption. We shall do so, in fact, by invoking the Laursen–Metzler effect. The import demand function will have total income as its scalar variable. We shall offer two specifications of the money demand function which demonstrate how crucial its structure can be for the impact of a general tariff under perfect capital mobility if the monetary authorities do not expand the money stock *pari passu* with the increase in income generated by the tariff.[3]

For simplicity we shall keep to the situation where a newly-imposed tariff is being evaluated. In that case if the money demand function assumes the format given in equation (4.6) in the MMM, it is transparent that if there is no expansion of the money stock after the general tariff has been levied, output must fall in the new equilibrium as the advocates of the MMM proclaim. Thus, by equation (4.20), if $e = \dot{r}/r = 0$ and $i = \bar{i}$ in equilibrium, if $\bar{i}$ *per se* does not alter, and M^S is fixed, it follows that y which was hitherto equal to the maximum attainable level of output V^* must now equal that level of output plus the tariff revenue. Hence, the new equilibrium output V must be lower than V^*, *ex definitione*, as it were. This is an ineluctable conclusion given the binding 'arithmetic' of the quantity theory equation that (4.6) becomes when $i = \bar{i}$.

However, let us consider the demand for money function

$$\frac{M}{P} = L(i, Y) \tag{4.21}$$

within this model

$$V = A(y, r(1 + t), i) + X(r) - rI - R \tag{4.22}$$

$$y = PY \tag{4.23}$$

$$Y = \frac{V + R}{P} \tag{4.24}$$

$$R = trI \tag{4.25}$$

$$P = r^\delta (1 + t)^\delta \tag{4.26}$$

$$I = I(y, r(1 + t), i) \tag{4.27}$$

Using the conditions for money market equilibrium (4.21) (the LM curve), the commodity market equilibrium (4.22) (the IS curve), as well as equations (4.7) and (4.8), we have, assuming $i = \bar{i}$ under perfect capital mobility, the following

$$\begin{bmatrix} a_{11} & a_{12} \\ a_{21} & a_{22} \end{bmatrix} \begin{bmatrix} \mathrm{d}V \\ \mathrm{d}r \end{bmatrix} = \begin{bmatrix} K_1 \\ K_2 \end{bmatrix} \qquad (4.28)$$

The parameters are

$$a_{11} = A_1 - rI_1 - 1$$

$$a_{12} = X_1 - rI_2 - A_1I$$

$$K_1 = r^2(II_1 + I_2)\,\mathrm{d}t$$

$$a_{21} = \frac{L_2}{r^\delta}$$

$$a_{22} = \delta r^{-1-\delta}M(1-\eta)$$

$$K_2 = \frac{-r^{-\delta}M}{V+R}\,[(1-\eta)R + rI]\,\mathrm{d}t$$

The initial tariff rate has been set at zero, but, of course, not R. Explicit use has been made of the Laursen–Metzler condition to factor out A_2 as $(1-A_1)I$. Finally, η is the income elasticity of money demand, that is $\eta = (YL_2/L) = (yL_2/M)$.[4]

After some tedious algebra, we get

$$\frac{\mathrm{d}V}{\mathrm{d}t} = \frac{r^{-\delta}M\delta}{\Delta}\,[(X_1 - A_1I)(1-\theta\eta)$$

$$+ rI_2\eta(\theta - 1) + rII_1(1-\eta)] \qquad (4.29)$$

where $\Delta = a_{11}a_{22} - a_{12}a_{21}$, the determinant of the Jacobian, and $\theta = (R/rI + R)$, the share of tariff revenue in total value of imports.[5] Clearly $\theta < 1$.

Stability analysis of the implicit dynamics of the MMM helps us to sign the determinant Δ as negative.[6] However, it is clear that the sign of $\mathrm{d}V/\mathrm{d}t$ is indeterminate, and it is possible to have $\mathrm{d}V/\mathrm{d}t$ to be positive – an expansionary tariff.

Consider the special case of the simple quantity theory equation discussed earlier, where $\eta = 1$. Then (4.29) becomes

$$\frac{\mathrm{d}V}{\mathrm{d}t} = \frac{1}{\Delta}\,[(X_1 - A_1I - rI_2)(1-\theta)] \qquad (4.30)$$

Given the Marshall–Lerner condition $(X_1 - I - rI_2) > 0$ and $A_1 < 1$, dV/dt must be negative. This indicates that the existence of contractionary tariffs depends very much on the specific assumptions made about the form of the money demand function.

The importance of η can be seen clearly if we assume further that the price elasticity of exports $x = (rX_1/X)$ is greater than unity. This is, of course, a more stringent condition than required for the case where the Metzler paradox will *not* hold.[7] Then, at full equilibrium, trade balance being equal to zero, we get $X = rI$ and the first term in (4.29) $(X_1 - A_1 I) = I(x - A_1)$ is positive. Now, *if* $\eta < 1$, then $dV/dt < 0$. Thus, the three sufficient conditions for a (newly imposed) general tariff to reduce output are (a) current account balance $(X = rI)$, (b) export elasticity greater than one $(x > 1)$; and (c) income elasticity of money demand less than unity $(\eta < 1)$.

The economics of the effect of tariffs can be seen from figure 4.4 which gives the IS and LM curves on the (i, V) space. The full equilibrium is at E_1 with the domestic interest rate being equal to world interest rate $\bar{i}$. Initially, with a (new) tariff, expenditure switching towards the domestic product, as well as expenditure increasing via the Laursen–Metzler effect, will shift the IS curve to the right (IS_1) as demand for V expands. The domestic interest rate will rise causing net capital inflow which will put pressure on the exchange rate to appreciate. A fall in r will start shifting the IS curve to the left again (see IS_2 in figure 4.4).

The new final equilibrium will depend on the intersection of the LM and $i = \bar{i}$ curves. This is similar to what happens in the classic Mundellian case of fiscal and monetary policy effectiveness under flexible exchange rates and perfect capital mobility. Now suppose $\eta = 1$. Rewrite the LM equation

$$\frac{M}{r^\delta(1 + t)^\delta} = L\left(\bar{i}, \frac{V + R}{r^\delta(1 + t)^\delta}\right) \tag{4.31}$$

For a given nominal income, the effect of price $[r(1 + t)]$ changes will be the same for the supply of and demand for real money balances. But tariff revenue has risen (R is now positive), thus nominal income $(V + R)$ is higher. Excess demand for money ensues and to correct the disequilibrium, given $\bar{i}$, output V must fall.

Now consider the case where $\eta > 1$. Suppose the Metzler paradox does not hold, that is the tariff inclusive relative price is greater than the previous level. Since $r(1 + t)$ is now *higher*, it will affect both the demand and supply of real balances, and both will fall. But $\eta > 1$ ensures that demand falls more, relative to supply. Excess supply of real money can be corrected by an increased $V + R$. Thus even with a rise in R it is possible for V to increase, for any given i. LM may shift *rightwards*. Figure 4.4 shows this possibility, with LM moving to LM_1 and the new equilibrium at E_2, with higher output. Note that $\eta > 1$ is not sufficient, other effects such as the size and share of tariff revenue (R, θ) are important too. Additionally, if the monetary authorities pursue an active policy, when $dM/dt > 0$, we 'add' a negative term to the numerator of equation (4.29), rendering it more likely that output will respond favourably to the imposition of a general tariff. Again, there will be combinations of (dM, dt) that will produce target levels of dV for the government: one-off policies may not, in general, be superior to each other, if there are other targets such as the exchange rate.

Why have we managed to obtain this favourable impact on output (and employment) even under perfect capital mobility? The answer is straightforward, even though we do not have anything more than a pseudo-dynamic framework to aid our understanding. The demand for nominal money function, *ceteris paribus* is no longer of unit elasticity with respect to nominal income: that unit elasticity meant that the demand for real money balances was constant with respect to real disposable income. Equation (4.21) is such that the demand for real money balances is not homogeneous of degree one in the consumer price index. Thus, if indeed i is fixed, so that the *ceteris paribus* does obtain, the lack of an accommodatory monetary policy by the government will not necessarily prevent real income and domestic output from increasing with the general tariff. The MMM exploits the 'Cambridge k' nature of the Keynesian money demand function (4.6) when i is fixed; it removes, therefore, once again the possible impact on the economy of the 'effectiveness terms of trade' P, creating a simple budget restraint, in effect, to which the macroeconomy must comply.

4.4 *Concluding Comments*

We have seen that the negative views expressed or produced in the literature by those authors who have developed the monetary analogue of the MM, such as Boyer (1977), Chan (1978), Eichengreen (1981) and Krugman (1982), are not of universal

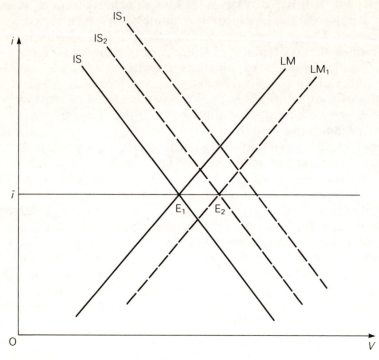

FIGURE 4.4

validity. Although the models they have employed have had different features in the case of perfect capital mobility, they have been predicated on the quantity theory of money representation of the model. That view or the slightly more sophisticated version of it embodied in the 'Cambridge k equation' leads inexorably to the conclusion that a general tariff (or a general quota) can only serve to reduce output. Under capital immobility the utilization of the Cambridge k version of the money demand function leads to the inevitable conclusion that nominal income cannot be affected (with a fixed money stock) by a general tariff: a result obtained by Sohmen (1958, 1969) in his extensive work on the role of flexible exchange rates.[8] That approach to money holdings is a common vein in the work of Boyer (1977), Krugman (1982) and others, even though their models contain individual refinements.

Apart from highlighting the fact that accommodatory changes in the money stock can improve the chances of a general tariff being able to rejuvenate economic activity, we have focused on the limitations of the Cambridge k specification of the money demand function, especially in a world of perfect capital mobility. We have also demonstrated that a general tariff (and *in extenso* an increase in an already-present general tariff) can have beneficial effects on output and employment under capital immobility, even if the money demand function (which includes the interest rate) is still of unit nominal income elasticity as is the Cambridge k equation. Additionally, perfect capital mobility does not render commercial policy otiose: the effect of protectionism depends upon the properties of the domestic economy's demand for money function. Even in the absence of ancillary government policies, protectionism can have beneficial repercussions on the real economy.

Notes

1 Δ in this case becomes

$$\Delta = H_1(H_1 - 1)\frac{\delta}{P}(I + rI_2 - X_1)yL_1(\log r) - H_1I_1\left(\frac{y}{P}\right)\delta yL_1$$

$$-\left[\frac{H_1 yL_1}{P} + L(i)H_2(H_1\delta \log r - 1)(I + rI_2 - X_1)\right]$$

2 The consequence of letting $I(.)$ include i and $L(.)$ assume the form given in equation (4.18) (with $\partial I/\partial i = I_3$); using $A = A(Y, r(1 + t), i)$, (with $\partial A/\partial i = A_3$), rather than $H(.)$ to make the role of variables clearer; and of invoking equation (4.8) for dP/P; is, with $t = 0$ *originally*, that

$a_{11} = A_1 - 1 - rI_1$

$a_{12} = A_2 + X_1 - I - I_2r$

$a_{13} = A_3 - rI_3$

$K_1 = [I_2r^2 - (A_1 - 1 - rI_1)rI - A_2r]\, dt$

$a_{21} = rI_1$

$a_{22} = I + I_2r - X_1$

$a_{23} = I_3r$

$K_2 = -r^2(I_1I + I_2)\, dt$

$a_{31} = L(i)$

$$a_{32} = -yL_2 \left(\frac{W}{P}\right)\frac{\delta}{r}$$

$$a_{33} = yL_1$$

$$K_3 = \left(1 - \frac{yL_2}{P}\right) dM^S - \frac{yL_2}{P} dB^S - \left[L(i)rI - yL_2\left(\frac{W}{P}\right)\delta\right] dt$$

If $L_2 < 0$, $|J| < 0$ as required; but on the conventional hypothesis that $L_2 > 0$, we have, in fact, that

$$|J| < 0$$

iff

$$(A_1 - 1)\left[(I + rI_2 - X_1)yL_1 + yL_2\left(\frac{W}{P}\right)\delta I_3\right] - rI_1 A_2 yL_1$$

$$-I_1 yL_2\left(\frac{W}{P}\right)\delta A_3 + L(i)[A_2 I_3 r - A_3(I + I_2 r - X_1)] < 0$$

These conditions that permit $|J| < 0$ do not rule out the possibility that $dV/dt \gtrless 0$ and $dr/dt \gtrless 0$, even when $dM^S = dB^S = 0$.

3 In the latter part of the preceding section, and note 1 above, we have indicated the possible importance (via W/P), of the money demand function in a world of capital immobility.

4 The model in excess demand form is

$$A[V + trI, r(1 + t), \bar{i}]$$

$$+ X(r) - r(1 + t)I[V + trI, r(1 + t), \bar{i}] - V = 0$$

$$L\left(i, \frac{V + trI}{r^\delta(1 + t)^\delta}\right) - \frac{M}{r^\delta(1 + t)^\delta} = 0$$

Taking total differentials of the first equation, assuming $A_2 = (1 - A_1)I$ and setting initial $t = 0$, we get

$$(A_1 - rI_1 - 1) dV + (X_1 - rI_2 - A_1I) dr = [r^2(II_1 + I_2)] dt$$

which gives a_{11}, a_{12}, K_1 in the text.

The second equation requires a more complex analysis. Taking the total differentials of L only (with $d\bar{i} = 0$)

$$dL = L_2[r^\delta(1 + t)^{-\delta}(dV + rI \, dt) + (V + trI)(-\delta)r^{-\delta-1}(1 + t)^\delta \, dr$$

$$+ (V + trI)r^{-\delta}(-\delta)(1 + t)^{-\delta-1} \, dt]$$

Put $\delta = [r(1 + t)I/V + R]$, the share of imports *with* tariffs

$$dL = L_2\{[r^{-\delta}(1 + t)^{-\delta}] \, dV + [-L_2 r^{-\delta-1}(1 + t)^\delta(rI + R)] \, dr$$

$$+ [L_2 r^{-\delta}(1 + t)^{-\delta} rI - L_2 r^{-\delta}(1 + t)^{-\delta-1}$$

$$\times rI - L_2 r^{-\delta}(1 + t)^{-\delta-1} R] \, dt\}$$

Set $t = 0$, but $R \neq 0$, then

$$dL = (L_2 r^{-\delta})\, dV + [-L_2 r^{-\delta-1}(rI + R)]\, dr + (-L_2 r^{-\delta} R)\, dt$$

Similarly, the total differential of the term for real money supply M/P is, with $t = 0$,

$$\left(-Mr^{-\delta-1}\frac{rI + R}{V + R}\right) dr + \left(-Mr^{-\delta}\frac{rI + R}{V + R}\right) dt$$

Therefore

$$d\left(L - \frac{M}{P}\right) = (L_2 r^{-\delta})\, dV$$

$$+ \left[-L_2 r^{-\delta}(rI + R) + Mr^{-\delta-1}\frac{rI + R}{V + R}\right] dr$$

$$+ \left[-L_2 r^{-\delta} R + Mr^{-\delta}\frac{rI + R}{V + R}\right] dt = 0$$

This gives, as in the text, the following

$$a_{21} = L_2 r^{-\delta}$$

$$a_{22} = \frac{rI + R}{V + R} Mr^{-\delta-1}\left[1 - \frac{L_2(V + R)}{M}\right]$$

$$= \delta Mr^{-\delta-1}(1 - \eta)$$

and

$$K_2 = r^{-\delta}(L_2 R - \delta M)$$

which can be rewritten as

$$K_2 = \frac{-r^{-\delta} M}{V + R}\,[(1 - \eta)R + rI]$$

5 Solving the system we get initially

$$\frac{dV}{dt} = \frac{1}{\Delta}\,\{[r^2(II_1 + I_2)\delta Mr^{-\delta-1}(1 - \eta)]$$

$$+ [\delta r^{-\delta} M(X_1 - A_1 I - rI_2)]$$

$$+ [-r^{\delta} L_2 R(X_1 - A_1 I - rI_2)]\}$$

$$= \frac{r^{-\delta} M\delta}{\Delta}\,\{[r(II_1 + I_2)(1 - \eta)] + (X_1 - A_1 I - rI_2)\}$$

$$+ \frac{r^{-\delta} M\delta}{\Delta}\left[-(X_1 - A_1 I - rI_2)\frac{L_2 R}{\delta M}\right]$$

The final term can be written as

$$\frac{r^{-\delta}M\delta}{\Delta}\left\{-(X_1-A_1I-rI_2)\left[\frac{L_2}{M}(V+R)\right]\left(\frac{R}{rI+R}\right)\right\}$$

$$=\frac{r^{-\delta}M\delta}{\Delta}[-(X_1-A_1I-rI_2)\theta\eta]$$

where, remember, $\theta = (R/rI + R)$. Then

$$\frac{dV}{dt}=\frac{r^{-\delta}M\delta}{\Delta}\{(X_1-A_1I)-(rI_2\eta)$$

$$+[rII_1(1-\eta)]-(X_1-A_1I)\theta\eta+(rI_2\theta\eta)\}$$

$$=\frac{r^{-\delta}M\delta}{\Delta}[(X_1-A_1I)(1-\theta\eta)$$

$$+rI_2\eta(\theta-1)+rII_1(1-\eta)]$$

This is equation (4.29) in the text.

6 The implicit dynamics of the MMM are the following: (a) the nominal interest rate rises when there is excess demand for money; (b) aggregate output rises when there is excess demand for it; and finally (c) the exchange rate depreciates (r rises) when the world interest rate is above the domestic interest rate. The first two are obvious. The last follows standard treatment also, see Dornbusch (1980), '... our interest rate has fallen below that in the rest of the world. There is a tendency for capital to flow out, creating a deficit in the balance of payments and thus leading to exchange depreciation'. Since there are three variables adjusting in disequilibrium (i, V, r), the Jacobian determinant Δ must be negative for stability.

7 See chapter 2.

8 As Tower (1973, p. 437) has stated: 'Sohmen's demonstration is a flawless statement about life in a 'quantity theory' world, with perfectly flexible wages and prices, a constant money supply, and a constant ratio of money holdings to money expenditure.'

5

Tariffs under Capital Mobility
and Rational Expectations

Introducing a money market and a rate of interest allows us, as we have already seen, to extend the basic framework to include capital mobility. The earlier concern, in the Mundell–Keynes model, on the trade balance is now replaced by the emphasis on the balance of payments and concomitant implications for capital flows induced by the imposition, or change, of the tariff structure.

The classic Mundell–Fleming model, discussed in the last part of chapter 4, assumes in addition, static expectations and fixed prices. We analyse here the more general dynamic version[1] allowing for price flexibility out of steady-state equilibrium as well as rational expectations. This gives us an opportunity to analyse explicitly the dynamics of the system, specifically the movement of exchange rates, price and output over time, after a tariff has been imposed (or increased). The case of fixed price level and static expectations may be seen as a special form of this more general model.

We maintain two assumptions of the model in chapter 4 which strictly speaking should be relaxed in an extended dynamic analysis. The money stock is assumed to be fixed throughout. Further absorption and hoarding depends on the nominal, and not the real, rate of interest. As Dornbusch (1980) points out, the latter assumption does not really change any substantive conclusions but adds considerably to the tractability of the model. As we shall see later, assuming that hoarding depends on the real rate of interest will actually *strengthen* the output/employment augmenting role of tariffs.[2] These effects will be pointed out in due course. Constancy of money supply may also be changed, at the cost of some complex algebra, particularly if we wish to consider accommodating monetary policy. The appendix, to this chapter, points out how this can be done.

5.1   *The Basic Model*

We start off with the case of zero tariffs and investigate the effect of the imposition of a tariff regime. Since expectations are a crucial ingredient of the analysis, the consequences of an anticipated or unanticipated tariff will generally be different and need to be properly discussed. Further, if the equilibrium is characterized by saddle path stability (as is often the case with rational expectations models), we shall have to allow for discontinuities and 'jumps' in variables. The two dynamic variables in the model are the domestic price level and the *nominal* exchange rate. We make the (now) conventional assumption that the exchange rate is a jump or non-predetermined variable which adjusts rapidly at any point of time when unanticipated changes occur. On the other hand there are rigidities in the domestic price level, which is therefore a predetermined variable at any point of time and can only change in response to the adjustment mechanism postulated.[3]

Without tariffs, the model is given by the following equations

$$H = H\left(\frac{qV}{P}, i\right) \quad H_1 > 0, H_2 > 0 \tag{5.1}$$

$$X = X\left(\frac{r}{q}\right) \qquad X_1 > 0 \tag{5.2}$$

$$I = I\left(V, \frac{r}{q}\right) \qquad I_1 > 0, I_2 < 0 \tag{5.3}$$

$$B = qX - rI \tag{5.4}$$

$$H = \frac{B}{P} \tag{5.5}$$

$$M = L(i)(qV) \qquad L_1 < 0 \tag{5.6}$$

$$\frac{\dot{q}}{q} = \lambda(V - \bar{V}) \qquad \lambda > 0 \tag{5.7}$$

$$i = i^* + \frac{\dot{r}}{r} \tag{5.8}$$

$$P = q^{1-\delta} r^{\delta} \tag{5.9}$$

The new notations introduced are q, the domestic price level; $i*$, the foreign interest rate; $\bar{V}$, the level of full employment or potential output. Also note that i is the nominal rate of interest.

The first equation is the standard one for hoarding, except to note that real value of output is now defined as qV/P, since domestic price level is no longer equal to unity. A more general formulation would be to have (5.1') instead of (5.1)

$$H = H\left(\frac{qV}{P}, i - \frac{\dot{q}}{q}\right) \tag{5.1'}$$

Thus hoarding is a function of the real interest rate. Unfortunately, this complicates the diagrammatics since changes in many dimensions have to be considered using only two-dimensional figures. But the general algebraic solutions will be pointed out.

Equations (5.2)–(5.4) once again give exports, imports and the nominal value of the balance of trade B. Commodity market eqilibrium is postulated by (5.5) where real hoarding is equal to the real value of B. Money market equilibrium comes from (5.6), again the demand for nominal money is a function of the nominal income qV – as well as, of course, the nominal interest rate i. We assume, for expositional simplicity, unitary income elasticity; more discussion on this is given later.

Explicit dynamics are given by equations (5.7) and (5.8). If V is the demand for domestic output and $\bar{V}$ the potential level, then $V - \bar{V}$ is an index of excess demand, and it is assumed that domestic price responds positively (negatively) over time to excess demand (supply) in the output market. Equation (5.8) is the standard one for covered interest parity where the expected rate of currency depreciation is equal to the difference between domestic and foreign interest rates. Under rational expectations (perfect foresight with no uncertainty), the expected and actual exchange depreciation coincide and we get (5.8).

Making suitable substitutions, the system can be whittled down to four equations in the four unknowns, V, i, r and q. We get

$$H\left(\frac{qV}{P}, i\right) = \frac{1}{P}\left[qX\left(\frac{r}{q}\right) - rI\left(V, \frac{r}{q}\right)\right] \tag{5.10}$$

$$M = L(i)(qV) \tag{5.11}$$

$$\frac{\dot{q}}{q} = \lambda(V - \bar{V}) \tag{5.12}$$

$$\frac{\dot{r}}{r} = i - i^* \tag{5.13}$$

P is of course known from the definitional equation (5.9). Equations (5.10) and (5.11) are the IS/LM representations while (5.12) and (5.13) give the dynamics.

The solution trick is to use (5.10) and (5.11) to determine V and i as parametric functions of q and r. Then substitute these into (5.12) and (5.13) to derive explicit dynamical equations for q and r. Thus we would get

$$V = V(r, q) \quad \text{and} \quad i = i(r, q) \tag{5.14}$$

to finally end up with

$$\frac{\dot{q}}{q} = \lambda[V(r, q) - \bar{V}] \tag{5.15}$$

$$\frac{\dot{r}}{r} = i(r, q) - i^* \tag{5.16}$$

All dynamic analysis as well as that of steady-state equilibrium (where $V = \bar{V}$ and $i = i^*$) can be done in terms of (5.15) and (5.16), provided of course we can sign the partials of V and i with respect to r and q. Since these are derived functions, we shall use the convention here that $V_r = \partial V/\partial r$, etc. Note that V_r gives the effect on V for a change in r given q constant. It is determined from the solution to the IS/LM model, therefore, the interest rate i changes simultaneously. For a given value of q, as r changes by a specified amount, instantaneous equilibrium in commodity and money markets, equations (5.10) and (5.11), determines the change in V which is represented by V_r. The corresponding change in i is given by i_r. Similarly for V_q, i_q.

For *given* values of q and r, the model can be solved at any point of time for V and i using the IS and LM functions (5.10) and (5.11). Taking total differentials we get

$$a_{11} \, dV + a_{12} \, di = K_1 \, dq + K_2 \, dr \tag{5.17}$$

$$a_{21} \, dV + a_{22} \, di = K_3 \, dq \tag{5.18}$$

$$a_{11} = qPH_1 + rPI_1 > 0$$

$$a_{12} = P^2H_2 > 0$$

$$a_{21} = qL > 0$$

$$a_{22} = qVL_1 < 0$$

$$K_1 = \frac{1}{q^2} [q(1-\delta)(H_1 qV - B) - q^2 P(VH_1 - X)$$

$$+ rP(rI_2 - qX_1)]$$

$$K_2 = \frac{1}{rq} [\delta q(qVH_1 - qX + rI) + rqPX_1 - rqPI - Pr^2 I_2$$

$$= \frac{1}{rq} \left[\delta q(qVH_1 - B) + rqP\left(X_1 - I - \frac{r}{q}\right)I_2 \right]$$

$$K_3 = -VL < 0$$

The signs of a_{ij} are clear, so also is the determinant of the Jacobian

$$\Delta = (a_{11}a_{22} - a_{12}a_{21}) < 0$$

However, K_1 and K_2 cannot in general be signed. There is no supposition in a model with perfect capital mobility that the balance of trade will be zero. However, if we *assume* that $B = 0$, then $K_2 > 0$ (provided the Marshall–Lerner condition holds, that is $[X_1 - I - (r/q)I_2] > 0]$, but once again the sign of K_1 is unknown.

The inability to sign these coefficients and thus to find the effect of r and q on V and i have been faced before. The best way of intuitively understanding the problem is to go back to the schedule of internal balance in chapter 2. There we assumed it to be upward rising, so that a rise in the exchange rate (both real and nominal since domestic price level was unity) would cause domestic output to rise. If we maintain the same framework, then in this case, once again, a rise in the *real* exchange rate should make output rise. The real exchange rate is defined as the nominal rate r divided by the domestic price level q. Thus, a fall in q or a rise in r should increase V, provided the internal balance line slopes upwards on the $(r/q, V)$ plane, which is reasonable. We should then have

$$\left. \frac{\partial V}{\partial r} \right|_{IS} = \frac{K_2}{a_{11}} > 0$$

$$=> K_2 > 0$$

and

$$\left. \frac{\partial V}{\partial q} \right|_{IS} = \frac{K_1}{a_{11}} < 0$$

$$=> K_1 < 0$$

Equation (5.10) (and (5.17)) is essentially the formal representation of the IS schedule. The foregoing signs of K_1 and K_2 therefore imply that a rise in the exchange rate or a fall in domestic price level shifts the IS curve outwards.

For the LM schedule given by (5.11) (and (5.18) in differential form), the situation is more clear cut. A rise in r has no effect on the position of the LM curve. On the other hand, an increase in q shifts the LM curve leftwards (or upwards).

What then are the final effects on V and i for changes in q and r?. Equations (5.17) and (5.18) give

$$dV = \frac{1}{\Delta} [(qVL_1K_1 + VLP^2H_2) \, dq + (qVL_1K_2) \, dr] \qquad (5.19)$$

$$di = \frac{1}{\Delta} \{-[(qPH_1 + rPI_1)(VL) + qLK_1] \, dq - (qLK_2) \, dr\}$$

$$(5.20)$$

It is clear that

$$V_r = \frac{\partial V}{\partial r} > 0 \quad \text{and} \quad V_q = \frac{\partial V}{\partial q} < 0 \qquad (5.21)$$

However, the sign of the partial derivatives of the i function (see (5.14)) are not that clear cut

$$i_r = \frac{\partial i}{\partial r} > 0 \quad \text{but} \quad i_q = \frac{\partial i}{\partial q} \qquad (5.22)$$

Krugman (1982) assumes that $i_q > 0$, and as we shall see many of his conclusions regarding the contractionary effects of tariffs are crucially tied up to this assumption. However, a priori there is nothing in the system which will give $i_q > 0$ always; the final outcome depends on a whole host of parameters and complex non-linear relationships. We shall demonstrate that with $i_q < 0$, the possibility opens up for expansionary tariff effects. Since the perfect capital mobility/rational expectations model has been used as the most sophisticated version of the Mundellian paradigm and concomitant critique of tariffs, it helps to be careful about the nature of the assumptions made. In what follows we assume $i_q < 0$ and contrast its implications with that of the previous literature, exemplified by Krugman, which has $i_q > 0$.

Since the sign of i_q is important for what follows, its meaning should be emphasized at the outset. There are various ways of

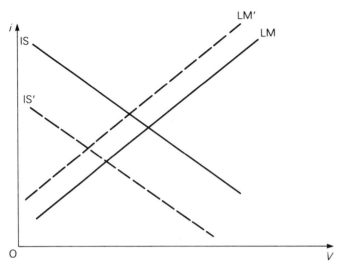

FIGURE 5.1   Increase in q

doing this. In figure 5.1, consequent to a rise in q, both IS and LM have shifted leftwards. Since we have assumed a unit (income) elastic money demand function, for a given interest rate, the fall in output V is equiproportionate to the postulated rise in domestic price q. Consider the implications, for the IS relation, of that particular point on the LM curve. Use equation (5.10). The value of qV has not changed, i is taken as a parameter for the exercise, thus a rise in q causing P to increase will lower hoarding. Rewrite the right-hand side of (5.10) as

$$\left(\frac{q}{r}\right)^{\delta}\left[X\left(\frac{r}{q}\right)-\frac{r}{q}I\left(V,\frac{r}{q}\right)\right] \qquad (5.23)$$

With an increase in q, by Marshall–Lerner, the trade balance becomes adverse, thus $[X-(r/q)I]$ falls. If this is sufficiently large then the whole expression $(q/r)^{\delta}[X-(r/q)I]$ will fall. To restore equilibrium in the commodity market it is necessary to know which of the two sides of (5.10) have fallen more. Suppose the trade balance effect is very strong. Therefore the right-hand side of (5.10) falls more than the left-hand side. Excess supply ensues which leads to a reduction in V to restore (commodity) equilibrium. Thus the specific point on the LM curve that we have been considering has excess supply and the IS curve cannot pass through it. The IS curve has to shift more leftwards, leading to a reduction in equilibrium i, hence $i_q < 0$.

If the current account responds strongly to a change in the terms of trade then we could get the situation depicted in figure 5.1. Essentially, an increase in q leads to a sharp worsening of the current account. Hoarding must fall to accommodate the new equilibrium. This may require both a fall in V and in i, contributing to a reduction in H (remember $H_1, H_2 > 0$).

The foregoing discussion concentrated on IS shifts and the current account. An alternative explanation would be in terms of the elasticity of the money demand function and the LM curve. Suppose the demand function for real balance is more general and we have in equilibrium

$$M = qL(V, i) \tag{5.11'}$$

instead of equation (5.11). Consider the case where the elasticity, $\eta = (qV/M)L_1$, is greater than unity. In the previous case we considered a shift in the LM with equiproportionate changes in q and V, since η from (5.10) is equal to one. But now a 1 per cent rise in q will require a less than 1 per cent fall in V, to equilibrate the money market, for given M and (parametric) i. Thus LM will need to shift *less* leftwards and this will strengthen the case for $i_q > 0$.

Finally consider the situation where hoarding depends on the real rate of interest. If we make hoarding a function of the real rate of interest, that is use (5.1') instead of (5.1), we get the internal balance or IS schedule as (instead of (5.10))

$$H\left(\frac{qV}{P}, i - \frac{\dot{q}}{q}\right) = \frac{1}{P}\left[qX\left(\frac{r}{q}\right) - rI\left(V, \frac{r}{q}\right) \right] \tag{5.10'}$$

Thus (5.20), giving the change in i for changes in (r, q), becomes

$$di = \frac{1}{\Delta}\left\{ -[(qPH_1 + rPI_1)(VL) + qLK_1 - VLH_2\lambda P] \, dq \right.$$

$$\left. -(qLK_2) \, dr \right\} \tag{5.20'}$$

It is easily verified that an additional negative term $(VLH_2\lambda P)/\Delta$ has been added to the term which will give the expression for i_q. This strengthens the case for making $i_q < 0$ since hoarding must in principle be made a function of the *real* interest rate.

To sum up at this stage, there are three situations where it is possible for interest rate to fall corresponding to a rise in domestic price level to equilibriate the commodity and money markets. Remember V will always fall under the postulated circumstances. If the current account deteriorates necessitating a fall in hoarding then interest rates may be pulled down in equilibrium. If the money demand function is highly elastic with respect to income, then a decline in the supply of real balances can be matched by a fall in output in spite of the money demand stimulation given by a fall in interest rate. Finally, if inflation rate decelerates consequent to lower demand, real cost of borrowing rises and creates excess supply. The interest rate needs to fall to stimulate demand. The final effect is difficult to predict a priori.

Diagrammatically the familiar IS/LM curves are now drawn on the basis of given r and q. Then these are made to change and the dotted line represents the new IS/LM schedules. The final effect on equilibrium i and V will give us the direction of change, that is allow us to sign for (V_q, V_r, i_q, i_r). Under the postulated conditions, an increase in r increases V by shifting the IS curve upward, while keeping the LM unchanged. This is equivalent to saying that the internal balance line is upward rising so that an increase in the exchange rate makes the domestic relative price more attractive, induces expenditure switching to the domestic output, thus raises demand and consequently supply of the domestic product. A rightward shift in aggregate demand (for each level of interest rate i) will obviously increase the equilibrium interest rate. Thus $V_r > 0, i_r > 0$ from figure 5.2.

An increase in q has an opposite effect. The relative price of the foreign good falls, demand is switched from domestic to foreign goods and output of V falls for each level of the interest rate. The IS curve shifts leftwards. The rise in q increases nominal demand for money which, faced with a fixed supply, forces the nominal interest rate to rise to equilibriate the money market, again for given levels of output V. The LM shifts upwards. The final effect on equilibrium output is unambiguous, $V_q < 0$. This is again the same as saying that the internal balance line slopes upwards so that a rise in q implies a fall in real exchange rates, thus reducing demand for domestic goods, both from exports and within the economy. The effect on the equilibrium interest rate is ambiguous. Figure 5.1 gives $i_q < 0$. The implication of putting the inflation rate (of domestic price level q) in the commodity market equilibrium condition (see (5.10′)) exacerbates the negative

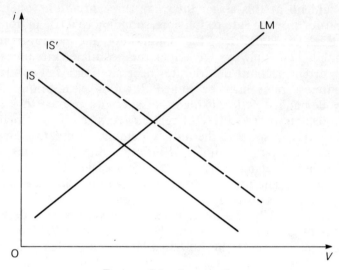

FIGURE 5.2   Increase in r

impact on i of a once and for all change in q. A rise in q reduces V. This reduces the inflation rate instantaneously and the real cost of borrowing $(i - \dot{q}/q)$ goes up. Absorption falls (hoarding rises) and the IS curve shifts even more leftwards to IS′. The commodity market effects then have a greater change of swamping the monetary effects since LM, drawn on the basis of i, remains unaffected.

We are now in a position to bring the pieces together and analyse the dynamics of the system.

The phase diagrams for the dynamic system (5.15), (5.16) using the signs of the derivatives in (5.21), (5.22) can be analysed now. Consider first the stationary solution for

$$\frac{\dot{q}}{q} = \lambda[V(r, q) - \bar{V}] \tag{5.15}$$

Thus

$$\left.\frac{dr}{dq}\right|_{(\dot{q}/q)=0} = -\frac{V_q}{V_r} \tag{5.24}$$

From (5.19) we get

$$\left.\frac{dr}{dq}\right|_{(\dot{q}/q)=0} = -\left(\frac{K_1}{K_2} + \frac{LP^2H_2}{qL_1K_2}\right)$$

Similarly for $\dot{r}/r$ we have

$$\frac{\dot{r}}{r} = i(r, q) - i^* \tag{5.16}$$

and

$$\left.\frac{dr}{dq}\right|_{(\dot{r}/r=0)} = -\frac{i_q}{i_r} \tag{5.25}$$

Using (5.20), this turns out to be

$$\left.\frac{dr}{dq}\right|_{(\dot{r}/r=0)} = -\left(\frac{K_1}{K_2} + \frac{PVH_1}{K_2} + \frac{rPVI_1}{qK_2}\right) \tag{5.26}$$

Equations (5.21) and (5.22) tell us that

$$V_r > 0, \quad V_q < 0, \quad i_r > 0$$

We also assume that

$$i_q < 0$$

Thus from (5.24) and (5.25)

$$\left.\frac{dr}{dq}\right|_{(\dot{r}/r=0)} > 0 \quad \text{and} \quad \left.\frac{dr}{dq}\right|_{(\dot{q}/q=0)} > 0 \tag{5.27}$$

Also, comparing (5.24) and (5.26) we see that the line depicting $\dot{q}/q = 0$ (QQ in figure 5.3) has a greater slope than the line depicting $\dot{r}/r = 0$ (RR in figure 5.3). The phase diagram for $\dot{q}/q$ and $\dot{r}/r$ is shown in figure 5.3.

Along QQ, output is constant at $\bar{V}$ and the domestic price level does not change. It is upward rising since an exchange rate depreciation (increase in r) raises demand and output, thus domestic price level q must rise to choke off the rise in V. Its slope is greater than unity, therefore along QQ r/q must rise to keep $V = \bar{V}$. To understand this, consider an equiproportionate rise in r and q, keeping V constant initially. Imports and exports are unchanged, so also is the real value of trade balance B/P and hoarding H (see (5.1)–(5.5)). However, LM will shift and, given money stock and output, a rise in q will cause a rise in interest

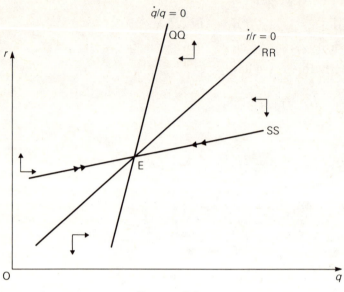

FIGURE 5.3

rate i. This increases hoarding, so to preserve equilibrium in the commodity market V must fall below $\bar{V}$. For $\dot{q}/q = 0$, V must be raised and this can be done by increasing r more than proportionately relative to q. The reasoning also explains why, to the right of QQ, $V < \bar{V}$ and $\dot{q}/q > 0$, thus q falls. Similarly, to the left of QQ, q rises.

Given our assumption that $i_q < 0$, so that the IS effect dominates the LM shift in figure 5.1, due to the influence of the real interest rate on H and the strong non-monetary effect of q on absorption and trade balance, RR in figure 5.3 also slopes upwards. Since i_r is unambiguously positive, above RR, the exchange rate depreciates. If we start initially from the point on RR where the exchange rate is constant ($i = i^*$), and let the exchange rate increase, then from the IS/LM model the interest rate will rise (see figure 5.2). This increases hoarding and to preserve equilibrium, the trade balance must increase too. Speculators expect the exchange rate to rise (since now $i > i^*$), and under perfect foresight r actually rises. This raises the trade balance and restores equilibrium.

Equilibrium E is characterized by a saddle path solution, so that there is one unique path SS that converges towards long-run equilibrium. We assume that the domestic price level is sluggish, thus q is predetermined, while the exchange rate is a 'jump' variable. At any point of time, given q, the exchange rate jumps to attain the stable saddle path and the system converges towards equilibrium E. The solution method therefore follows that of Dornbusch (1976).

If, alternatively, we assume that $i_q > 0$, so that the monetary effect dominates, the inflationary effects on the IS curve are insignificant and current account changes to relative price shifts are small, then $\dot{r}/r = 0$ slopes downwards and we get the phase diagram of figure 5.4. On the saddle path in figure 5.4, r and q move in opposite directions and this, as we shall see, may give diametrically opposite results for comparative dynamics.

What happens to the system if a positive tariff is now imposed? Note that the initial equilibrium is one with zero tariffs. The IS/LM instantaneous equilibrium is now given by

$$H\left(\frac{qV}{P} + \frac{trI}{P}, i\right) = \frac{1}{P}\left[qX\left(\frac{r}{q}\right) - rI\left(V + trI, \frac{r(1+t)}{q}\right)\right] \quad (5.28)$$

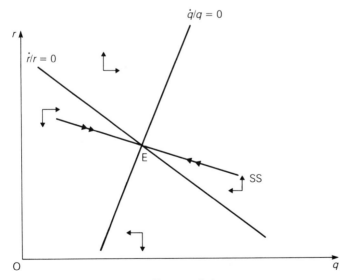

FIGURE 5.4

$$M = L(i)(qV + trI) \tag{5.29}$$

$$P = q^{1-\delta}r^{\delta}(1 + t)^{\delta} \tag{5.30}$$

Once again, the effect on the IS relation (equation (5.28)) is not unambiguous. The price level P will rise, but so also will nominal income $qV + trI$,[4] (remember we started from an initial position of zero tariffs) for a given level of V. If we assume that real income increases, thus increasing hoarding H, then to preserve commodity market equilibrium (IS), the interest rate should rise. Since V is parametrically held constant, the rate of inflation does not change, so that for all practical purposes, we can assume that i will increase to equilibrate the commodity market after a tariff has been imposed. Concentrating on the IS relation essentially takes us back to the model of chapter 2 where internal balance was assumed to shift *rightwards* with a tariff. We maintain the same condition here.

Starting from zero tariffs and imposing a positive one gives us an unambiguous movement of the LM curve. Nominal income has risen by the transfer of tariff revenue trI, so in the absence of accommodating monetary policy, $L(i)$ must fall from (5.29), thus i will rise given V. So LM shifts upwards.

The impact effects of a tariff on V and i for *given r and q* are shown in figure 5.5. Interest rate rises unambiguously, but the

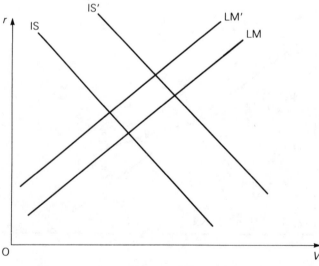

FIGURE 5.5

impact on output is unknown. Once again, if the monetary effect is weak so that LM does not shift much while the commodity market changes are more significant entailing a larger shift in IS, then V will rise. Intuitively, the condition for $\partial V/\partial t > 0$, that is V to rise after a tariff, will be similar to that of $i_q < 0$. Alternatively, if the parameter values are such that i_q tends to be negative, then there is a greater possibility that $\partial V/\partial t (= V_t)$ will be positive.[5] Remember V_t is the impact effect of tariffs from the IS/LM model.

We now have therefore

$$V = V(r, q, t) \quad \text{and} \quad i = i(r, q, t)$$

with

$$V_r > 0, \quad V_q < 0, \quad i_r > 0, \quad i_t > 0 \qquad (5.31)$$

the signs of V_t and i_q are unknown.

A very large number of cases are possible. Simply changing the signs of V_t and i_q give us four alternatives. Within each there will be sub-cases with various alternative possibilities. Without going through an extensive, and probably unfruitful, taxonomy, we will take some cases and examine the effects on equilibrium and transition paths when a tariff is imposed. The interested reader can then work out the other variants. We shall be careful about choice of cases emphasizing *both* contractionary and expansionary tariffs. It will be clear, as in chapter 2, that various possibilities exist depending on parameter values.

We continue with the assumption, in the light of our previous discussion, that $i_q < 0$ (as in figure 5.3). Consider first the case where $V_t > 0$. The RR line is given now by

$$\frac{\dot{r}}{r} = 0 = i(r, q, t) - i^* \qquad (5.32)$$

An imposition of tariffs t raises i. Thus r must fall given any predetermined value of q, to keep $\dot{r}/r = 0$, that is $i = i^*$. The RR line shifts downwards with positive tariffs. The QQ line is given by

$$\frac{\dot{q}}{q} = 0 = \lambda[V(r, q, t) - \bar{V}] \qquad (5.33)$$

Tariffs raise V ($V_t > 0$). To maintain $\dot{q}/q = 0$, V must fall to $\bar{V}$, needing a fall in r, again for given q. The QQ line also shifts downwards.

The long-run equilibrium, with full employment $V = \bar{V}$ and domestic and foreign interest rates equal, $i = i^*$, is given by the intersection of the new RR and QQ lines. In the following diagrams the pre-tariff and post-tariff curves are indexed by 1 and 2 respectively; thus we have $R_1 R_1$, $Q_2 Q_2$, etc. There are three possibilities here. The long-run equilibrium exchange rate and price level can both fall or rise. On the other hand we can have an increase in q with a corresponding fall in r. We will generally have real effects in the sense that the real exchange rate (r/q) will change. This is not surprising since, even in a monetary model, real shocks (such as a tariff) are expected to produce real changes and will not be 'neutral' in terms of relative prices.

To understand the nature of changes in q and r in the long run, it helps to solve (5.32) and (5.33). Let these equilibrium values be given by $\hat{q}$ and $\hat{r}$. Then we have

$$\frac{d\hat{q}}{dt} = \frac{i_t V_r - i_r V_t}{\Delta} \tag{5.34}$$

$$\frac{d\hat{r}}{dt} = \frac{(i_q V_t - i_t V_q)}{\Delta} \tag{5.35}$$

and

$$\Delta = i_r V_q - i_q V_r < 0 \tag{5.36}$$

The sign in (5.36) is guaranteed by the saddle point properties of equilibrium in the long run. As should be clear from (5.31) and (5.34)–(5.36), and the fact that $i_q < 0$, $V_t > 0$, $(\hat{q}, \hat{r})$ can move in the three directions mentioned above. Figures 5.6 to 5.8 depict these three alternatives. Initial full employment equilibrium, with zero tariff, is at E_1. Post-tariff equilibrium is at E_2.

Consider first figure 5.6. E_2 lies to the right of E_1, given the movement of RR and QQ. Thus at the initial E_1, *after* the tariff has been imposed, $\dot{q}/q$ is positive, implying V is greater than $\bar{V}$. Tariffs are expansionary and they lead to a short-run increase in national product. Of course, the way the model is set up, there is long run neutrality. Thus $\dot{q}/q$ becomes positive with $V > \bar{V}$, q rises and chokes off demand since $V_q < 0$. But that is not germane to the issue. What is important is that the effect of tariffs on the transition path towards the new steady state is expansionary.

The transitional dynamic path shows that overshooting is also possible. Assume that there is an unanticipated imposition of a tariff when the economy is at E_1. The new stable path is now $S_2 S_2$.

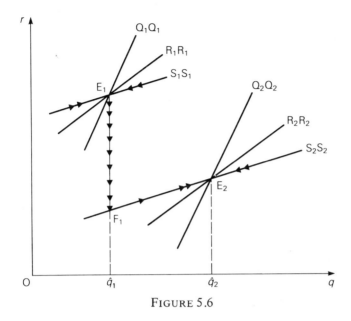

FIGURE 5.6

Given the level of predetermined variable $\hat{q}_1$, the exchange rate jumps to a lower level at F_1 on S_2S_2. The impact effect of the tariff, given by V_t, is positive and high. Output can rise; but exchange rate appreciation causes a decline in output. On the other hand, the nominal interest rate falls (remember $i_r > 0$) and this increases absorption. Further F_1 is to the left of Q_2Q_2, thus $\dot{q}/q$ is positive now. So the inflation rate has risen cutting the cost of borrowing, thus raising absorption even further. The net effect is an increase in output from its initial $\bar{V}$. Ultimately, the economy moves along F_1E_2 and reaches full employment equilibrium. The exchange rate overshoots at F_1 and then rises towards the point E_2.

Consider now the second possibility within this group depicted in figure 5.7. If the impact effect (from the previous analysis of the IS/LM models) of tariffs on output is low, then the fall in the exchange rate may not be compensated and output will decline. The QQ line shifts very little, since V_t is small, and this puts the new full employment equilibrium, at E_2, to the left of E_1. The fall in the exchange rate is sufficient to swamp the other beneficial effects. The effects of interest rate changes are also important. Tariffs cause the interest rate to rise on impact, but a fall in the

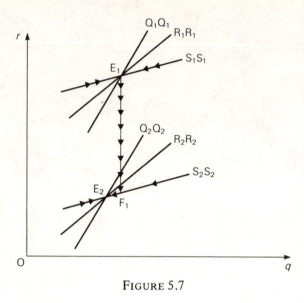

FIGURE 5.7

exchange rate makes the interest rate decline (see (5.31)). The former is assumed, implicitly, to be stronger than the latter, adding to the contractionary pressures.

The transitional dynamics from E_1 to E_2 via F_1 shows that there is no overshooting. But F_1 is to the right of Q_2Q_2, thus output is lower than full employment. Excess supply causes q to fall, and V to rise, until full employment is attained once again.

Figure 5.8 shows the possibility that the exchange rate may *rise* in the new full employment equilibrium. This is fully expansionary since the upward movement of the real exchange rate (remember q is sluggish, r 'jumps' upwards) causes the export multiplier to operate. Competitiveness *improves* with a tariff. The reason is transparent if one remembers that such models place the burden of adjustment of the exchange rate on the capital account. Thus, current account surpluses emanating from tariffs are less important than the interest differential consequent on protection. The impact effect of tariff on interest rate is positive ($i_t > 0$). On the other hand, the possibility of a rise in the domestic price level q may reduce the nominal interest i ($i_q < 0$). If the former is dominant, i will increase and the exchange rate must depreciate to induce speculators to hold foreign bonds.

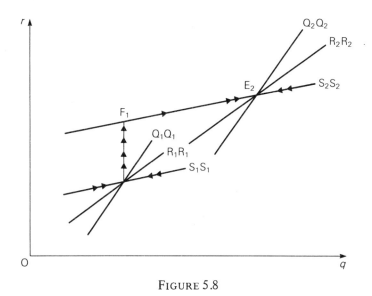

FIGURE 5.8

We draw attention to the fact that these alternative long-run possibilities were inherent in the simple Mundell–Keynes model. But the dynamic analysis there was sketchy and relatively *ad hoc*. Here, a richer analysis can be provided, about the behaviour of the economy, in terms of a wider class of variables and a better treatment of expectations. In principle, the QQ lines can be identified with full employment internal balance and RR may be similar to external balance.

The foregoing analysis regarding the impact of tariffs on the transitional path to new long-run equilibrium (figure 5.6), has been done on the basis of the assumption that $V_t > 0$. Thus for a *given* real exchange rate, the impact effect of tariffs on output is positive. This is similar to what was assumed in chapter 2 (as well as in Mundell and all the literature), that with tariffs the internal balance line shifts to the right. Tariffs increase the terms of trade $(r(1 + t)/q)$, thus there is a pure substitution effect in favour of the domestic product. Redistributed tariff revenue might also have an income effect, pushing demand and therefore output V up. Overall, $V_t > 0$ is a reasonable assumption.

A more important point is when the IS/LM configurations are such that an increase in the domestic price pushes the interest rate up. Then $i_q > 0$. This may be contractionary given RR is now downward sloping. We have

$$\frac{\dot{q}}{q} = \lambda [V(r, q, t) - \bar{V}] \quad V_r > 0, V_q < 0, V_t > 0$$

$$\frac{\dot{r}}{r} = i(r, q, t) - i^* \quad i_r > 0, i_q > 0, i_t > 0$$

Initial (zero tariff) equilibrium is given by the intersection of $R_1 R_1$ and $Q_1 Q_1$ at E_1. After the tariff the new long-run solution is at E_2 (figure 5.9).

The exchange rate overshoots from E_1 to F_1. Appreciation causes a decline in output ($V_r > 0$). The situation at F_1 is that $V < \bar{V}$ and q is falling. The interest rate falls ($i_q > 0$) thus stimulating aggregate demand. The stable path is $F_1 E_2$ and finally the economy reaches equilibrium along it at E_2 with a lower domestic price level and of course full employment $\bar{V}$.

The possibility of a contractionary tariff is increased considerably if we have $i_q > 0$. The exchange rate *must* decline, in long-run equilibrium, given the slope of the $\dot{r}/r = 0$ line, and the assumed shift of the QQ and RR lines downwards, consequent to a tariff (remember V_t, $i_t > 0$). The possibility that equilibrium $\hat{r}$ may be higher in the post tariff situation (as in figure 5.8) is no longer present. The definite appreciation of the exchange rate is one channel by which tariffs can have a negative effect on output.

Further insight can be gleaned by looking at the two overshooting cases for $i_q < 0$ and $i_q > 0$ (see figures 5.6, 5.9). The impact effect of tariffs (from IS/LM) raises the nominal interest rate. For long-run equilibrium, the domestic interest rate must fall to the constant world interest rate. If $i_q < 0$, then this will necessitate an *increase* in q on the stable (saddle) path. In the foregoing Dornbusch-type model a rise in q is equivalent to saying that output is higher than full employment (natural rate). Thus, consequent on a tariff, output must have risen since initially we had $V = \bar{V}$. On the other hand if $i_q > 0$, then a reduction in i requires q to fall along the transition path to the new equilibrium. Output must therefore be lower than full employment and the fall in q restores the economy to full employment equilibrium. Essentially the slope of the stable manifold determines the behaviour of prices and output outside of full equilibrium. Since the exchange rate has fallen below its long-run value, it rises along the saddle path SS and this is consistent with the fact that $i > i^*$.

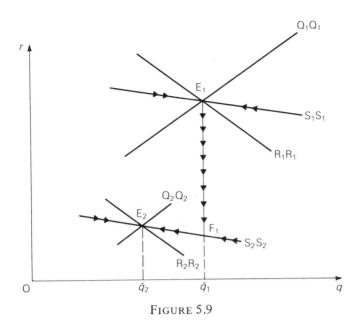

FIGURE 5.9

Once again we are forced to be eclectic. Depending on parameter values, it is quite possible that i_q will be negative. This
will be so if for a decrease in q (given r), the IS curve shifts
relatively more than LM, consequently the short-run equilibrium
interest rate rises. The postulated relative shift will occur if the
commodity market (real sector) effects are stronger than the
money market (monetary sector) effects, and/or the real interest
rate is explicitly introduced into domestic demand, absorption
and hoarding. Under these conditions,[6] tariffs are expansionary.

The importance of the sign and quantitative values of parameters in determining the final outcome of the imposition of
tariffs, is not surprising in the light of our general discussions.
The specific nature of i_q and the condition under which it is
negative (or positive) have already been discussed. Thus, under
reasonable assumptions, it is quite possible to have expansionary
tariffs in the sense that output increases after a tariff has been
imposed (or increased).

Instead of dealing with all possible alternatives, let us continue
with the analysis using one of the foregoing models. Henceforth
we shall discuss the case where, in long-run equilibrium, q rises

and r falls; the short run is characterized by overshooting; and tariffs have an expansionary effect. The relevant figure is 5.6, and we note that $i_q < 0$. All of these models in general analyse impact and long run effects starting from a point of initial steady-state equilibrium, that is $V = \bar{V}$. One may (and rightly) question the *relevance* of a tariff under these circumstances if we are already in a situation of full employment. However, the method used is simply for analytical tractability. There is nothing in the model *per se* that precludes us from starting off from a situation of initial unemployment, and observing the behaviour of the economy on the transition path. This is, of course, provided we are on the stable path, otherwise nothing really can be said since Samuelson's 'tulip mania' takes over.

Consider once again figure 5.6 which is redrawn in figure 5.10. As before, E_1 is the zero tariff *long-run* equilibrium while E_2 has positive tariff.

Initially the economy is either at G_1 or G_2, both to the right of $\dot{q}/q = 0$, hence $V < \bar{V}$ and q is falling. If now the tariff is imposed while we are at G_1, the impact effect (with q predetermined) is to move the economy to H_1 and then slowly towards E_2. Note H_1 is to the *left* of E_2, $\dot{q}/q > 0$, q is rising and $V > \bar{V}$. Thus output has increased above its potential level. The tariff has unambiguously

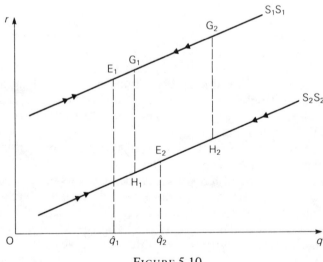

FIGURE 5.10

increased V. Alternatively, if we are at G_2, tariffs move the economy to H_2, given q. There is still unemployment since on the saddle path $\dot{q}/q < 0$. However, the transition path now entails moving from H_2 to E_2 rather than from G_2 to E_1 as in the zero tariff situation. A much lower reduction in q will produce full employment $\bar{V}$. Since $\bar{V}$ is constant and $V_q < 0$, this implies that the level of output at H_2 is closer to full employment output, than the level at G_2. Again tariffs are expansionary.

Until now the imposition of tariff was perfectly unanticipated. What if there is an anticipated or announced tariff, designed to come into effect T periods hence? Using Wilson's (1979) analysis, it can be shown that there will be less of a jump and overshoot. The exchange rate will reach the new stable path $S_2 S_2$ (see figure 5.11) in T periods time, rather than 'instantaneously'. Thus when the tariff is actually imposed, the economy is already on $S_2 S_2$ and moves towards the new equilibrium.

The path followed from E_1 to E_2 via F_1 and G_1 is shown in figure 5.11. The time taken to move from the initial equilibrium E_1 when the tariff is announced, and the point G_1 on the new saddle path $S_2 S_2$ when the tariff is actually implemented, is exactly T periods.

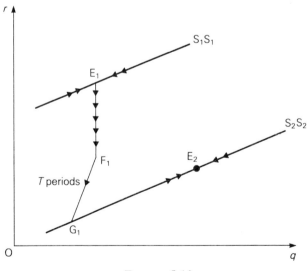

FIGURE 5.11

An interesting feature of the path $E_1F_1G_1$ should be noted. So long as the equilibrium is at E_1 (tariffs have not been implemented, though they have been announced), points on $E_1F_1G_1$ lie to the right of the stationary line $\dot{q}/q = 0$. In this region $\dot{q}/q < 0$, thus $V < \bar{V}$. Therefore output has *fallen* below its long-run full employment level $\bar{V}$ at E_1. This is the announcement effect, where even before implementation the expected exchange rate starts moving downwards, in anticipation of the new tariff-ridden equilibrium. As the nominal exchange rate appreciates, aggregate demand declines leading to a fall in domestic output and employment. Expenditure switching and demand augmenting effects of tariffs are absent since the tariff has not been imposed, only anticipated. This will continue until and unless the tariff has been actually instituted T periods later when the economy is at F_1. The new $\dot{q}/q = 0$ will pass through E_2, G_1 will be to the *left* of $\dot{q}/q = 0$, thus $V > \bar{V}$. From G_1 to E_2, output will be higher than full employment, with exchange rate depreciation and a rise in the price level, until the new equilibrium at E_2.

The shorter is T, the less time is the economy at less than full employment output. Thus tariffs to be effective should be unanticipated, or if anticipated and announced, then quickly implemented. The longer it takes for tariffs to come into force after speculators know about this, the stronger will be the contractionary effects. Thus maximum expansion is possible when there is a 'surprise' tariff.

The distinction between perfectly unanticipated and anticipated tariffs (announced to be imposed T periods hence) is quite important, and the results will be generally different. Another crucial distinction needs to be mentioned, that between permanent and temporary tariffs. We have assumed until now that tariffs are permanent, so that equilibrium shifts to E_2 and stays there. Consider the alternative, the government decides to impose a tariff for a specific period of time, and the public of course believes this. Let the tariff be imposed for $\hat{T}$ periods and then removed. Again we can distinguish between anticipated and unexpected tariffs.

Figure 5.12 gives the effect of an unanticipated but temporary tariff. Once again initial zero tariff equilibrium is at E_1 and the post-tariff equilibrium at E_2. However, E_2 is not forever; after $\hat{T}$ periods, tariffs will be removed and the economy will revert back to E_1. The exchange rate will fall as before, but it will not go down to the new saddle path S_2S_2. Rational speculators know

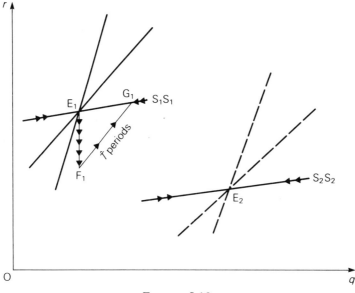

FIGURE 5.12

that though S_2S_2 is the relevant stable path now after the tariff
has been set, it will not be so after $\hat{T}$ periods. At the later date,
tariffs will be removed, so that the stable path after $\hat{T}$ will be
once again S_1S_1. Thus the exchange rate will fall instantaneously
along E_1F_1 and then move up along F_1G_1. Note that along the
path F_1G_1, the economy is obeying the new laws of motion
pertaining to E_2. But its objective is to reach S_1S_1 by $\hat{T}$ periods,
so that once the tariff is removed it can coast downwards along
the stable path S_1S_1. There is no need for a second jump. The
implicit idea behind this and all other models of the same genre
is of course the fact that agents wish to achieve the stable saddle
path. Though no explicit optimization is analysed in usual macromodels, the desire to achieve the saddle path can be rationalized
in terms of the Mangasarian (1966) theorem and the economic
example given by Brock (1975).

Since points on E_1F_1 and F_1G_1 are to the left of the new
(dotted) $\dot{q}/q = 0$ line (remember, from figure 5.3, that this is the
steeper line), they represent points where $V > \bar{V}$. Thus tariffs
raise output so long as it is operative and E_2 is the relevant equili-

brium point. However, once tariffs are removed at G_1, the relevant equilibrium becomes E_1, thus $\dot{q}/q < 0$ and $V < \bar{V}$. Then output falls sharply, and the deflationary forces reduce q. Of course, long-run neutrality assures that output finally will be $\bar{V}$, but this is merely a simplification (of a minor order). The major point to note is that output rises with a tariff and falls when it is removed. A tariff is expansionary even when it is temporary; however, the increase in output is also temporary.

Consider, finally, the case of anticipated and temporary tariffs. The government announces a tariff to be instituted T periods hence and then to be removed after a further $\hat{T}$ periods. The anticipation of future tariff induced exchange rate appreciation will cause the exchange rate to start falling immediately (see figure 5.13). Given equilibrium at E_1 between periods 0 and T, the laws of motion pertaining to E_1 are in force, thus a movement along $E_1F_1G_1$ will take place. Anticipation of exchange rate fall will actually cause r to decline. Again the movement on $E_1F_1G_1$ will last T periods, whence the tariff will be imposed and equilibrium will shift to E_2, with S_2S_2 as the stable path. Why then does the economy not go on the new saddle path? Since it knows that E_2 is not permanent, after $\hat{T}$ periods, equilibrium reverts back to E_1, it is optimal to reach the path leading to E_1 at the point

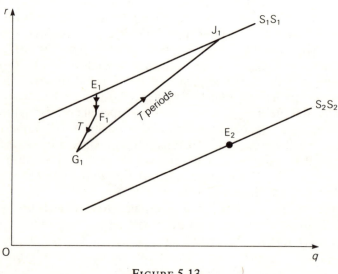

FIGURE 5.13

$T + \hat{T}$. Thus G_1 will be determined by the fact that the path $G_1 J_1$ will last for $\hat{T}$ periods, given the laws of motion pertaining to E_2.

Again along $E_1 F_1 G_1$ there is unemployment, and output is less than full capacity. After the tariff is imposed, there is expansion, output rises above $\bar{V}$ and the expansionary effects of a tariff are shown in rising q. From J_1, with tariffs removed, output remains below $\bar{V}$ until full equilibrium at E_1. Thus tariff imposition causes output to rise, removal causes output to fall.

The dynamics analyses for this particular case gave a rich story of the effects of a tariff on output dependent on whether it is (a) unanticipated permanent, (b) anticipated permanent, (c) unanticipated temporary, and (d) anticipated temporary. Note the importance of anticipation and permanence. In effect we have a similar result to the familiar Lucasian one for monetary policy. If agents have perfect foresight and policies are known beforehand, they will react to neutralize their prospective effects. Unanticipated shocks matter, whether nominal as in the new-classical doctrine, or real as here. This is also in line with recent work in the open economy literature (Turnovsky, 1981). The analysis here deals with one case. Similar classification with the other models is also possible and once again gives interesting results, some of them opposite to those we have discussed. We leave the interested reader to analyse the other possibilities.

We may conclude by claiming that it is not at all clear within a fully specified Mundell–Fleming–Dornbusch model that tariffs will be contractionary. Previous literature has tried to show that tariffs reduce aggregate output and employment within the framework of perfect capital mobility. However, as we have demonstrated, there are plausible sufficient conditions under which tariffs may be expansionary. In particular, if a rise in the domestic price level reduces the nominal interest rate, given the IS effect dominates the LM effect, then it is quite possible to have an expansionary tariff in the sense that an unanticipated imposition of a general tariff will raise output and employment.

APPENDIX

Consider the capital mobility model when the money stock is changing at a fixed rate determined by the monetary authorities. Thus

$$\frac{\dot{M}}{M} = \mu \qquad (5\text{A}.1)$$

The rate of domestic price inflation depends on the 'core' rate of inflation μ and also on the excess demand for domestic output. We get

$$\frac{\dot{q}}{q} = \mu + \lambda(V - \bar{V}) \tag{5A.2}$$

It is easier to analyse the model in terms of absorption defined in terms of home goods rather than in 'real' terms as in the exposition of the main chapters. Recalling our discussion from chapter 2, with tariffs, we get the IS function as

$$V = A\left(V + rtI, \frac{r(1 + t)}{q}, i - \frac{\dot{q}}{q}\right) + X\left(\frac{r}{q}\right) - \frac{r(1 + t)I}{q} \tag{5A.3}$$

The import function is given by

$$I = I\left(V + trI, \frac{r(1 + t)}{q}, i - \frac{\dot{q}}{q}\right) \tag{5A.4}$$

Here absorption is made to depend on disposable income (including tariff revenue), relative price, and the *real* rate of interest. Similarly for the import demand function.

The demand for real money is given by

$$\frac{M}{q} = L(V + trI, i) \tag{5A.5}$$

Money market equilibrium implies that demand and supply of money are equal. Using (5A.2) in (5A.3) and (5A.4) we get the short-run equilibrium of the IS/LM type as

$$V = A\left(V + trI, \frac{r(1 + t)}{q}, i - \mu - \lambda V + \lambda \bar{V}\right)$$
$$+ X\left(\frac{r}{q}\right) - \frac{r(1 + t)I}{q} \tag{5A.6}$$

$$I = I\left(V + trI, \frac{r(1 + t)}{q}, i - \mu - \lambda V + \lambda \bar{V}\right) \tag{5A.7}$$

$$\frac{M}{q} = L(V + trI, i) \tag{5A.8}$$

It is useful to work in terms of two variables; these are the log of real balances, $l = \log(M/q)$, and the real exchange rate $c = (r/q)$.

Then we have, using (5A.1) and (5A.2)

$$\dot{l} = \frac{\dot{M}}{M} - \frac{\dot{q}}{q}$$

$$= \lambda(\bar{V} - V) \tag{5A.9}$$

Further

$$\frac{\dot{c}}{c} = \frac{\dot{r}}{r} - \frac{\dot{q}}{q}$$

$$= i - i^* - \mu - \lambda(V - \bar{V}) \tag{5A.10}$$

From (5A.6), (5A.7) and (5A.8) we can solve for V and i for the two relevant endogenous variables l and c, as well as for the exogenously given tariff rate t. Thus

$$V = V(l, c, t) \tag{5A.11}$$

$$i = i(l, c, t) \tag{5A.12}$$

Substituting these in (5A.9) and (5A.10) and choosing units such that $\bar{V} = 0$, we get

$$\dot{l} = -\lambda V(l, c, t) \tag{5A.13}$$

$$\frac{\dot{c}}{c} = i(l, c, t) - \lambda V(l, c, t) - i^* - \mu \tag{5A.14}$$

The dynamic solution of these two equations then gives the time path of all variables in the model. Since we have assumed long-run constancy of output $\bar{V}$, the main interest is to analyse short-run adjustments. The solution is very complex, but qualitatively not different from that presented in the text.

Notes

1 Similar models are used by Dornbusch (1976), see also Dornbusch (1980).
2 It can be shown that Krugman's (1982) contractionary tariff result is partly due to ignoring this distinction between the real and nominal rate of interest.
3 In the language of the rational expectations literature we can also call the exchange rate and domestic price level, forward-looking and backward-looking variables.
4 The tariff revenue is distributed to the private sector, so that transfer income is trl.
5 Compare the IS/LM shifts in figures 5.2 and 5.5.
6 Another condition of course is that $V_t > 0$, which is very plausible.

6
Commercial Policy and the Portfolio Model

6.1 *Basic Concepts*

The previous chapter analysed commercial policy, in particular tariffs, under perfect capital mobility. Using a Mundell–Fleming–Dornbusch model with interest parity and rational expectations, we found that tariffs may be expansionary particularly when relative price effects on aggregate demand (IS schedule) are large. The basic structural assumption behind that model is that domestic and foreign bonds are perfect substitutes, and (financial) capital is perfectly mobile between the home country and the rest of the world. The assumptions behind expected interest parity models are of course rather strong but they give a useful insight into exchange rate movements.

Interest parity (as well as purchasing power parity) models fall within the general class of the monetary approach to balance of payments theory. The monetary approach emphasizes the role of stocks of assets rather than the flow of funds and views the equilibrium exchange rate as the relative price of domestic and foreign money (stock). Mussa (1976), criticizing 'Keynesian' theories of the balance of payments, claims that 'the traditional theory ... contains two serious conceptual errors. First it views the exchange rate as the relative price of national outputs, rather than as the relative price of national monies. Second, it assumes that the exchange rate is determined by the conditions for equilibrium in the market for flows of funds, rather than by the conditions for equilibrium in the markets for stocks of assets'.

Given the basic concepts of monetary models of the balance of payments, it is logical at this stage to analyse a broader structure of assets. A more general view than that taken in previous chapters is to consider a portfolio of assets denominated in different currencies. It is also plausible to assume that these stocks of assets are imperfect substitutes. Perfect substitution can then be seen to be special cases when relevant derivatives or elasticities tend to infinity. The portfolio approach is increasingly popular with open economy macroeconomists and Eichengreen (1981) gives an early, though simplified, example of an application to tariffs.

In an interesting recent paper Gylfason and Helliwell (1983) have shown that *both* Keynesian and monetary approaches can be construed as special cases of a properly formulated portfolio model of the balance of payments. Though their paper has no direct connection with commercial policy, it is an important contribution in integrating the various approaches to balance of payments analysis which often end up with diametrically opposite policy prescriptions. We shall use some of the structural characteristics of their model to highlight the expansionary effect of tariffs.

The basic concepts of commercial policy effects within a portfolio model can be understood readily in the context of a simplified model. Ignoring real capital which is constant in the short run, there are three financial assets held by economic agents: (a) domestic money M; (b) domestic bonds Z (measured in domestic currency), which are non-traded and not held by foreigners; as well as (c) foreign bonds F which are traded and denominated in foreign currency. Z and F are measured in nominal units. We leave out for tractability the holding of foreign money. The asset structure is similar to that of Branson (1979). The supply of money stock and domestic bonds are given. Thus demand must adjust to the given levels of M and Z, for equilibrium. The value of foreign bonds rF may change either through exchange rate movements or through balance of trade disequilibrium and international capital movements. The three assets are imperfect but gross substitutes (the cross-price elasticities are positive).

The portfolio structure is given in equation form (without tariffs) as

$$M = VL(i) \tag{6.1}$$

$$Z = b(i, i^*, V, W) \tag{6.2}$$

$$rF = f(i, i^*, V, W) \tag{6.3}$$

$$W = M + Z + rF \tag{6.4}$$

With the domestic price equal to unity, V is both real and nominal income as well as total output. Equation (6.1) is the simplest version of the money demand function, used previously. The demand for domestic and foreign bonds depends upon domestic and foreign interest rates as well as income (output) and wealth. These are given by equations (6.2) and (6.3). The wealth constraint gives (6.4), where W is nominal wealth measured in domestic currency.

Consistency requires that at any point of time, given the value of wealth W

$$VL_1 + b_1 + f_1 = 0 \tag{6.5}$$

$$b_2 + f_2 = 0 \tag{6.6}$$

$$L(i) + b_3 + f_3 = 0 \tag{6.7}$$

$$b_4 + f_4 = 1 \tag{6.8}$$

where b_i is the ith partial derivative of b etc.

The signs of the partials of b and f are important. It is standard that

$$L_1 < 0, \quad b_1 > 0, \quad f_1 < 0$$

$$b_2 < 0, \quad f_2 > 0 \tag{6.9}$$

$$1 > b_4 > 0, \quad 1 > f_4 > 0$$

The signs of b_3 and f_3 are not clear a priori. Essentially these are income effects on the demand for domestic and foreign bonds (remember $b_3 = \partial Z/\partial V$, $f_3 = \partial F/\partial V$). We assume following Gylfason and Helliwell that there is a negative income effect on foreign bonds so that a rise in domestic income reduces the demand for F. Further, we also *assume* an increase in income, for given wealth, increases the demand for money and reduces the demand for foreign bonds, and this leaves the demand for domestic bonds unchanged. Thus we have $f_3 < 0, b_3 = 0$.

Throughout the analysis it is assumed that M and B are exogenously fixed. The value of foreign bonds F is predetermined at any point of time but changes over time, due to international capital movements and as domestic residents acquire foreign assets. Nominal wealth changes correspondingly. It should be noted that the financial wealth constraint (6.4) is akin to a balance sheet, so that only two out of equations (6.1)–(6.3) are independent. In what follows we choose to work with the money and foreign bond 'markets'.

In a fully specified model, there should be a link between the current and capital accounts, as well as between the real and financial sectors of the economy. Since our task in this section is expository, we do not emphasize these links explicitly, rather we concentrate on the portfolio structure. The full model is left for the next section. Rather we will assume the internal balance equation used previously. In principle, it should be remembered, that at any given point of time, given (fixed) M and Z, as well as (predetermined) F and i, the exchange rate adjusts quickly to give portfolio equilibrium. The resulting impact of the exchange rate on the current account causes a change in the trade deficit (or surplus), and this allows the stock of foreign assets to adjust. The conditions for internal balance also change consequent on the trade balance and this affects output. As we shall see in section 6.2, the resulting effects are quite complex.

Coming back to our simple model, consider the asset market equation (6.1)–(6.4). Dropping the (dependent) bond market equation, and noting that M, Z and F are given, we can derive a relation between output V and the exchange rate r, that satisfies portfolio balance. Taking total differentials and eliminating di and dW we get

$$(1 - f_4) F \, dr = \left(-\frac{f_1 L}{V L_1} + f_3\right) dV \tag{6.10}$$

which, using the assumptions made on the partial derivatives, shows that dr/dV must be negative for asset equilibrium. The AA lines in figures 6.1 and 6.2 depict this relationship. A rise in output increases the demand for money, thus the domestic interest rate must rise to equilibriate the money market (equation (6.1)). An increase in i causes nominal demand for foreign bonds to fall. Since all assets must be willingly held, asset equilibrium requires the exchange rate to fall.[1] This reduces the value (in domestic currency) of the supply of foreign bonds.

If the internal balance line is given, as in chapter 2, as IB, then E_1 is the initial pre-tariff equilibrium. The stage is now set for the introduction of a tariff, the revenue R from it being disbursed to domestic residents, thus raising their nominal income by R. Equations (6.1)–(6.3) can now be written as

$$M = (V + R) L (i) \tag{6.11}$$

$$Z = b (i, i^*, V + R, W) \tag{6.12}$$

$$rF = f(i, i^*, V + R, W) \tag{6.13}$$

where $R = rtI$, and t is the tariff rate as before.

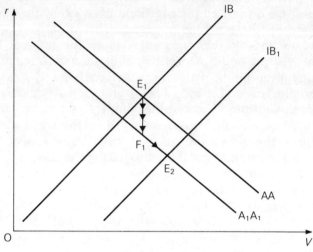

FIGURE 6.1

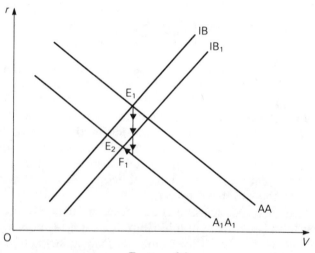

FIGURE 6.2

Once again using (6.11), (6.12) and (6.13) we get a relation between the differentials of r, V and R, eliminating di and dW in the process. Thus

$$(1 - f_4) F \, dr = \left(-\frac{f_1 L}{V L_1} + f_3 \right) dV + \left(-\frac{f_1 L}{V L_1} + f_3 \right) dR \quad (6.14)$$

From (6.14) it is clear that for a given V, an increase (or imposition) of a tariff will reduce r to maintain portfolio equilibrium. The reason is similar; tariffs being redistributed causes income to rise, the interest rate to increase and the exchange rate to fall in the short run, if we require asset markets to clear. Diagrammatically the AA line shifts downwards to A_1A_1. Tariffs will also move the IB line rightwards to IB_1, as discussed in previous chapters. The new equilibrium is established at E_2. Two alternative possibilities are depicted in figures 6.1 and 6.2.

As is clear from the first case given by figure 6.1, output rises and the exchange rate falls. The rightward shift of the IB line compensates for the opposite movement of AA, and the final outcome is that V increases. Tariffs are expansionary. Figure 6.2 shows, on the other hand, that tariffs can lead to a reduction in national product. The exchange rate always appreciates since the revenue effect lowers the AA schedule and the balance of trade effect on IB does the same. The relative shifts of AA and IB will depend of course on parameter values.

The dynamics are interesting. Consider output as a sluggish or predetermined variable that responds to excess demand (or supply). The exchange rate moves instantaneously to clear asset markets. At the initial equilibrium E_1, tariffs are introduced and the revenue redistributed to increase domestic income. Money market equilibrium requires the domestic nominal interest rate to rise. The exchange rate falls, to reduce the nominal supply of foreign bonds, since the demand for overseas bonds has fallen consequent on a fall in the price of domestic bonds (and corresponding rise in its demand). Remember assets are gross substitutes. The instantaneous equilibrium is at F_1 on the new $A_1 A_1$ line, the locus of V and r giving portfolio balance after tariffs are introduced. The exchange rate has appreciated but not significantly to offset the expansionary effects of tariffs emanating from additional income (tariff revenue) and a rise in the domestic terms of trade (Laursen-Metzler). F_1 lies above IB_1, thus there is excess demand for output which pulls up V and final equilibrium is reached along the path F_1E_2.

Figure 6.2 shows the case where the fall in the exchange rate is much higher and thus more contractionary. In fact overshooting occurs as r falls below its new equilibrium consequent on a tariff. Fall in demand due to currency appreciation causes excess supply and output falls along F_1E_2.

The analysis here, though simple, brings out clearly that a portfolio model definitely allows for the possibility of a rise in output subsequent to a general tariff. Once again, the conclusions are in line with our previous chapter; unlike the pessimism in the literature, there is nothing *per se* contractionary about protection under flexible exchange rates. We now consider this result in a more general model noting carefully all the implications and interconnections that portfolio models entail.

6.2   A General Model

Essentially, a general portfolio model will have some specification of goods market equilibrium tagged on to the asset market conditions already specified as well as a well-defined link between the capital and current account. Using the commodity market specification of the previous chapters we therefore get the following

$$H\left(\frac{y}{P}, i\right) = \frac{B}{P} \tag{6.15}$$

$$B = X(r) - rI[y, r(1 + t)] \tag{6.16}$$

$$y = V + trI \tag{6.17}$$

$$P = r^\delta (1 + t)^\delta \tag{6.18}$$

$$M = yL(i) \tag{6.19}$$

$$Z = b(i, i^*, y, W) \tag{6.20}$$

$$rF = f(i, i^*, y, W) \tag{6.21}$$

$$W = M + Z + rF \tag{6.22}$$

We have assumed for simplicity that the domestic price level is unity, thus reverting to the Keynesian models. It is quite a simple extension to include endogenous domestic prices, no substantive conclusions differ.

A more serious omission is that of expectations. In principle all asset demand functions given by (6.11)–(6.13) should contain the expected exchange rate depreciation. Not only is this realistic, it allows also for a richer class of dynamics. The reason for leaving it out is tractability. Since we concentrated on expectations formation in the last chapter and discussed the large variety of results that are possible in the short and medium term, using (rational) expectations, here we concentrate on the essential features of the portfolio structure only. Thus we extend the model in one direction (a richer menu of assets), and simplify in another (static expectations). Exchange rate change is expected to be zero by assumption, and is thus left out from the various asset demand functions.

Equations (6.15)–(6.18) give the internal balance (noting that B is the nominal value of the balance of trade) for the system; t is as usual the tariff rate so that $t = 0$ effectively gives the pre-tariff situation. Equations (6.19)–(6.21) are the conditions for portfolio equilibrium. The allocation of financial wealth W among the three different assets gives the budget constraint (6.22).

As we have seen, in the short run, the above model gives a value of various endogenous variables which preserve equilibrium in the goods and assets markets. However, since we have capital mobility and the possibility of acquiring foreign bonds, balance of trade surplus (deficit) entails capital outflows (inflows) into the economy, thus leading to net accumulation of foreign bonds in the hands of domestic residents. We therefore postulate

$$\dot{RS} = X(r) - rI - r\dot{F} = 0 \tag{6.23}$$

where RS is reserves measured in domestic currency and $\dot{F}$ is the change in domestic holding of foreign bonds, measured in foreign currency. Equation (6.23) tells us that the balance of payments is the sum of net exports and net capital inflows, thus export revenue is used to finance imports and acquisition of foreign assets. This then links the current and capital accounts of the balance of payments.

How does the model, given by (6.15)–(6.23), work? Instantaneous equilibrium obtains when the goods and assets markets clear. This determines the short-run value of nominal output, income and exchange rate. These values are dependent on the predetermined level of foreign asset F. (Remember domestic money and bond supply are fixed.) Current account balance from (6.16) and (6.24) gives the change in F over time. In the next period a new instantaneous equilibrium is again established. For the long-run stationary state we require

$$\dot{F} = 0 \tag{6.24}$$

which simply implies $B = X - rI = 0$, that is external balance of the Keynesian model. Thus the long-run behaviour of the portfolio model is akin to our basic Keynesian one, extensively discussed in chapter 2.

Let us now consider the solution to this model. Using our previous analysis, equations (6.15)–(6.19) may be used to derive the IB line in the (r, V) space. Internal balance requires goods market (IS) and money market (LM) equilibrium. A rise in V requires i to increase for a given supply of money (see (6.19)). Both these factors raise hoarding H. To achieve goods market equilibrium (6.15), trade balance must rise. An increase in V has already caused B to fall. Thus r must rise to compensate (Marshall-Lerner ensures that B will rise too), and make B equal to the increased H. Of course we know that P will also rise, but as assumed throughout, this is not sufficient for H to fall consequent on an increase in V. Thus on the IB line, V and r move together. Note for future reference that by virtue of our simple money demand function, the stock of foreign assets F does not enter the goods and money market equilibrium conditions, thus IB is independent of F[2].

Using the same analysis as in section 6.1, asset equilibrium can be depicted by the downward sloping AA line. Eliminating i from (6.19), (6.21) and (6.22) and noting that M and Z are constants, portfolio balance requires that when V rises, r must fall. An increase in output raises the domestic interest rate from the money market. The consequent reduction in nominal demand for foreign bonds, forces the exchange rate to appreciate (r falls), thus clearing the market for foreign bonds. Note that AA is held in position by the predetermined value of F. An increase in F will shift AA downwards, for a given output (income), r must fall (from (6.21)).

Instantaneous or short run equilibrium once again obtains when IB and AA intersect. But now the story proceeds one step further, since F changes by (6.23). Our major concern then is to establish the conditions for *long-run* equilibrium and observe the effects of a tariff. It is necessary to demonstrate that long-run equilibrium is (at least locally) stable and for this we require

$$\left.\frac{\partial \dot{F}}{\partial F}\right|_{B=0} < 0 \tag{6.25}$$

(remember $B = 0$ is external balance and thus the stationary state). Noting

$$\dot{F} = \frac{B}{r}(V, r), \qquad B_1 < 0, B_2 > 0 \tag{6.26}$$

and also the fact that at each point of time V and r are determined by F itself (intersection of IB and AA) we have

$$\dot{F} = \frac{B(\hat{V}(F), \hat{r}(F))}{\hat{r}(F)} \tag{6.27}$$

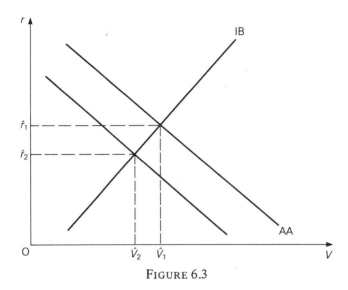

FIGURE 6.3

In figure 6.3, $\hat{V}$ and $\hat{r}$ are the instantaneous values of these variables, given F.

Now consider a rise in F. IB is unchanged and AA moves leftwards. Both $\hat{V}$ and $\hat{r}$ fall. Thus we have

$$\left(\frac{\partial \hat{V}}{\partial F}, \frac{\partial \hat{r}}{\partial F}\right) < 0 \tag{6.28}$$

For stability we need

$$\left.\frac{\partial \dot{F}}{\partial F}\right|_{B=0} = \frac{1}{\hat{r}}\left(B_1 \frac{\partial \hat{V}}{\partial F} + B_2 \frac{\partial \hat{r}}{\partial F}\right) < 0 \tag{6.29}$$

But (6.29) is not necessarily negative, given (6.28) and the signs of B_1 and B_2. Assuming therefore that the negative term dominates the positive, we postulate that the dynamic system for F is stable and the system converges to $\dot{F} = 0$.

Long-run equilibrium requires $\dot{F} = 0$, alternatively $B = 0$. This gives the upward sloping EB line whose slope as analysed in previous chapters is less than the slope of IB. Figure 6.4 then shows this equilibrium at D with the intersection of IB, EB and AA.

The effect of tariffs can now be easily seen. The basic building blocks are all there. Tariffs shift IB rightwards, EB and AA down-

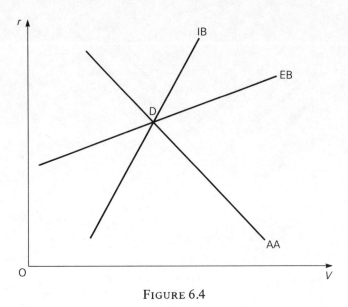

FIGURE 6.4

wards. One possibility is drawn in figure 6.5, with the post-tariff curves labelled IB_1, EB_1 and A_1A_1. It is possible to have an increase in output, thus tariffs can be expansionary. The new post-tariff long-run equilibrium is at G and as is clear from the figure, the exchange rate must fall, but output rises.

Again, the dynamics can be easily interpreted. Suppose the level of output V is slow to respond to excess demand; thus it is predetermined at any point of time. The exchange rate r adjusts rapidly to preserve equilibrium in asset markets. A possible transition path, in figure 6.5, would be given by DFG. Consequent on tariffs, the exchange rate appreciates, r falls and the economy moves quickly from D to F. At F, there is excess demand for domestic output (remember the new long-run equilibrium is at G on IB_1). The impact effect of the tariff is to create a trade surplus; the appreciation of the exchange rate is not sufficient to eliminate this. The point F lies to the left of EB_1, thus it represents a point of (current account) surplus. Output rises, the exchange rate falls, to eliminate excess demand and restore the trade balance in full equilibrium at G.

Tariffs can also, given parameter values, be contractionary. In figure 6.6, the internal balance line shifts less than the external

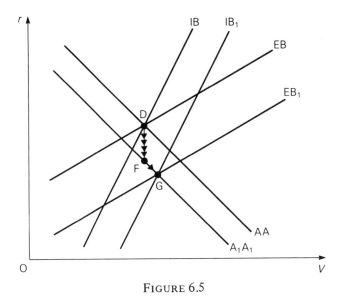

FIGURE 6.5

balance; this leads to a fall in output in long-run equilibrium. The exchange rate overshoots to F, provided output is sluggish. After the impact effect, the economy is characterized by a trade *deficit*, since the appreciation of the exchange rate is high enough to swamp the initial beneficial response to tariffs. Exports fall substantially and we have, at F, excess supply of output and a deficit in the current account. The response is to lower output and increase the rate of exchange to correct the imbalance. The final post-tariff full equilibrium is at G.

It is interesting to contrast our expansionary result with that of Eichengreen (1981), whose formal analysis was the first (to the best of our knowledge) to derive the effects of tariffs in a portfolio model. He found that tariffs may increase output in the short run (as in section 6.1), but would definitely reduce output in the long run. However, his stationary state is characterized by a quantity theory equation

$$vM = y = V + trI \tag{6.30}$$

where v is the income velocity, *assumed* to be constant. Thus starting from a zero tariff, imposition of $t > 0$ implies that the right-hand side of (6.30) increases, the left-hand side remains

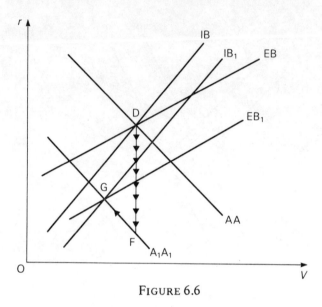

FIGURE 6.6

constant, consequently V has to fall. Tariffs reduce output. However, it is clear that this result hinges on the very simplifying assumption that velocity is constant. If we have assumed $v = 1/L(i)$ (see equation (6.19)), then with the interest rate going up and V rising, it is possible to have V increasing together with trI and still get equilibrium in the asset markets.

The overall conclusion then is similar to what we have consistently maintained. It is possible to have expansionary tariffs both in the short and long run and there is nothing inherently contractionary in macroeconomic protection, as the literature would have us believe. It is of course possible for output to fall, but the final outcome must depend on parameter values.

Notes

1 This is essentially the message of the portfolio approach, see Krueger (1983), 'the exchange rate is the price at which individuals willingly hold the stocks of domestic and foreign assets'.
2 This is a simplification that does not change any conclusions that follow.

7
Commercial Policy, Government Stabilization Policy, Output and Employment under Rigid Real Wages

Calls for protection have increased recently, especially in the UK since 1977 (and the US has always had a strong protectionist lobby). As far as the UK is concerned the protectionist case has been most persistently and vehemently argued by the Cambridge Economic Policy Group (Cripps and Godley, 1976, 1978; Godley and May, 1976; Featherston and Godley, 1978; Godley, 1979; Hindley, 1979) who have provided most of the intellectual justification for the introduction of quotas or more-or-less comprehensive tariffs.

The CEPG's position is that any adjustment of the exchange rate, in a world of 'fixed exchange rates' or of a 'managed float', will not remove the balance of payments constraint that a country such as the UK faces; and so exchange rate adjustments will not permit stimulatory policies to be pursued. The reason for this is real wage resistance. Thus, a devaluation of a country's currency (a rise in r under our definition of the exchange rate) will cause import prices to rise, *ceteris paribus*, and, so the argument goes, cause wages to appreciate accordingly. In effect, through the view that workers are no longer subject to money illusion, the attempt to bargain for a level of real wages by workers will lead to a situation where as far as possible money wages are appreciating *pari passu* with the rise in the cost of living (which is dependent upon import prices). The consequence is that we have economies now, certainly in the Western world, where we do have real wage rigidity. This, naturally, is a special case of the familiar hypothesis advanced by Keynes (1936) that *money* wages are likely to be rigid in a downward direction.

147

The view *is* prevalent, amongst Western politicians as well as neo-classical economists, that real wages are a major factor in determining the level of employment in an economy. Certainly, in an open economy, the level of real wages, given technology and hence productivity, can be a key element in determining the level of economic activity through its influence on the country's competitive position. The kind of pronouncements that emanate from CEPG about real wage rigidity are seen increasingly to be realistic. Therefore, if real wages are important determinants of the level of employment, they argue that exchange rate adjustments will not alter (radically) the real wage and, as a consequence, will not in fact improve the balance of trade. In effect, real incomes will have been so adjusted that under conventional assumptions about the economy's import demand function (of the sort we have made so far) and about the demand for the country's exports (dependent upon the real exchange rate), there will be no change in either imports or exports, and hence, in the balance of trade. Thus with the adjustments of wages to compensate fully for the change in prices generated by exchange rate movements, the real income of the domestic residents remains unaltered; so too do the terms of trade. Any possible boost to domestic output that could arise through a 'devaluation' type promotion of exports has been dissipated by the compensating variation in the domestic price of home-produced goods due to the equivalent variation in money wages.

Now, in a world that is somewhat less than the ideal for exchange rates to be fully flexible, there will be exchange rate adjustment occurring which will lead, in a world of real wage rigidity, to the kind of scenario, *à la* CEPG, pictured above. So the balance of payments, even if only in the 'short run', will be a constraint on the conduct of macroeconomic stabilization policies. That constraint can be circumvented by the government imposing a *general* tariff or a quota (although in reality, as CEPG advocate, it is likely to exclude intervention in the food and raw materials markets).

As Cripps and Godley (1978) have written, to give just a flavour of their cogently argued opinions on this issue:

Fiscal expansion accompanied by direct control of imports (whether through tariffs or quotas) is the only practical means by which the UK, and probably several other industrial countries, can sustain expansion of national output sufficient to restore full employment in the next decade...

Effective devaluation raises both import and export prices relative to home costs and prices. In so doing it cuts real wages and raises export profits. This highly inflationary transfer of income occurs whether or not there is any deterioration in the external terms of trade, and it occurs before there is any significant gain to real national income in aggregate. It is not possible for the government to suppress the effect by redistributive taxation without destroying the mechanism through which devaluation stimulates exports... The inflationary consequences of devaluation are such that at best only minor adjustments can be achieved by this means, and even these may require uncomfortably large falls in the nominal exchange rate...

Control of imports... need to have no inflationary consequences... Imports themselves may be more expensive to final buyers when their volume is controlled, but if tariffs or auctioned quotas are used as the mechanism of the restriction, the additional domestic cost of imports accrues as revenue to the government and can be handed back to consumers through general tax reductions or subsidies without in any way destroying the beneficial effect on import propensities and aggregate demand... If control of imports is ruled out and the policy choice lies between deflation and devaluation, the notion of a steep trade-off between inflation and unemployment has substance because of the impact of devaluation on import costs and money wages. The choice between deflation and devaluation presents a genuine dilemma and is very much a question of preferences. Control of imports has become a significant policy option precisely because it offers an escape from this dilemma. (Cripps and Godley, 1978, pp. 327, 331)

These views have tended to meet hostile reactions at the hands of political leaders and they have been challenged in the recent literature on commercial policy and the macroeconomy in a world of flexible exchange rates (Krugman, 1982). Strictly, as expressed, they should be evaluated in a world where exchange rates are 'fixed' or where the floating rates exist but they are 'managed', rather than being permitted to reflect fully excess demand/supplies in the foreign exchange market. Under a *truly* flexible exchange rate regime, naturally, almost *ex hypothesi*, the balance of payments can present no problem to economic policy makers.

However, rather than develop a framework to consider a managed float, we retain the limiting case of a fully flexible exchange rates world utilized hitherto, which permits us to examine the view that if there is real wage resistance the kind of policy options advocated by the CEPG are not propitious to the macroeconomy.

In the next section we shall consider the effect of import restrictions in a rigid real wages model. The discussion and analysis will consider both a general tariff and a quota. Ensuing sections of this chapter will extend the model of section 7.1 to incorporate in more detail the presence and role of the tariff revenue, the effect of quotas, subsidies and government stabilization policy, in the macroeconomy. Additionally, in section 7.5, we shall investigate the further propositions that have been propounded by the CEPG on the (favourable) effects of the adoption of import-restricting policies; such as the effect on the 'rest of the world' that emerges through the home country's changed import demand as a consequence of the trade restrictions.

7.1   *A Fixed Real Wages Model under Flexible Exchange Rates*

The model that we shall use as the foundation of our analysis is that described by Modigliani and Padoa-Schioppa (1978) as their framework for investigating the effects of wage-indexation in an open macroeconomy.

The essential situation is identical with that which we have portrayed in the comparative statics models of previous chapters. We are, in effect, considering a small open macroeconomy. It is posited to produce a bundle of goods which it consumes (invests as necessary) and exports. The rate of exchange is flexible; and it is determined by the balance of payments equilibrium. The latter occurs when the value of exports equals the value of imports in domestic currency; the assumption being, therefore, that there are no capital flows between countries. It is also supposed that there is no explicit money sector.

Equilibrium in the real goods market obtains, as usual, where (*ex ante*) aggregate demand for domestic production equals (*ex ante*) supply. The demand comprises domestic residents' demand for home goods and export demand. We can also incorporate, quite easily, a government sector.

The central difference between this model and that used hitherto is that we now have an equation for domestic *supply*. The internal equilibrium is determined jointly by demand and supply and is not demand determined as it is in the basic Mundellian (Keynesian) paradigm. The supposition is, in effect, that aggregate output (supply) V depends solely upon the real wage in terms of 'the' domestic good, by the classical profit maximization property. Consequently we can write the domestic price of 'the' domestic good P_d as

$$P_d = \tilde{W}f(V) \quad f_1 > 0 \tag{7.1}$$

where $\tilde{W}$ is the money wage. The notion of *real wage rigidity* can now be introduced by the Modigliani–Padoa-Schioppa (1978) assumption that the money wage is indexed.[1] Let it be indexed to the consumer price index P as we have called it hitherto; or the price of absorption, or the price of the bundle of goods consumed by the home economy.

Therefore

$$\tilde{W} = \bar{w}P \tag{7.2}$$

the money wage is a constant $\bar{w}$, scaled up by the overall price level. Now, as previously, let

$$P = P_d^{1-\delta} r^\delta (1 + t)^\delta \tag{7.3}$$

since we are still normalizing the foreign currency price of importables at unity, but are permitting the domestic price of the home-produced bundle P_d to vary. That price, therefore, will appear in the terms of trade.

The model then consists of these equations in addition to (7.1)–(7.3)

$$V = C\left(Y, \frac{r(1 + t)}{P_d}\right) + X\left(\frac{r}{P_d}\right) \tag{7.4}$$

$$P_d X\left(\frac{r}{P_d}\right) = rI\left(Y, \frac{r(1 + t)}{P_d}\right) \tag{7.5}$$

$$Y = \frac{P_d V + R}{P_d} \tag{7.6}$$

$$R = trI\left(Y, \frac{r(1 + t)}{P_d}\right) \tag{7.7}$$

Y is disposable income measured in term of the home good, R is nominal tariff revenue. Equations (7.4) and (7.5) are the conditions for internal and external balance respectively. The right-hand side of equation (7.4) specifies the total demand for home output as the sum of $C(.)$, domestic demand, and $X(.)$, foreign demand.[2] V in equation (7.4) is the supply of output, which is determined by equation (7.1), the inverse of the supply equation. If we substitute equation (7.2) into equation (9.1) we have

$$P_d = \bar{w} P f(V) \tag{7.8}$$

or

$$\bar{w} \left(\frac{r}{P_d} \right)^\delta (1 + t)^\delta f(V) = 1 \tag{7.8$'$}$$

The model, given by (7.4), (7.5) and (7.8), has three endogenous variables V, Y and (r/P_d). In our previous analysis, in chapter 2, we had two endogenous variables, output and the (real) exchange rate. Disposable income y could be derived *after* the determination, through internal and external balance, of aggregate output and the rate of exchange. The endogeneity of Y makes the redistribution of tariff revenue less relevant since it does not appear *explicitly* in the formulation. Thus, as we shall see later, whether the government spends the tariff revenue (in nominal terms), or gives it back to the households as a transfer, the final conclusions remain invariant.

The model also has some interesting classical properties. There is an implicit dichotomy; real variables are determined by the system given above while nominal variables are indeterminate. We have the famous homogeneity property, where if all nominal variables changed proportionately, real variables would be unchanged. Thus nominal shocks to the system cannot affect real values of output, income and prices. Monetary and fiscal parameters denominated in money terms are ineffective in expanding output since their impact will be crowded out by price changes. There is a one-to-one correspondence between real and nominal shocks on the one hand and real and nominal variables on the other. Thus macroeconomic policies using nominal instruments will affect nominal variables but not real ones. It is in this context that real shocks become necessary to stimulate the economy. Tariffs, by changing relative prices, are therefore potentially useful policy instruments. However, it is the relative price change that really matters. As mentioned earlier, government expenditure of the nominal tariff revenue, *per se*, cannot change the conclusions that emanate from those pertaining to real price effects.

The other characteristic worth noting is the major emphasis put on the supply side. Equation (7.8') shows that real disposable income, a major determinant of aggregate demand, does not figure in the determination of the supply of output. It is true, of course, that relative prices (P/P_d) or (r/P_d) will be affected by demand considerations. We do not have the old classical dichotomy. What we do have is the independence, directly, of aggregate supply from income changes. This will have major implications for the analysis that follows. In particular, government policies which affect the supply side will prove to be more effective than usual policy models would suggest. In principle, of course, the authorities can generate real demand shocks, say, by commandeering a proportion of total output. However, if the government's expenditure is adjusted in nominal terms, this may not be translated into real demand effects. We proceed to a formal analysis of the role of the general tariff t in the economy characterized by equations (7.3)–(7.5) and (7.8). From these equations, substituting for $d(P/P_d)$ we discover that

$$
\begin{bmatrix}
-1 & C_1 & C_2(1+t)+X_1 \\[2em]
0 & \dfrac{r}{P_d}I_1 & I_2(1+t)\dfrac{r}{P_d}+I-X_1 \\[2em]
\dfrac{-f_1}{f(V)}\dfrac{r}{P_d}^{\delta} & 0 & -\delta\dfrac{r}{P_d}^{\delta-1}
\end{bmatrix}
\begin{bmatrix}
\dfrac{dV}{dt} \\[2em]
\dfrac{dY}{dt} \\[2em]
\dfrac{d(r/P_d)}{dt}
\end{bmatrix}
=
\begin{bmatrix}
-C_1\dfrac{r}{P_d} \\[2em]
-I_2\dfrac{r}{P_d}^{2} \\[2em]
\dfrac{\delta}{1+t}\dfrac{r}{P_d}^{\delta}
\end{bmatrix}
$$

$$(7.9)$$

Hence

$$
\frac{\partial V}{\partial t} \gtreqless 0 \quad \text{as} \quad \frac{r}{P_d}I_1 X_1 - C_1(I-X_1) \lesseqgtr 0 \tag{7.10}
$$

This condition holds even if we set *the* initial tariff at zero. The determinant of the Jacobian in equation (7.9) is uniquely positive on the standard assumption about the signs of the behavioural parameters and on the presumption that the Marshall–Lerner condition $(X_1 - I_2(1+t)(r/P_d) - I) > 0$ is satisfied.

Given that the price elasticity of exports is x

$$
x = \frac{r}{P_d}\frac{X_1}{X} > 0 \tag{7.11}
$$

Condition (7.10) can be written as, in equilibrium,

$$\frac{\partial V}{\partial t} \gtreqless 0 \quad \text{as} \quad C_1 I(1-x) - \frac{r}{P_d} X_1 I_1 \gtreqless 0 \tag{7.12}$$

Thus a sufficient condition for a contractionary tariff is that $x > 1$. On the other hand a necessary condition for an expansionary tariff is given by $x < 1$. We can also deduce that

$$\text{sign}\,\frac{\partial Y}{\partial t} = \text{sign}\left\{\left[\frac{\delta}{1+t} + \frac{f_1 C_2}{f(V)}\frac{r}{P_d}\right](I - X_1) - \frac{f_1}{f(V)}\left(\frac{r}{P_d}\right)^2 I_2\right\} \tag{7.12a}$$

$$\text{sign}\,\frac{\partial (r/P_d)}{\partial t} = \text{sign}\left[\frac{f_1}{f(V)}\frac{r}{P_d}(C_1 I_2 - C_2 I_1) - \frac{I_1 \delta}{1+t}\right] \tag{7.12b}$$

$$\text{sign}\,\frac{\partial (r(1+t)/P_d)}{\partial t} = \text{sign}\left(-\frac{\partial V}{\partial t}\right) \tag{7.12c}$$

Therefore r/P_d falls uniquely as a tariff is imposed or is increased; and if $x < 1$, real income will definitely increase under the general tariff, even if the value of x is not sufficient to produce an increase in domestic output. The domestic relative price of importables moves in the opposite direction to V.

It is a straightforward matter to illustrate these results diagrammatically. We can telescope the four equation system characterized by equations (7.3)–(7.5) and (7.8) into one of two equations in two variables. Thus from (7.3) and (7.8) we obtain

$$\frac{r}{P_d} = \frac{1}{(1+t)[\bar{w}f(V)]^{1/\delta}} \tag{7.13}$$

and from equations (7.4) and (7.5) solving implicitly for Y in terms of V and r/P_d from the IB schedule we can write the EB schedule as

$$V = F\left(\frac{r}{P_d}, t\right) \tag{7.14}$$

Equation (7.13) provides us with a negative relationship, for given t, between r/P_d and V. It also informs us that when a tariff is imposed the relationship shifts to the left in $(V, r/P_d)$ space. Thus a tariff, or an increase in the level of the tariff, will reduce the level of output at a given terms of trade and given $\bar{w}$; because under those conditions the real wage to labour has increased in terms of the domestic good since $\tilde{W}$ increases to match the pure effect of the tariff.

The partial derivatives of the behavioural equations in (7.4) and (7.5) reveal that F_1 and F_2 in equation (7.14) are positive. V and r/P_d are positively related; the levying or increasing of a tariff increases V, at given terms of trade, because it stimulates home and foreign demand for domestic production. The situation is illustrated on figure 7.1, where W_1W_1 depicts equation (7.13) under a tariff (or an increased tariff). Similarly, D_1D_1 depicts equation (7.14). The new equilibrium Z evidently, can be directly below E, to the right of E, or to the left of E. But one outcome is clear: r/P_d must fall as the formal analysis has shown.

It is to be noted that the current model, because of its homogeneity property, has the attribute that we can consider the levying of a tariff as we would a structural change.

As we have seen in the formal solution, the disbursement of tariff revenues plays no *explicit* role in the final outcome. Disposable income Y and output V are jointly determined; so also is the real exchange rate r/P_d, the index of competitiveness; therefore nominal tariff revenues fall out almost as a residual, from equations (7.6) and (7.7), in level being such as to be consistent with values of Y and V. Thus, in principle, the conditions which generate the sign of dV/dt should not change when

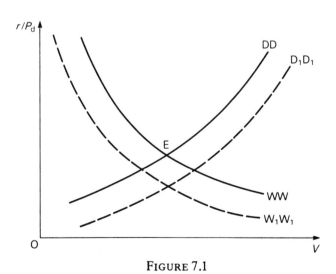

FIGURE 7.1

an alternative scheme of revenue distribution is considered. Suppose the government wishes to spend the whole revenue on the domestic product, rather than passing it on to households as a transfer. There will be some expansion of domestic demand since households do spend part of their disposable income on imports. But the final conclusion regarding the effect of tariffs on output will remain the same. Remember government spending, from tariff revenue, is denominated in nominal terms rtI. This is therefore an alternative way of stating that fiscal expansion in *nominal* terms cannot *change* the direction in which the economy will move consequent on a real shock.

Under the postulated conditions we have, instead of equations (7.4) and (7.6), the following

$$V = C\left(Y, \frac{r(1+t)}{P_d}\right) + X\left(\frac{r}{P_d}\right) + t\left(\frac{r}{P_d}\right)I\left(Y, \frac{r(1+t)}{P_d}\right) \quad (7.4')$$

$$Y = V \quad (7.6')$$

(7.12) then becomes, after solving the system,

$$\frac{\partial V}{\partial t} \lesseqgtr 0 \quad \text{as} \quad C_1 I(1-x) + \frac{r}{P_d}I_1(1-x) \lesseqgtr 0 \quad (7.12')$$

Once again if the export elasticity is greater than unity, $x > 1$, a tariff causes output to fall.

It should also be noted that if $x > 1$, then from (7.5) the volume of imports will also decline. Alternatively, since the world price is given by unity, the value of imports in foreign currency will fall. The appreciation of the real exchange rate causes a decline in export volume. If the price elasticity of exports is greater than one then the foreign currency value of exports will fall. Under balanced trade, imports measured in foreign prices must therefore go down. In this sense, under real wage resistance, and provided $x > 1$, we have an international trade contraction and a sort of beggar-my-neighbour policy (which also happens to harm the home economy). Such a suicidal protectionist race can be Pareto inferior for the world. But as we shall see shortly, the conclusions are predicated by the specific structure of the model. In addition, there will always be countervailing interventionist policies in addition to the protection given above which can increase output all round. More discussion on this issue can be found later.

There is some empirical evidence that export price elasticities of a single small open economy may be greater than one. Thus the contractionary tariff argument could be valid in an economy with real wage rigidity. However, since we have mentioned the international economy here, it is fair to point out that if a group of countries are operating tariffs the export elasticities for each will probably go down with protection. If x then becomes less than unity and real wages are fixed in a classical world then we have a quite different picture. Output expands, the real exchange rate depreciates, exports increase in volume and import value rises. Of course, this *cannot* happen if *all* countries pursue the same protectionist policies. To paraphrase Krugman (1982), in a world of Englands protectionism will fail worldwide; however, if there are some Englands, for historical reasons or otherwise, and they are allowed to rejuvenate under the protectionist umbrella, then the international economy can gain.

It is important, and interesting, to note the relevance of the elasticity assumption, as well as to compare it with the results obtained for the Mundell–Keynes model of chapter 2. Basically, $x > 1$ or $(X_1 - I) > 0$ implies that the Metzler paradox does not hold. Therefore, the tariff induced relative price, of importables with respect to the domestic product $(r(1 + t)/P_d)$, rises. Since the nominal wage is indexed to the price of importables, the real wage *relevant to the firm* also increases. The supply equation, (7.8) or (7.8'), shows that output *must* fall. The supply effects are dominant. Tariffs raise demand for the home good, thus putting a pressure from the demand side on P_d/r to rise, but this is insufficient, in equilibrium, to counteract the inflationary forces on inputs emanating from protection. Since the supply side is independent of real income, given an increase in $(r(1 + t)/P_d)$, output has to decline; this is clearly seen from (7.8'). To be consistent, demand must follow supply. Expenditure switching and possible reimbursement of tariffs do indeed raise domestic demand for the home product C. But exports fall substantially due to the inevitable exchange rate appreciation (remember they have a high elasticity). Thus (reduced) supply creates its own (lower) demand. As figure 7.1 shows, the WW curve representing the supply side moves leftwards. Conversely, the DD curve embodying demand effects moves rightwards. Under the implicit elasticity assumption, the contractionary supply side wins.

In the analysis of chapter 2, the supply side was effectively absent. Tariffs caused expenditure switching towards the domestic product. But this was not enough to compensate for the increase in hoarding (saving) that took place due to redistribution of tariff revenues to households. The Metzler non-paradox implied that the aggregate price level went up; this reduced hoarding and created demand. It was possible to have a final expansionary effect; aggregate demand could be stimulated by tariffs. The crucial importance of the supply side, *à la* classicals, denies this channel from operating. Demand still rises here, but supply falls more.

7.2   Fiscal and Commercial Policy with Real Wage Rigidity

The CEPG position (as we have partly seen) is that there will be suitable fiscal policies that can be implemented alongside the imposition of controls on imports to improve the output/employment prospects of the economy under real wage rigidity. Krugman (1982) has attempted to tackle this general proposition by a simple procedure. He has assumed that initially, under free trade, the government has imposed an *ad valorem* tax on the price level P, or 'the price of absorption', in effect there is a tax of θ per cent levied on P.

Consequently, we write

$$P = P_d^{1-\delta} r^\delta (1 + t)^\delta (1 + \theta) \tag{7.15}$$

His argument is that when t is introduced (or increased), θ is lowered to offer a compensating variation in P; so that the aim is to lower the money wage, thus lowering the real wage in terms of the price of domestic output. Such an outcome would stimulate the supply of domestically-produced goods.

The analysis of such a situation should embody consideration of the distribution of the sales tax. In the Krugman (1982) presentation it is not clear how that issue is being handled. Without any explicit government budget constraint,[3] the implication has to be that the sales tax revenue is handed back to domestic residents since nowhere in the model is there any form of government demand. The sales revenue is being reimbursed to domestic residents in just the same manner as is the tariff revenue. We can also implicitly assume that the government maintains a balanced budget, paying for the loss in sales tax revenue with the revenue earned from tariffs. We therefore ignore the complications raised in Blinder and Solow (1973, 1974) since we wish to focus on tariffs.

With a sales tax the pre- and post-tariff versions of equation (7.13) become

$$\frac{r}{P_d} = \frac{1}{[\bar{w}f(V)(1 + \theta)]^{1/\delta}} \tag{7.16}$$

$$\frac{r}{P_d} = \frac{1}{[\bar{w}f(V)(1 + \theta)]^{1/\delta}(1 + t)} \tag{7.17}$$

Thus the tariff would shift WW to W_1W_1 on figure 7.1 for unchanged θ. If θ is reduced then W_1W_1 will be moved back towards WW. Since the DD schedule is unaffected by the sales tax the chances of an improvement in output and employment consequent upon the imposition of a general tariff are that much higher. Clearly, there will be an optimum combination of tariff and sales tax reduction which will enable the government to lift output to a target level.

From the system incorporating a sales tax[4] we can deduce that if output is to remain constant, that is $dV = 0$, we need the absolute value of the change in θ with respect to a change in t to be

$$\frac{1 + t}{1 + \theta}\left|\frac{d\theta}{dt}\right| = \left|\frac{\delta[C_1(I - X_1) - \lambda I_1 X_1]}{C_1[I + \lambda(1 + t)I_2 - X_1] - [C_2(1 + t) + X_1]\lambda I_1}\right| \tag{7.18}$$

The initial tariff rate is set at zero. $\lambda = r/P_d$ is the real exchange rate or the index of international competitiveness.

For a given change in t, if the absolute value of the fall in θ is greater than that given by (7.18), we have a situation where output expands after the imposition of tariffs. The numerator of the expression is well known (see (7.10) and note $\lambda = r/P_d$). The denominator tells us that there are two possible effects of the reduction in the tax rate θ. For a given real exchange, a fall in θ means that nominal wages can be reduced since the price of the absorption basket is now reduced. Firms respond by increasing employment and thus output; real income rises, but so does the budget deficit; this puts pressure on the real exchange rate which depreciates; demand increases to match supply. The effect of domestic income on aggregate demand and thus output is given by two components; the first is through the marginal propensity to spend C_1 and the second through the trade balance changes or Marshall–Lerner $(X_1 - \lambda I_2 - I)$. The effect of the rise in the real exchange rate in boosting local and foreign demand works through C_2 and X_1.

It is apparent that there will be some scope for the government to select a combination of θ and t to achieve a preassigned level of output (employment). But rather than investigate the range of situations over which that conjecture will be valid, and so deduce situations where one extreme policy or the other might be appropriate, we can examine briefly the analogous situation when the government is considering the imposition of a new policy or alteration of any existing one, to bolster output and employment, and it is thus concerned with changes in those variables. Such consideration parallels that undertaken previously in this book, and it avoids the immense degree of complexity, and hence indeterminacy, that can arise, as we have noted, from endeavours to solve these models for the levels of the variables.

The differential equations of the complete system with a pre-existing tariff are set out in general in equation (7.17a) (note 4).

In general, then, for given $dV/dt = Z$, we have

$$d\theta = \frac{\Delta Z}{\gamma_2} - \frac{\gamma_1}{\gamma_2}\, dt \tag{7.19}$$

where Δ is the determinant of the Jacobian in equation (7.17a), which is positive; (and where $\lambda = r/P_d$)

$$\left. \begin{aligned} \gamma_1 &= \delta\lambda^\delta\left[\lambda(I_1 C_2 - I_2 C_1) + \frac{1+t}{A}\right] \gtreqless 0 \\[2ex] \gamma_2 &= \frac{\lambda^\delta A}{1+\theta} < 0 \\[2ex] A &= C_2[I_2(1+t)\lambda + I - X_1] - \lambda[C_2(1+t) + X_1]\,I_1 < 0 \end{aligned} \right\} \tag{7.20}$$

Therefore, equation (7.20) can be plotted in the manner illustrated on figure 7.2. At any given t, the higher the required change in output ($Z_1 > Z_2 > Z_3$) the bigger must be the reduction in θ for any given increase in the tariff.

Since the model allows the authorities to expand output by supply side changes emanating from a reduction in indirect taxation, is there really any need for a tariff which may be contractionary under the assumption that export elasticity is greater than unity? The answer is positive for at least two reasons. Tariffs allow the underlying aggregate demand function (DD in figure 7.1) to shift rightwards, thus there are expenditure switching, absorption raising, demand creating, factors at work. An indirect tax only affects the supply side directly, though of course there are indirect demand effects. If the government believes that lack of domestic demand expansion is the main culprit behind stagnation, it may stimulate it through protection. The adverse supply side effects are then mitigated through compensating tax changes. Secondly,

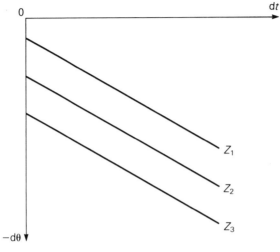

FIGURE 7.2

there need not be real budgetary effects for the postulated policies. The new tariff revenue exactly balances the loss in sales revenue, thus balanced budget policies can be followed. If indirect taxes are reduced *per se* there will be concomitant difficulties with the money supply and public sector borrowing which may create a new set of policy problems.

The 'second-best' argument against tariffs has been conducted along these lines. It has been claimed, and rightly so, that export/import taxes affect both the consumption and production side when it may be necessary only to control either side separately. But, as we have just noted, it is often the desire of governments to affect both demand and supply simultaneously. If, for example, the export elasticity is less than one, then beneficial supply *and* demand effects can operate together. Further, the budgetary arguments should be considered carefully. Tariffs may be introduced, together with a tax/subsidy policy as described, to correct for domestic distortions, say, caused by unemployment. The budgetary effects are neutral. On the other hand, a pure tax/subsidy policy may require a deficit in the government sector causing, possibly, another distortion like higher inflation. Both types of policies are then second best and it is problematic to compare them.

In the previous analyses and discussions we have seen that the tariff revenue and the taxation reductions have no *explicit* role to play. Should the government transfer the revenue receipts to the personal sector, the homogeneity property of the system masks the implications of those transfers. To ascertain the likely part played by such transfers we should permit the government itself to play an active, demand-creating, role in the economy.

However, before we turn our attention to that kind of consideration, we shall comment on a situation where the government intervenes to lessen any unfavourable impact of a general tariff by a subsidy scheme, without the government itself undertaking any direct expenditure on home or imported goods.

We would expect that the government would be seeking to maximize the success of its policy strategy in expanding the economy and that it would not be so blinkered as to concentrate on one-off policies. Thus, it would see immediately that one obvious way in which to increase the likelihood of boosting output by its imposing a general tariff would be for it to offer a subsidy to domestic producers. Such a device would mean that P_d was lower at any given level of output; the 'effective' mark up on costs would always be lower than hitherto. So, at any given P_d, output would be expanded (profitably). The subsidy *per se* would then have the effect of shifting the WW schedule on figure 7.1 to the right. Essentially, the real wage in domestic goods falls and so employment and output are stimulated. Yet the subsidy (because of the properties of this type of model) do not impinge on the DD schedule. A general tariff will shift DD to the right and so enhance the *ceteris paribus* effect of the subsidy. But the tariff itself acts as a countervailing force to the favourable shift of the WW schedule imparted by the subsidy. So there will be an optimum combination of subsidy and tariff; or an optimum combination of changes in those two variables, as relevant.

Thus, as a simple example, take the case where wages are subsidized by a factor S, $(0 < S \leqslant 1)$. Then the price of domestically-produced goods will obey the equation

$$P_d = \bar{w}P(1 - S)f(V) \tag{7.21}$$

Making use of the definition of P, we have

$$\delta\left(\frac{r}{P_d}\right)^{\delta-1} d\left(\frac{r}{P_d}\right) = \frac{-f_1(r/P_d)^\delta}{\delta(V)} \, dV - \frac{\delta(r/P_d)^\delta}{(1+t)} \, dt + \frac{(r/P_d)^\delta}{1-S} \, dS \tag{7.22}$$

This is identical, as expected, with the derivation of r/P_d with respect to V, t and θ, with $1 + \theta$ and $d\theta$ being replaced by $1 - S$ and $-dS$ respectively (see equation (7.17a), note 4). Thus, referring back to equation (7.19), the 'trade-off' between dS and dt is identical with that drawn on figure 7.2, with $-d\theta$ set as dS; again, the outcome is intuitively appealing. The implication being, naturally, that if the model is solved (numerically) for the levels of the variables, there will exist an optimum combination of tariff and subsidy to produce specific levels of output and employment (not just a tariff or a subsidy).

7.3   Government Expenditure and the Impact of a General Tariff Under Rigid Real Wages

We shall now rescind the supposition that the government plays only a passive role in the economy. We shall presume that, at the most general level, the government will spend its revenue on home and foreign goods; the limiting possibilities always being present in the model, namely that it decides to allocate all of its expenditure to home-produced goods and none to imports or vice versa. The government's budget constraint must now be taken as an integral part of the model. We commence by assuming that the government only raises revenue by means of the general tariff. Thus the following condition must be satisfied

$$P_\text{d} G_H + G_I = (1 - \mu)\, R \tag{7.23}$$

where G_H is the level of *real* expenditure by the government on home-produced output, G_I is the domestic currency value of its expenditure on imported goods, R is the domestic currency value of the tariff revenue and μ is the proportion of that revenue transferred to the personal sector. We thus assume that the government levies no direct or indirect taxes.

We further let

$$G_H = \frac{\alpha(1 - \mu)\, R}{P_\text{d}} \quad \text{and} \quad G_I = (1 - \alpha)(1 - \mu)\, R \tag{7.24}$$

So, α is the proportion of its revenue that the government spends on home-produced goods. The system is still one that exhibits the zero-homogeneity characteristic so that in differential form it can be set out in terms of dY, dV, $d(r/P_d)$ and $d(P_d/P)$. Having solved for $d(P_d/P)$ the system becomes

$$
\begin{bmatrix} a_{11} & a_{12} & a_{13} \\ a_{21} & a_{22} & a_{23} \\ a_{31} & a_{32} & a_{33} \end{bmatrix} \begin{bmatrix} dV \\ dY \\ d(r/P_d) \end{bmatrix} = \begin{bmatrix} b_1 \\ b_2 \\ b_3 \end{bmatrix} dt \tag{7.25}
$$

where

$$
a_{11} = -1, \quad a_{21} = 0, \quad a_{31} = \frac{-f_1(r/P_d)^\delta}{f(V)}, \quad a_{32} = 0
$$

$$
a_{12} = C_1 + \alpha(1 - \mu)\left(\frac{r}{P_d}\right) t I_1
$$

$$
a_{13} = C_2(1 + t) + X_1 + \alpha(1 - \mu)\left(\frac{r}{P_d}\right) t I_2(1 + t) + \alpha(1 - \mu) It
$$

$$
a_{22} = \left[\frac{r}{P_d} + (1 - \alpha)(1 - \mu) tr\right] I_1
$$

$$
a_{23} = \left[\frac{r}{P_d} + (1 - \alpha)(1 - \mu) tr\right][I_2(1 + t)] + I - X_1
$$

$$
a_{33} = -\delta\left(\frac{r}{P_d}\right)^{\delta - 1}
$$

$$
b_1 = -\frac{r}{P_d}\left[C_2 + \alpha(1 - \mu) I + \alpha(1 - \mu) t I_2\left(\frac{r}{P_d}\right)\right]
$$

$$
b_2 = -\left[\frac{r}{P_d} + (1 - \alpha)(1 - \mu) tr\right] I_2\left(\frac{r}{P_d}\right) - (1 - \alpha)(1 - \mu) Ir
$$

$$
b_3 = \frac{\delta(r/P_d)^\delta}{1 + t}
$$

In these conditions a_{23} is the negative of the Marshall–Lerner condition. Assuming that that condition is satisfied and that $a_{13} > 0$, it follows that the determinant of the Jacobian of equation (7.25) is positive. Hence we deduce, with the initial tariff set at zero, that

$$
\frac{\partial V}{\partial t} \gtreqless 0 \quad \text{as} \quad -I_1 X_1\left(\frac{r}{P_d}\right)^2 + \frac{r}{P_d} C_1(I - X_1) + \left(\frac{r}{P_d}\right)^2 I_1 I\alpha(1 - \mu)
$$
$$
- Ir(1 - \alpha)(1 - \mu) C_1 \gtreqless 0 \tag{7.26}
$$

In essence this is the condition presented in equation (7.10) with the addition of the two terms involving I (which appear through the medium of the tariff revenue). If $I > X_1$, such that x is sufficiently small to generate a positive dV/dt in the case where the government plays no active role in the economy, we see from equation (7.26) that as α approaches unity, for given μ, the beneficial impact on output will be greater than in the variant of the model wherein the domestic residents spend all of the tariff proceeds. In essence, the general result supports the basic intuition that the expending of the revenue by the government, biased towards home-produced goods, must improve the chances of the general tariff's having a beneficial effect on the level of economic activity even under rigid real wages. Should the government spend most of the tariff revenue itself and on home-produced goods, the schedule DD will be shifted further to the right on figure 7.1, with the imposition of (or increase in) a general tariff, than in the case where the revenue is recycled back to the personal sector.

The more interesting form of the basic model is one wherein the government also raises *general*, as opposed to indirect, taxes. Naturally, in principle we can have two possible versions of the model; the one is where taxes are raised by a poll tax (equal to T in *nominal* units of domestic currency); the other is where taxes are generated via an income tax of τ per cent of the value of domestic output.

The case where government expenditure is introduced via a poll tax is of intrinsic importance because it brings a nominal variable into the model that can, in theory, influence the real variable output, real disposable income, and relative prices including the terms of trade. The general conclusion that has emerged from the utilization of this model structure has been that the conventional weapons of government policy, namely fiscal-policy inspired expenditures and changes in the money supply, can only have (classical) neutrality effects on real variables. Changes in monetary variables such as government expenditure and the money supply affect only nominal variables, but do so by the same proportionate amount. Hence, for example, any impact on the exchange rate r will be transmitted equally to, say, the domestic price of domestic output (see Modigliani and Padoa-Schioppa (1978); their view is repeated by Krugman (1982) and incorporated implicitly by Eichengreen (1981).[5]

Unfortunately, the results derived from the imposition of a poll tax, even if μ is set to unity and the initial tariff is set equal to zero, cannot be unscrambled by any meaningful economic interpretation; so we omit them, since they would only complicate the text for no useful purpose.[6] All that can be said is that there do exist sets of circumstances when there can be a trade-off between a change in poll taxes and a change in the general tariff; such that with an increase in the general tariff there will be changes in taxes that will enhance the output repercussions of the change in the general tariff. Mitigating fiscal policy is possible. The essential difficulty produced by the incorporation of a poll tax in the model is that it rescinds the zero degree homogeneity of the equation explaining the real variables; that fact makes the analysis of even this small model unduly complex. But it is that fact which creates the possibility that expansionary fiscal policy can affect real variables. We shall content ourselves with some analysis of fiscal policy via income taxes, with τ being the marginal rate of tax. We need now to specify the government's budget constraint, which can be written in its most general form as

$$P_d G_H + G_I = \alpha[(1 - \mu) R + T] + (1 - \alpha)[(1 - \mu) R + T]$$

$$(7.27)$$

Aggregate demand for home-produced output becomes

$$V = C\left(Y^D, \frac{r(1 + t)}{P_d}\right) + X\left(\frac{r}{P_d}\right) + \alpha(1 - \mu) t\left(\frac{r}{P_d}\right)I + \frac{\alpha T}{P_d}$$

$$(7.28)$$

where we have utilized the definition of R. Also we have

$$Y^D = \frac{P_d V + \mu tr I - T}{P}$$

$$(7.29)$$

with

$$T = \tau(P_d V)$$

$$(7.30)$$

Thus, the zero homogeneity property is retained.

Solving for $d(P/P_d)$ we can write the system in general format as

$$\begin{bmatrix} a_{11} & a_{12} & a_{13} \\ a_{21} & a_{22} & a_{23} \\ a_{31} & a_{32} & a_{33} \end{bmatrix} \begin{bmatrix} dV \\ dY^D \\ d(r/P_d) \end{bmatrix} = \begin{bmatrix} B_1 \\ B_2 \\ B_3 \end{bmatrix}$$

$$(7.31)$$

Here, letting $\lambda = r/P_d$

$$a_{11} = \alpha\tau - 1$$

$$a_{12} = C_1 + \alpha(1 - \mu) t\lambda I_1$$

$$a_{13} = C_2(1 + t) + X_1 + \alpha(1 - \mu) t\lambda I_2(1 + t) + \alpha(1 - \mu) It$$

$$a_{21} = (1 - \alpha) \tau$$

$$a_{22} = \lambda[1 + (1 - \alpha)(1 - \mu) t] I_1$$

$$a_{23} = \lambda I_2(1 + t)[1 + (1 - \alpha)(1 - \mu) t] + I - X_1$$
$$+ (1 - \alpha)(1 - \mu) It$$

$$a_{31} = -\frac{f_1\lambda}{f(V)}$$

$$a_{32} = 0$$

$$a_{33} = -\delta\lambda^{\delta-1}$$

$$B_1 = -[C_2\lambda + \alpha(1 - \mu) t\lambda^2 I_2 + \alpha(1 - \mu) \lambda I] dt - \alpha V d\tau$$

$$B_2 = -[(1 - \alpha)(1 - \mu) I\lambda + \lambda^2 I_2(1 + (1 - \alpha)(1 - \mu) t)] dt$$
$$+ (\alpha - 1) V d\tau$$

$$B_3 = \frac{\delta\lambda^\delta}{1 + t} dt$$

Should the Marshall–Lerner condition be satisfied ($a_{23} < 0$) and should $a_{13} > 0$, the determinant of the Jacobian Δ will be positive. If there is no increase in the general tariff but the government endeavours to expand the economy by means of fiscal policy we deduce that (with $\Delta > 0$)

$$dV \gtreqless 0 \quad \text{as} \quad [\alpha a_{22} + (1 - \alpha) a_{12}] d\tau \gtreqless 0 \tag{7.32}$$

$$\therefore dV \gtreqless 0 \quad \text{as} \quad [\alpha\lambda I_1 + (\alpha - 1) C_1] d\tau \gtreqless 0 \tag{7.33}$$

Equation (7.33) informs us that should the government devote all of its receipts to expenditure on home-produced output, that is $\alpha = 1$, then if it raises the marginal rate of income tax the fiscal outcome on output in the new equilibrium will be positive; the government's marginal propensity to spend on domestic output being higher than that of the domestic personal sector out of its real disposable income.

Should the government seek to evaluate the wisdom of introducing changes in both commercial and fiscal policy it would discover that

$$\frac{\partial V}{\partial t} \gtreqless 0 \quad \text{as} \quad (a_{22}a_{33})(q_1) - (a_{12}a_{33})(q_2)$$

$$- (a_{12}a_{23} - a_{22}a_{13})(q_3) \gtreqless 0 \tag{7.34}$$

Here $q_1 = B_1/dt$, $q_2 = B_2/dt$ and $q_3 = B_3/dt$. As α approaches unity the likelihood is that q_1 becomes negative and q_2 is positive; q_3 is negative. Therefore, given the signs of the coefficients on $q_1 - q_3$, as α approaches unity, for a positive value of $d\tau/dt$, output responds positively to an increase in the tariff. Likewise, the same result is obtained if $d\tau/dt = 0$; and in both cases, from a situation where initially $t = 0$.

7.4   An Extended Footnote on the Role of the Money Stock

We mentioned previously that the rigid real wage models that have been utilized to assess the impact of policy choices on the macro-economy, especially in respect of commercial policy, have ignored the money sector explicitly. The introduction of a money sector renders the model difficult to analyse and it is largely intractable without the use of a numerical, simulation model.

This is because, no matter how we specify a well-defined money demand function (and even if we omit reference in it and accordingly, in the expenditure function, to the rate of interest) it removes the zero homogeneity characteristic of the model, in terms of prices, that is so central to the path by which a tractable solution can be found. It is not possible to offer a heuristic assessment of the impact of money on the model, even if we do not permit the government to have an active role in the economy and do not explicitly model tariff revenue. Adopting a Cambridge k approach to money demand may be the only way available. We can then have

$$\bar{M} = kP_\text{d}Y$$

where, remember, Y is measured in home goods and P_d is the price of the domestic product. Since Y is determined from the real system, this equation gives us a value for P_d for a given stock of money. Knowledge of P_d helps us derive the nominal exchange rate r and aggregate price level P.

7.5   A Brief Look at the CEPG Propositions

Four key propositions have figured in the views expressed by CEPG and these have underlain, or played an overt role in, all of their several published studies of the effects of protectionism. One of those we have encountered in the preamble to this chapter.

Two of the others cannot be accommodated in the analyses we are presenting in this particular book: so we shall not detain ourselves with them.[7]

The proposition that we shall consider in part is this:

The use of import controls with fiscal expansion to raise the level of activity need not be a 'beggar-my-neighbour' policy. The total volume of other countries' trade will not be diminished, provided that there is no retaliation, that the country introducing import controls does not use them to secure a larger trade surplus or smaller deficit than it would otherwise have done, and that the composition of its imports does not shift in favour of 'surplus' countries. Indeed, if the composition of its imports is shortened *against* 'surplus' countries and the latter do not retaliate, the total volume of world trade will rise enabling the rest of the world to expand production; 'surplus' countries will regain elsewhere trade which they have lost in the country which discriminates against them and *therefore will have no valid reason for retaliation.* (Cripps and Godley, 1978, p. 327; original italics)

By the nature of our theoretical constructs, centred as they are also on flexible exchange rates (or more-or-less floating rates of exchange), we cannot strictly analyse the validity of this proposition. However, we can gauge its strength in the confines of our type of paradigm by analysing the impact on the foreign country's (or the 'rest of the world's') exports as a consequence of the domestic country's imposing a general tariff. It will then be possible to judge whether or not retaliation is necessary.

We can investigate that conflated interpretation of the above CEPG proposition in the simple multiplier model of real wage rigidity utilized in section 7.1. We thus ignore the possible (positive) amplifying effect of fiscal policy on the macroeconomy. So we concentrate on the weakest form of model as far as the CEPG are concerned; we again ignore overtly the role of government activity and assume that the money market is adjusted in sympathy with the needs of industry by the monetary authority's operating an accommodatory money stock policy.

Consider then the change in the quantity of the home country's imports as

$$\frac{\mathrm{d}I}{\mathrm{d}t} = I_1 \frac{\mathrm{d}Y}{\mathrm{d}t} + I_2 \frac{r}{P_\mathrm{d}} + I_2(1 + t) \frac{\mathrm{d}(r/P_\mathrm{d})}{\mathrm{d}t} \qquad (7.35)$$

Using the expressions for dY/dt and $d(r/P_d)/dt$ derived from equations (7.9) or (7.17a) (note 4), we can deduce, after much manipulation, that

$$\frac{dI}{dt} \gtreqless 0 \quad \text{as} \quad 0 \gtreqless f_1 X [C_1(x-1) + I_1 x] \tag{7.36}$$

So, a *necessary* condition for the quantity of imports to increase (since f_1, X, C_1, x and I_1 are all positive) is that the export-'price elasticity' of demand x be less than one. We saw in section 7.1 that that was also a necessary condition for a general tariff to produce an increase in domestic output and employment. Thus, should x be less than $C_1/(C_1 + I_1)$, a tariff (or a small increase in any prevailing tariff level) will increase the demand for the foreign country's, the rest of the world's, exports.

In the instances where the government exercises a presence in the economy by spending some of the tariff revenue and, as a consequence, amplifying any beneficial repercussion on output/ employment of a tariff (or of its increase), the change in the tariff-imposing country's import level is also likely to be enhanced. But a priori we cannot be certain of this because of the terms of trade adjustments that we set in motion by the concomitant government fiscal policy, which will affect exports, hence home output, the domestic price level, imports, the tariff revenue, disposable income, and hence, further the demand for imports, the terms of trade, as the whole multiplier process works itself out.

The analysis is also rudimentary, of course, in that it does not have an explicit dynamic framework and it does not embody the feedback effects from the rest of the world that would be stimulated by the increased demand for its products. In essence, 'world income' is omitted, as is customary in these small open economy macromodels, from the home country's export demand schedule.

It should be remembered also that our result is based on the assumption that the exchange rate is determined solely by the current account trade balance. Thus we need to have in equilibrium $I = X/(r/P_d)$, where the right-hand side of the equality is a function only of the real exchange rate. In a more complicated model with a stronger role given to balance of payments and to the capital account, it is possible, in the medium term and without full equilibrium, for the burden of adjustment to be shifted away from the current account. Since it is not necessary for exports to be equal to imports (valued appropriately), in such a model, it is possible that even if the foreign currency value of exports falls (with $x > 1$) we can have an increase in imports. Since tariffs are not expected to last 'forever', the Dornbusch-type model discussed in chapter 5 can be extended to a world of real wage resistance and the effect of tariffs noted.

Therefore, a thorough assessment of the CEPG propositions would require us to extend the structure of our model. It would also require some recognition of the social welfare functions of the relevant countries. Such an exercise would be very complex even for the small aggregate models we have been employing. It probably could not be accomplished without extensive numerical analysis.

7.6 Quotas and Real Economic Activity with Rigid Real Wages

We now turn to a consideration of quotas under inflexible real wages. The problems of equivalence are again relevant here. In principle the model can be *constructed* such that equivalence will hold almost by definition. However, the adjustment mechanism and the nature of endogenous variables may be different between quotas and tariffs. This has been extensively discussed in chapter 3; there is little reason to cover this ground once again.

Even though the theoretical constructs can guarantee a form of equivalence, in practice there are, of course, major dissimilarities. The practical difference between quotas and tariffs, as opposed to the purely analytical ones, is pointed out clearly by Caves and Jones (1977):

> The difference is that import duties raise tariff revenue which, if the government does not immediately spend it, leaks out of the income circuit and reduces the money supply. Tariffs are thus an expenditure-switching policy with a heavy clout for expenditure reduction. An increase in government saving raises the hoarding function ... [quota] effects may differ, however, if the quotas are doled out to domestic importers, or if imperfectly competitive foreign exporters will not raise their home-currency prices (for fear of long run adverse effects on their sales). If the importers get the windfall profits permitted by the [quotas], they presumably spend them and thus recycle the purchasing power into the domestic income circuit. If exporters simply fail to take advantage of the chance to shore up their prices,

the windfalls are handed over to domestic consumers lucky enough to secure the rationed imports, and frustrated buyers presumably channel their purchasing power elsewhere in the domestic income circuit. [Quotas] thus may perform an expenditure-switching function, but they are more likely to increase expenditure than are other import duties ... They are also more costly to administer. (Caves and Jones, 1977, pp. 333–334)

The essential point to note is that in *practice*, quotas and tariffs may behave differently, particularly if the structure of the market changes consequent on their imposition. This may also alter the relevant aggregate demand and supply functions. But again, as already noted, given competition and invariant behavioural parameters, we can construct a model where the effects of quotas and tariffs on the macroeconomy will be similar.

In one of the few detailed considerations of the quota in a model constrained by real wage rigidity, Krugman (1982) has concluded that, like a tariff, a quota will shift the line DD to the left on figure 7.1 and the schedule WW to the left, for the simple reasons we advanced earlier for the case of the tariff. Therefore output, ostensibly, can rise or fall with a newly introduced or a more stringent quota if there is no compensating variation in fiscal policy.

Consider then figure 7.3. The original, no quota WW line shifts to W_1W_1 when the quota restriction is imposed on imports. The argument is that DD will shift to intersect W_1W_1 to the left of Z; the central question being whether Z represents a point of surplus or deficit in the balance of payments. If it indicates a deficit then V must fall to reduce the value of imports (the quantity has been reduced, of course, *ex hypothesi*) and cause r/P_d to appreciate to increase the value of exports.

Krugman's position is this:

An import quota will reduce output as long as the price elasticity of export demand exceeds one. To see this, consider the extent of the [downward] shift in the two schedules. At an unchanged level of output, the WW schedule must shift down by the same proportion as the equivalent tariff . . .

The question which remains is whether the [DD] schedule shifts more or less than this; i.e. is point Z . . . a point of surplus or deficit? Notice that since P_d/P_m has not changed,

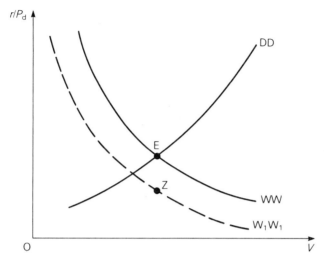

FIGURE 7.3

neither have imports, so the sole question is whether the real appreciation has increased or reduced the foreign exchange value of exports. At any rate, rX will rise if the export demand elasticity is less than one, fall if it is more than one. (Krugman, 1982, p. 168; original italics)

In terms of our notation, P_m is the domestic price of a unit of the importable, being equal to $r(1 + t)$, in the case of an *ad valorem* general tariff. For such a tariff it is straightforward to demonstrate that with a newly instituted tariff, WW (on figure 7.1 or figure 7.3) shifts as Krugman stated.[8] In that eventuality, $P_d/r(1 + t)$ remains fixed. But even with a general tariff this does not permit us to deduce that, at a point such as Z (with V identical with that at the pre-tariff equilibrium E) imports also will be the same as at E. Only if the income variable in the import demand function is domestic output will that be the case, provided P_d/P_m is fixed at the preassigned level of V. Krugman, in fact, has imports dependent upon real absorption (which can be proxied by real disposable income in terms of the price of absorption). With such a scalar variable even at given levels of P_d/P_m and V we cannot state whether imports would be the same at Z as they are at E, with a general tariff. There is a percentage change in the consumer price index (the price of absorption), equal to the percentage change in the exchange rate plus the change in the tariff (which is the tariff level, of course, if we are thinking of a newly-imposed tariff) (see note 8). We also have to contend with the fact that there is now some tariff revenue to add to domestic output; despite the fact that the percentage change in the domestic price is equal to the percentage change in the price of absorption under the defined conditions (see note 8), which means that the absorption basket value of domestically-generated income (P_dV/P) is constant at given V and is the same at E and Z, the percentage change in the absorption basket value of the tariff revenue cannot be deduced a priori: a full, formal analysis is required.

Suppose, however, that the import demand function is of the (anti-tariff-biased) kind used in the traditional version of the MM; that is, it depends only upon V and P_m/P_d. We can now demonstrate the validity of Krugman's proposition in that much simpler version of the model we have adopted. At Z the quantity of imports would be the same as at E, but their value is likely to have fallen owing to a reduction in r; but of that we cannot be certain because the model cannot solve, even formally, for the absolute level of the rate of exchange. Nevertheless, if imports have fallen in value it is possible that the fall in r/P_d given the elasticity of export demand, coupled with the rise in P_d, has caused the value of exports not to fall *pari passu* with the value of imports. The consequent balance of payments surplus at Z would mean that the equilibrium position of DD would have to be to the right of Z on W_1W_1 after the tariff had been levied.

Now we have

$$B = P_d X \left(\frac{r}{P_d} \right) - rI \left(V, \frac{P_m}{P_d} \right) \qquad (7.37)$$

$$P_m = r(1 + t) \qquad (7.38)$$

Thus:

$$dB|_V = P_d X_1 \, d\left(\frac{r}{P_d} \right) + X \, dP_d - Ir \left(\frac{dr}{r} \right) \qquad (7.39)$$

but from note 8 we can write

$$dB|_V = (XP_d - X_1 r) \, dt = (1 - x) \, XP_{dt} \qquad (7.40)$$

if *initially* $B = XP_d - Ir = 0$. This is the Krugman result. If $x < 1$, there is a balance of payments surplus at Z on figure 7.3: it can only be removed by an increase in V, given $I(.)$.

The above is a summary of the special case of the general tariff for $I = I(V, (r(1 + t)/P_d))$ discussed in section 7.1. But it was meant to be for the case of a quota. We note that Krugman refers to t (which for him as for us denotes the general tariff) as the equivalent tariff under the quota. We can only define an equivalent tariff, or an implicit tariff for a quota, that is equivalent to the general tariff in the way that Krugman means if we do have $I = I(V, (r(1 + t)/P_d))$. In his case, in essence, an equivalent tariff under a quota is one which at given $(V, r/P_d)$ produces the same value of I as 'the' alternative general tariff. Such an equivalence will imply, in this rigid wage model, where we can only solve for relative prices and other quantities, that the quota set at the I level generated by 'the' general tariff, will have the same configuration of real variables as would that general tariff.

However, that form of equivalence has little meaning in an economy where I depends upon the revenue produced by the tariff itself; and it has little operational value in providing data on the comparative impacts of a unit change in a quota and in a general tariff.

Let us consider the general case of a quota in the rigid real wages model of section 7.1. We shall denote the implicit tariff associated with the quota as z and the quota as $\bar{I}$. Then we can write

$$V = C\left(Y^D, \frac{r(1 + z)}{P_d}\right) + X\left(\frac{r}{P_d}\right) \tag{7.41}$$

$$X\left(\frac{r}{P_d}\right) = \left(\frac{r}{P_d}\right)\bar{I} \tag{7.42}$$

$$\frac{r(1 + z)}{P_d} = F(Y^D, \bar{I}) \tag{7.43}$$

$$\left(\frac{r}{P_d}\right)^\delta = \frac{1}{\bar{w}f(V)(1 + z)^\delta} \tag{7,44}$$

$$Y^D = \frac{P_d V + zr\bar{I}}{P_d} \tag{7.45}$$

$$P = P_d^{1-\delta} r^\delta (1 + z)^\delta \tag{7.46}$$

$F(.)$ is the inverse import demand function. We discover that

$$\begin{bmatrix} -1 & C_1 + C_2 F_1 & X_1 \\ 0 & 0 & \bar{I} - X_1 \\ \dfrac{f_1 \lambda}{f(V)} & \dfrac{\delta\lambda^{\delta-1}F_1}{1+z} & 0 \end{bmatrix} \begin{bmatrix} dV \\ dY^D \\ d\lambda \end{bmatrix} = \begin{bmatrix} -C_2 F_2 \\ -\lambda \\ \dfrac{-\delta\lambda^{\delta-1}F_2}{1+z} \end{bmatrix} d\bar{I} \quad (7.47)$$

where $\lambda = r/P_d$, $F_1 > 0$, $F_2 < 0$ and $f_1 > 0$. We observe that the sign of the determinant of the Jacobian Δ in equation (7.47) takes the sign of $I - X_1$. We deduce that if $z = 0$ initially

$$\frac{\partial V}{\partial \bar{I}} = \frac{\delta\lambda^{\delta-1}F_2 C_1(X_1 - I) - X_1 \delta\lambda^{\delta}F_1}{\Delta} \quad (7.48)$$

Now, if $X_1 - I > 0$, $\Delta < 0$, $\partial V/\partial \bar{I} > 0$; thus as $\bar{I}$ increases, that is as the quota becomes less stringent, output increases and vice versa. A quota *is* contractionary if the export price elasticity of demand does exceed one. We have also seen from equations (7.9) and (7.10) that so too is a general tariff in those conditions. In both cases it is necessary for $x < 1$ for output to respond positively to a tariff or a quota. However, we can conclude that in this variant of the model with I dependent upon Y^D, it is not *sufficient* for a quota (or a tariff) to increase output that $x < 1$.

Indeed, if we specify $I(.)$ as a linear function we can derive the parameters of $F(.)$ in terms of those for $I(.)$ and deduce that even the conditions that generate a positive dV/dt will necessarily provide a negative $dV/d\bar{I}$. Thus, for example, let

$$I = I_0 + I_1 Y^D + I_2 \frac{r(1+t)}{P}$$

$$\therefore F_1 = \frac{-I_1}{I_2} > 0 \quad \text{and} \quad F_2 = \frac{1}{I_2} < 0$$

Then

$$\frac{\partial V}{\partial \bar{I}} = \frac{\delta\lambda^{\delta-1}(C_1/I_2)(X_1 - I) + X_1 \delta\lambda^{\delta}(I_1/I_2)}{\Delta} \quad (7.49)$$

If $x < 1$, the condition for a quota to increase output ($\partial V/\partial \bar{I} < 0$) is

$$C_1(X_1 - I) + \lambda X_1 I_1 > 0 \quad (7.50)$$

(since $I_2 < 0$).

The condition for $\partial V/\partial t > 0$ is

$$\lambda X_1 I_1 + C_1(X_1 - I) > 0 \quad (7.51)$$

Notes

1 In their closed economy model they hypothesize that the domestic price level P is based on a mark-up equation, namely

$$P = \frac{mWs}{\pi} t \tag{1}$$

$$m = m(Q), \quad m' \geqslant 0 \tag{2}$$

where m is the mark up, W is the hourly money wage, $s = 1 + $ social security tax rate, π is output per man hour, Q is output and t is $1 +$ rate of indirect taxation. Then, having transformed equation (1) into a dynamic form to allow for adjustment costs

$$P = g \left(\frac{mWs}{\pi} t \right) + (1 - g) P_{-1} \tag{3}$$

W is assumed to be *indexed* to P to the effect that

$$W = \mu P_{-1} \tag{4}$$

2 We note, in line with our discussion in chapter 2 on units of measurement and the correct specification of the economic system, that it is meaningful to describe the real demand for home goods in terms of real income with respect to absorption or 'the basket of goods consumed' by domestic residents. Additionally, we draw our attention to the fact that Krugman (1982, p. 166) writes C and I as a function of (total) real *expenditure* measured in terms of the basket of goods, or of absorption. Strictly, the determining variable is real income rather than real expenditure, which is dependent upon real income. However, by that implicit functional relationship (or the Laursen–Metzler effect) it is of no consequence as to which real variable is entered in $C(.)$ and $I(.)$.

3 In his intuitive analysis Krugman has no such constraint. However, in his numerical simulation model that omission is rectified. Yet it is not certain what his specification means for he has set

$$R + P\theta A = trI + P\theta A = 0$$

where A is absorption.

4 The differential of the system is

$$\begin{bmatrix} -1 & C_1 & C_2(1+t) + X_1 \\ 0 & \lambda I_1 & I_2(1+t)\lambda + I - X_1 \\ \dfrac{-f_1 \lambda^{\delta}}{f(V)} & 0 & -\delta \lambda^{\delta-1} \end{bmatrix} \begin{bmatrix} dV \\ dY \\ d\lambda \end{bmatrix}$$

$$= \begin{bmatrix} -C_2\lambda & 0 \\ -I_2\lambda^2 & 0 \\ \dfrac{\delta\lambda^\delta}{1+t} & \dfrac{\lambda^\delta}{1+\theta} \end{bmatrix} \begin{bmatrix} dt \\ d\theta \end{bmatrix} \qquad (7.17a)$$

where $\lambda = r/P_d$. The determinant of the Jacobian is uniquely positive provided the Marshall-Lerner condition holds.

5 But we should be careful in drawing full comparison with the M-P-S findings. Their model is cast in dynamic form by equations (3) and (4) specified in note 1 above; so that they can locate the NIRO (non-inflationary rate of output). It is that output (and the excess of actual output over that NIRO) that they allege cannot be affected 'by the standard fiscal instruments (government expenditure and income taxes) or by monetary policy' (Modigliani and Padoa-Schioppa, 1978, p. 3). Additionally, they do note that the NIRO might be affected by *direct* government policies; presumably of a microinterventionist nature.

6 Let

$$\begin{bmatrix} a_{11} & a_{12} & a_{13} & dV \\ a_{21} & a_{22} & a_{23} & dY^D \\ a_{31} & a_{32} & a_{33} & dr \end{bmatrix} = \begin{bmatrix} B_1 \\ B_2 \\ B_3 \end{bmatrix}$$

Then for $\mu = 1$ and any t, for what they are worth we have

$$a_{11} = 1 - P_d \frac{C_1}{P - trI_1}$$

$$a_{12} = \frac{C_1}{P^2 - PtrI_1}\left[y\delta\frac{P}{r} - PIt\right] - \left|\frac{C_2(1+t) + X_1}{P_d}\right| - \frac{C_1 trI_2(1+t)}{P - trI_1}$$

$$a_{13} = \frac{C_1}{P - trI_1}\left(y\frac{1-\delta}{P_d} - V\right) + \frac{\alpha T}{P_d^2} + \frac{r}{P_d^2}$$
$$\times \left[\frac{C_2(1+t) + X_1}{P_d} + \frac{C_1 trI_2(1+t)}{P - trI_1}\right]$$

$$a_{21} = \frac{rI_1}{P - trI_2}$$

$$a_{22} = I - X_1 + \frac{I_2 r^2(1+t)\, tI_1}{P_d(P - trI_1)} + \frac{Itr}{P_d(P - trI_1)} - \frac{yr\delta}{P_d^2(P - trI_1)}$$

$$a_{23} = \frac{rI_1}{P_d(P - trI_1)}\left(V - \frac{y(1-\delta)}{P_d}\right) - \frac{r^3 tI_2(1+t)}{P_d^3(P - trI_2)}$$

$$a_{31} = \bar{w}f'$$

$$a_{32} = \bar{w}\delta \frac{P}{r} f(V)$$

$$a_{33} = \bar{w}f(V)(1-\delta)\frac{P}{P_\mathrm{d}} - 1$$

$$B_1 = \left[\frac{C_1}{P-trI_1}\left(\frac{I_2 tr^2}{P_\mathrm{d}} + Ir\right) + \frac{C_2 r}{P_\mathrm{d}} - \frac{C_1 y\delta}{(P-trI_1)(1+t)}\right]\mathrm{d}t$$
$$+ \left[\frac{\alpha}{P_\mathrm{d}} - \frac{C_1}{P-trI_1}\right]\mathrm{d}T$$

$$B_2 = \left\{\frac{r\delta y}{P_\mathrm{d}(P-trI_1)(1+t)} - \left[I_2\left(\frac{r}{P_\mathrm{d}}\right)^2 + \frac{r}{P_\mathrm{d}(P-trI_1)}\right.\right.$$
$$\left.\left. \times \left(trI_2\frac{r}{P_\mathrm{d}} + Ir\right)\right]\right\}\mathrm{d}t + \left[\frac{r}{P_\mathrm{d}(P-trI_1)} - (1-\alpha)\right]\mathrm{d}T$$

$$B_3 = \bar{w}f(V)\,\delta\,\frac{P}{1+t}\;\mathrm{d}t$$

7 Rather than leave this matter with such an oblique reference, we should perhaps just note what these two contain. The one argues that protectionism need not lead to 'featherbedding' of domestic industries; the other maintains that spreading protectionism could reduce world trade if it operated in a discriminating fashion against weak suppliers and it also could lead to inefficiency if it implied the subsidization of obsolete production methods (Cripps and Godley, 1978, p. 327).

8 Thus, if V is fixed

$$\frac{\mathrm{d}P_\mathrm{d}}{P_\mathrm{d}} = \frac{\mathrm{d}P}{P} \tag{5}$$

from the definition of P, given an initial t of zero

$$\frac{\mathrm{d}P}{P} = (1-\delta)\frac{\mathrm{d}P_\mathrm{d}}{P_\mathrm{d}} + \delta\frac{\mathrm{d}r}{r} + \delta\,\mathrm{d}t \tag{6}$$

(5) and (6) imply that

$$\mathrm{d}\left(\frac{r}{P_\mathrm{d}}\right)\bigg|_V = \frac{r}{P_\mathrm{d}}\left(\frac{\mathrm{d}r}{r} - \frac{\mathrm{d}P_\mathrm{d}}{P_\mathrm{d}}\right) = -\frac{r}{P_\mathrm{d}}\,\mathrm{d}t \tag{7}$$

8
Commercial, Monetary and Fiscal Policy in a Dynamic Macromodel with Flexible Prices and Wages

In the preceding chapters we have endeavoured to follow as logical a development of the structure of our models as was feasible. The end point of that sequence being an open economy macromodel that has flexible prices and wages, with the possibility of flexible real wages, incorporates a money-bonds sector, allows government activity to occur, can assimilate capital mobility and is truly dynamic. It is such a model that we will be considering in this chapter.

The dynamic model of the open economy that we shall employ to investigate the effect of 'commercial policy' on macroeconomic activity embodies the basic assumption of the static and pseudo-dynamic models discussed in earlier chapters, in that the country with which we shall be concerned is posited to operate in a perfectly competitive market for its imports but it can determine the price of its exports. That price is equal to the price of the basket of commodities which the economy produces. The dynamic model consists of the same set of financial markets as did the most sophisticated of our previous models, namely domestic money, domestic bonds and foreign exchange. The domestic market for labour is subsumed in that for output via our use of the Phillips curve or neo-classical supply hypothesis, as we shall see. International trade in commodities enters the model, naturally, through the domestic economy's demand for imports and the foreign demand for its exports. The Government's role in the economy can arise from several sources: its own expenditure on domestic output and on imports, but without a general tariff there is the

need for it to levy taxes in order to meet its budgetary requirements; its intervention in the money/bonds market, since it will
be concerned to take on the role of central bank in our *fiat
money* economy; and from the imposition of tariffs or quotas
on imports.[1] These several forms of government presence in the
economy will be considered in our analysis.

The dynamic model will be set out in conventional fashion.[2]
Thus we shall first of all describe the elements of the model and
produce a set of equations that will permit us to determine the
instantaneous equilibrium values of the endogenous variables, for
preassigned values of the exogenous and policy variables as well
as for the given values of the dynamic variables that drive the
system. The next stage is to solve for the short-run multiplier
effects, including those emanating from monetary, fiscal and
commercial policy. This is followed by a look at stability. We then
proceed to an evaluation of the steady-state and the multiplier
effects that obtain in the long run. The technical analysis is completed by some observations on the solution of the differential
equation system *per se*. The analytical evaluation of the properties
of the model is complemented in section 8.5 by the results obtained
for the imposition (or alteration) of a general tariff, from the
construction of a numerical version of it.

8.1   *The Model*

Domestic output

The description of the demand for domestic output is identical
with that in our previous models. Thus, we shall assume, so that
our model has wider application, that the government purchases
some domestic output. The latter is purchased in addition by
private domestic residents whose demand is described by $C(.)$ and
by foreigners by way of exports. Thus equilibrium in the domestic
market for output is given by

$$Q = C + X + G_d \tag{8.1}$$

where Q is *real* domestic output, the price deflator for the nominal
value of output is the price of domestically produced commodities,
P_d, C is *real* private demand for domestic output, X is *real* exports
of domestically produced goods and G_d is *real* government expenditure on domestic goods, with the subscript d used to denote
that fact.

Assume that

$$C = C\left(Y^D, r - \rho, \frac{FE\lambda}{P_d}, W\right), \quad 0 < \frac{P_1 C_1}{P} < 1, \tag{8.2}$$

$$C_2 < 0, C_3 > 0, C_4 > 0$$

$$X = X\left(\frac{FE}{P_d}\right) \quad X_1 > 0 \tag{8.3}$$

where Y^D is *real* private disposable income derived from nominal income by deflating by the domestic cost of living index P, r is the domestic nominal rate of interest, ρ is the *expected* rate of inflation of the domestic cost of living index P, P_d is the price of domestically produced goods in domestic currency units, F is the price of foreign goods in foreign currency, E is the exchange rate, being the price of foreign exchange in terms of domestic currency, W is *real* private domestic wealth, being nominal wealth deflated by P and $\lambda = 1 + t$, where t is the *ad valorem* tariff imposed on imported goods. Note once more the definition of E (hitherto denoted r); consequently, a 'devaluation' of the currency is represented by an appreciation of E.

Domestic prices and wages

The domestic cost of living index is defined as previously, so it is dependent upon both domestic and foreign prices

$$P = \phi(P_d, FE\lambda), \quad \phi_1 > 0, \phi_2 > 0 \tag{8.4}$$

with $\phi(.)$ such that (following Samuelson and Swami (1974))

$$P = P_d^\delta (FE\lambda)^{1-\delta} \tag{8.5}$$

Thus, taking logs of equation (8.5)

$$p = \delta p_d + (1 - \delta)(f + e + \lambda^*) \tag{8.6}$$

where

$$p_d = \frac{\dot{P_d}}{P_d} = \frac{dP_d/dt}{P_d}, \quad t \text{ is time}$$

$$f = \frac{\dot{F}}{F}$$

$$e = \frac{\dot{E}}{E} = \text{rate of exchange depreciation}$$

$$p = \frac{\dot{P}}{P}$$

$$\lambda^* = \frac{\dot{\lambda}}{\lambda}$$

The rate of inflation of domestically produced goods p_d is given by

$$p_d = \alpha_0 + \alpha_1(Q - \bar{Q}) + \alpha_2 p + \alpha_3(f + e + \lambda^*) \qquad (8.7)$$

$$\alpha_1 > 0, \quad 0 \leqslant \alpha_2 \leqslant 1, \quad 0 \leqslant \alpha_3 < 1, \quad 0 < \alpha_2 + \alpha_3 \leqslant 1$$

where $\bar{Q}$ is full capacity output. This equation follows from two familiar hypotheses: the first is that the rate of inflation of domestically produced goods will be affected by the degree of excess capacity in the economy, the expected rate of *wage* inflation and the expected inflation in the price of foreign goods, the second hypothesis is that the Phillips curve holds.

Thus if we take these hypotheses *seriatim* we have

$$p_d = a_0 + a_1(Q - \bar{Q}) + a_2 w + a_3(f + e + \lambda^*) \qquad (8.8)$$

where w is the rate of wage inflation. The term in expected price inflation of importables $(f + e + \lambda^*)$ can be justified on either or both of two grounds. These are that domestic producers will find it easier to raise their prices if foreign producers are expected to do so and the possibility that the basket of importables might enter the production process. The Phillips curve hypothesis (or we could say the Neo-classical supply hypothesis for that matter) gives us

$$w = b_0 + b_1 U + b_2 p, \quad b_1 < 0, 0 \leqslant b_2 \leqslant 1 \qquad (8.9)$$

where U is the rate of unemployment. Assuming a version of Okun's (or Keynes's) law

$$U = c_0 + c_1(Q - \bar{Q}), \quad c_0 \geqslant 0, c_1 < 1 \qquad (8.10)$$

Inserting (8.10) into (8.9) and the resulting expression into (8.8) produces equation (8.7) with the given restrictions on its coefficients.

In equations (8.2) and (8.3) we have hypothesized that domestic and foreign demand respectively are functions of relative prices; these are the terms of trade and in our 'baskets of goods' model they denote the *real* exchange rate. Let us define

$$\frac{FE\lambda}{P_d} = \sigma \qquad (8.11)$$

Then, from (8.5), it follows that

$$\frac{P}{P_d} = \phi(\sigma) = \sigma^{1-\delta} \tag{8.12}$$

The money and bonds market

There are assumed to be only two financial claims that can be held by domestic residents, namely domestic fiat money and bonds. The latter are variable interest rate bonds which can be issued by both domestic and foreign governments, with investors seeing the bonds as perfect substitutes under the assumption we shall make that there is perfect mobility of capital (which is much truer in reality than is the opposite assumption). Residents in neither country, however, hold foreign money as an asset.

The assumption of perfect capital mobility means, of course, that

$$r = \bar{r} + \hat{e} \tag{8.13}$$

where $\bar{r}$ is the foreign interest rate and $\hat{e}$ is the expected rate of depreciation of the home currency. If we assume, whether because of RE (rational expectations) or whatever, that movements in the rate of exchange are anticipated perfectly then

$$r = \bar{r} + e \tag{8.14}$$

with e, as previously defined, being the actual rate of depreciation of the home currency.

The supply of money and bonds have already been assumed to be exogenously determined by the authorities. It is necessary now, therefore, to specify the domestic demand for these assets. The demands for *real* holdings of these assets (L and B) are of standard form, namely when written in terms of financial market equilibria

$$\frac{L}{P} = L(Q, \bar{r} + e - \rho, -\rho, W), \quad L_1 > 0, L_2 < 0, L_3 > 0, \tag{8.15}$$
$$0 < L_4 < 1$$

$$\frac{B}{P} = B(Q, \bar{r} + e - \rho, -\rho, W), \quad B_1 < 0, B_2 > 0, B_3 < 0, \tag{8.16}$$
$$0 < B_4 < 1$$

where L is the nominal stock of domestic money (held by domestic residents) in domestic currency and B is the nominal stock of bonds held by domestic residents in domestic currency. Since it is assumed in this specific model that the capital stock is fixed, the wealth constraint consists only of money and bonds

$$W = \frac{L + B}{P} \tag{8.17}$$

In (8.15) and (8.16), L_4 and B_4 must be so signed, of course, by the balance sheet constraint on W and, in effect, given the definition of W we must have, by the Engel aggregation condition

$$L_4 + B_4 \equiv 1 \tag{8.18}$$

also by the Cournot aggregation condition

$$L_i + B_i \equiv 0, \quad i = 1, 2, 3 \tag{8.19}$$

Additionally, because of the definition of W, since it is included in the model, only one of (8.15) and (8.16) can also be incorporated in the model since the one implies the other, given W. They are not independent equations; we follow convention and omit (8.16).

Real disposable income of the private sector and the tariff revenue

We have still to specify the remainder of the budget constraints of the domestic private sector and the budget constraint of the government. Since the latter is a concomitant of the former and since it involves the *dynamics* of the model it is left until the next section. We now concentrate on the private sector's income constraint.

In the model without the tariff this would be specified as

$$Y^D = (1 - \tau)\left(\frac{P_d Q}{P} + r\frac{B}{P}\right) - \rho W, \quad r = \bar{r} + e \tag{8.20}$$

where τ is the marginal (average) income tax rate. So real disposable income equals the real value of factor income plus bond interest less the expected capital gain or loss on wealth ρW. But, naturally, when a tariff is present we have to add to this measure of real disposable income a term equal to the value of the transfer payment (deflated by P) that a government makes to the domestic private sector from the tariff revenue it, the government, receives. Now let R be the *real* tariff revenue, namely the nominal value of the tariff revenue in domestic currency deflated by P. Then to (8.20) we add

$$T = \mu R, \quad 0 \leqslant \mu \leqslant 1 \tag{8.21}$$

where T is the real value of transfers to the domestic private sector in cost-of-living units.

We shall define R in the next section, but it has essentially the same specification as that used hitherto, except that we shall generalize R to include the possibility that government's own purchases of imports are subject to the tariff.

The dynamics of the system: balance of payments, the governmental budget and the tariff revenue

The *nominal* balance of payments (BP) in units of domestic currency is given by

$$BP = P_d X - FE[I(.) + G_I] + \dot{A} + \dot{B} + (\bar{r} + e)(B - A) \quad (8.22)$$

Here I and G_I represent respectively the *real* import demands of the domestic private sector and of the government. We posit that

$$I = I(Y^D, r - \rho, \sigma, W), \quad 0 < \frac{FE\lambda}{P} I_1 < 1, I_2 < 0, I_3 < 0,$$

$$I_4 > 0 \quad (8.23)$$

Recall that δ includes the tariff $(\lambda - 1)$; and remember that the tariff does not affect the balance of payments except via its impact upon $I(.)$ and G_I if $G_I = G_I(\sigma)$.

When taken in conjunction with the government's budget constraint (Blinder and Solow, 1973, 1974; Tobin, 1980), this enables us to describe the accumulation of assets (in effect of W) in the model. That constraint is, in nominal units of domestic currency

$$\dot{A} + \dot{D} = P_d G_d + FE\lambda G_I + rA - \tau(P_d Q + rB) + PR + PT$$

$$\therefore \dot{A} + \dot{D} = P_d G_d + FE\lambda G_I + (\bar{r} + e)A - \tau[P_d Q + (\bar{r} + e)B]$$

$$+ (\mu - 1)PR \quad (8.24)$$

where A is the stock of bonds debt of the domestic government in nominal units of domestic currency and D is the domestic component of L, the monetary base, in nominal units of domestic currency.

$$R = \frac{\sigma(\lambda - 1)}{\phi(\sigma)\lambda} (I + G_I) \quad (8.25)$$

so that the government is assumed here to pay the tariff on its imports.[3]

Since

$$PB \equiv \dot{K} \tag{8.26}$$

where K is the level of foreign reserves in terms of domestic currency, and, *ex definitione*

$$\dot{L} = \dot{D} + \dot{K} \tag{8.27}$$

we have, by adding (8.24) and (8.26) and using (8.22) and (8.27), that

$$\dot{L} + \dot{B} = \{P_d G_d + FE\lambda G_I + (\bar{r} + e)A - \tau[P_d Q + (\bar{r} + e)B]$$
$$+ (\mu - 1)RP\} + [P_d X - FE(I + G_I)$$
$$+ (\bar{r} + e)(B - A)] \tag{8.28}$$

The accumulation of nominal wealth by the domestic private sector equals the government's nominal budget deficit plus the nominal balance of payments on *current account* (the net inflow of new capital $(\dot{A} - \dot{B})$ having been factored out). We need to turn equation (8.28) into an expression in $\dot{W}$, the accumulation of *real* wealth. The result is that we have[4]

$$\dot{W} = \left(\frac{G_d + \sigma G_I - Q}{\phi(\sigma)}\right) + \left(\frac{\lambda X - \sigma(I + G_I)}{\lambda\phi(\sigma)}\right)$$
$$+ (1 - \tau)(\bar{r} + e)b + (\mu - 1)R - pW \tag{8.29}$$

where $b = B/P$.

In the particular case of flexible exchange rates, of course, $\dot{K} = 0$, and we shall need to amend (8.29) eliminating b, as we shall see.

It is necessary to supplement the equation for $\dot{W}$ with one for $\dot{\sigma}$ and $\dot{\rho}$, since the change in the terms of trade and in inflationary expectations, *ceteris paribus* (for given government policies) cause the system to evolve over time. The dynamic equation for σ is easy to obtain. We merely differentiate σ, given by (8.11) with respect to time. Hence

$$\dot{\sigma} = (f + e + \lambda^* - p_d)\sigma \tag{8.30}$$

We must advance some hypothesis about $\dot{\rho}$, so let us assume that

$$\dot{\rho} = \theta(p - \rho), \quad \theta > 0 \tag{8.31}$$

Expectations formation using RE could be incorporated in the model as an alternative.

Transformation of the dynamic equation for $\dot{W}$

The equation for $\dot{W}$ can be written as

$$\dot{W} = S + (\rho - p)W \tag{8.32}$$

where S denotes saving by the domestic private sector. This means that, taken in conjunction with equations (8.30) and (8.31), the steady state of the system is attained when $S = 0$, a standard property of such a state. This is an equation that is intuitively sound as Turnovsky (1977) has pointed out. Thus, wealth accumulation equals planned saving plus unanticipated saving $((\rho - p)W)$, which arises in the model because of unanticipated changes in the value of real wealth due to unanticipated changes in inflation (since we have bonds with variable coupons). Further, because of the assumption that the goods market is in equilibrium, consumption plans must be realized *ex hypothesi*; therefore, any unexpected changes in real wealth must impinge upon the saving of the domestic private sector. It is postulated that

$$S = S(Y^D, \bar{r} + e - \rho, W), \quad 0 < S_1 < 1, S_2 > 0, S_3 < 0 \tag{8.33}$$

on the assumption that the domestic private sector's total real consumption is independent of σ (not its home demand *per se*, of course).

Turnovsky's (1977) proof of equation (8.32), adopted for the current model, is as follows.

The nominal national income identity states that

$$PY^D = P_d(C) + FE\lambda(I) + P(S) \tag{8.34}$$

Real saving plans S are

$$S = Y^D - \frac{\lambda C + \sigma I}{\lambda \phi(\sigma)} \tag{8.35}$$

Using the definition of Y^D, that is equation (8.20) plus equation (8.21), and using equation (8.1) which enables us to write C as a function of Q in Y^D, we discover that (8.35) becomes

$$S = (1 - \tau)\left[\frac{P_d}{P}(Q) + (\bar{r} + e)\frac{B}{P}\right]$$

$$-\rho W + \mu R - \frac{\lambda(Q - X - G_d) + \sigma I}{\lambda \phi(\sigma)} \tag{8.36}$$

Using the definitions of σ and of R we have

$$S = \frac{G_d - \tau Q + X}{\phi(\sigma)} + \frac{\sigma}{\phi(\sigma)} (\mu(\lambda - 1) - \lambda)I$$

$$+ \frac{\sigma}{\phi(\sigma)} \mu(1 - \lambda)G_I + (1 - \tau)(\bar{r} + e)b - \rho W \qquad (8.37)$$

If we insert the definition of R into (8.29) we have

$$\dot{W} = \frac{G_d - \tau Q + X}{\phi(\sigma)} + \frac{\sigma}{\phi(\sigma)} (\mu(\lambda - 1) - \lambda)I$$

$$+ \frac{\sigma \mu(1 - \lambda)G_I}{\phi(\sigma)} + (1 - \tau)(\bar{r} + e)b - pW \qquad (8.38)$$

Therefore, from (8.37) and (8.38)

$$\dot{W} = S + (\rho - p)W \qquad (8.39)$$

A summary of the model

The model can be summarized as follows

$$Q = C(Y^D, \bar{r} + e - \rho, \sigma, W) + X\left(\frac{\sigma}{\lambda}\right) + G_d \qquad (8.40)$$

$$p_d = \alpha_0 + \alpha_1(\bar{Q} - Q) + \alpha_2 \rho + \alpha_3(f + e + \lambda) \qquad (8.41)$$

$$p = \delta p_d + (1 - \delta)(f + e + \lambda^*) \qquad (8.42)$$

$$W = l + b \qquad (8.43)$$

$$l = \frac{L}{P} = L(Q, \bar{r} + e - \rho, -\rho, W) \qquad (8.44)$$

$$Y^D = (1 - \tau)\left(\frac{Q}{\phi(\sigma)} + (\bar{r} + e)b\right) - \rho W + \mu R \qquad (8.45)$$

These six equations can be solved (locally) for the values of Q, Y^D, p_d, p, b and l given the exogenous variables and parameters, as well as for *given* values of the *dynamic* variables W, σ and ρ. The latter have these equations

$$\dot{W} = S(Y^D, \bar{r} + e - \rho, W) + (\rho - p)W \qquad (8.46)$$

$$\dot{\sigma} = (f + e + \lambda^* - p_d)\sigma \qquad (8.47)$$

$$\dot{\rho} = \theta(p - \rho) \qquad (8.48)$$

The system can be reduced to one whereby we have four equations in Q, Y^D, p and b by our eliminating l through substitution of (8.44) into (8.43) and p_d by substituting (8.41) into (8.42). Thus $\dot{\sigma}$ is reformulated with p_d also being replaced by (8.41). Furthermore we note that

$$W \equiv \frac{D}{P} + \frac{K}{P} + \frac{B}{P} = d + k + b \tag{8.49}$$

where, we recall, K denotes reserves of foreign currency. Hence, given the definition of W in equation (8.43) we can also write

$$l = d + k \tag{8.50}$$

which we can also utilize when eliminating l. Therefore, we can write the model as

$$Q = C(Y^D, \bar{r} + e - \rho, \sigma, W) + X\left(\frac{\sigma}{\lambda}\right) + G_d \tag{8.51}$$

$$p = \gamma_0 + \gamma_1(Q - \bar{Q}) + \gamma_2\rho + \gamma_3(f + e + \lambda^*) \tag{8.52}$$

$$L(Q, \bar{r} + e - \rho, -\rho, W) = d + k, \quad L_2, L_3 \leqslant 0 \tag{8.53}$$

$$Y^D = (1 - \tau)\left[\frac{Q}{\phi(\sigma)} + (\bar{r} + e)b\right]$$

$$- \rho W + \frac{\mu\sigma(\lambda - 1)}{\phi(\sigma)\lambda}(I + G_I) \tag{8.54}$$

where

$$\gamma_i = \delta\alpha_i, \quad i = 0, 1, 2, \gamma_3 = [(1 - \delta) + \alpha_3\delta]$$

and

$$I = I(Y^D, \bar{r} + e - \rho, \sigma, W) \tag{8.55}$$

$$\dot{W} = S(Y^D, \bar{r} + e - \rho, W) + (\rho - p)W \tag{8.56}$$

$$\dot{\sigma} = [(1 - \alpha_3)(f + e + \lambda^*) - \alpha_0 - \alpha_1(Q - \bar{Q}) - \alpha_2\rho]\sigma \tag{8.57}$$

$$\dot{\rho} = \theta(p - \rho) \tag{8.58}$$

As it stands, provided e is set at zero, this characterization of the model is the correct form for the case of fixed exchange rates.

However, when the exchange rate is freely floating, and e consequently is determined endogenously, it is necessary to stipulate how the government finances its deficit; accordingly, we have an extra dynamic equation in the system. This situation arises because it follows by construction that $\dot{K} \equiv 0$ (i.e. foreign reserves cannot accumulate). Hence, $\dot{D} \equiv \dot{L}$ which implies a relationship between $\bar{d}$ ('the monetary base') and l. Any equation which describes the movements in l must clearly be consistent with the government's budget constraint given in equation (8.24), which in real terms and using $\dot{D} = \dot{L}$ can be written as

$$\frac{\dot{A} + \dot{L}}{P} = \frac{G_d + \sigma G_I - \tau Q}{\phi(\sigma)} + (\bar{r} + e)(a - \tau b) + (\mu - 1)R$$

(8.59)

$$\therefore \dot{a} + \dot{l} = \frac{G_d + \sigma G_I - \tau Q}{\phi(\sigma)} + (\bar{r} + e)(a - \tau b)$$

$$- (a + l)P + (\mu - 1)R \qquad (8.60)$$

Thus

$$\dot{a} + \dot{l} = G_\Delta \qquad (8.61)$$

Where G_Δ denotes government deficit.

Pure money financing occurs obviously if

$$\dot{l} = G_\Delta \qquad (8.62)$$

and pure bond financing occurs if

$$\dot{a} = G_\Delta \qquad (8.63)$$

In the case of pure bond financing, the dynamic path of a can be ignored and l set at $\bar{l}$; this is because a does not enter either the equilibrium relationships given in (8.51)–(8.54) or in the dynamic equations for W, σ and ρ. This is a special case, and arises because of the small country assumption together with that of perfect capital mobility. The situation is far more complicated if $\dot{l} = G_\Delta$ or if any fraction of G_Δ is met by $\dot{l} \neq 0$ (Turnovsky, 1977). Since our central purpose is to investigate the role of the tariff and of commercial policy – and to compare its effectiveness with that of monetary/fiscal policy only as a secondary exercise – we can assume that $\dot{l} = 0$ and that $\dot{a} = G_\Delta$.

Now, finally, the model set out in equations (8.51)–(8.54) has to be amended by our eliminating $d + k$ using the fact that it must equal l, by equation (8.50). Consequently equations (8.51)–(8.54) provide us with four equations in the four unknowns Q, Y^D, p and e for given values of the dynamic and exogenous variables, with b equal to $W - \bar{l}$.

8.2   Commercial Policy and Fiscal Policy in the Short Run

Once we have set $d + k = l$ in equation (8.53) we can, in principle, take the total differentials of equations (8.51)–(8.54), given the exogenous/dynamic variables, and evaluate the short run effects of different forms of policy choice on the economy. The policy choice variables are commercial policy (fixing $\lambda = 1 + t$ or adjusting it) and fiscal policy (determining or altering G_d and/or G_I).

Now let us define

$$\Pi_1 = \frac{\mu\sigma(\lambda - 1)}{\phi(\sigma)\lambda}, \quad \Pi_2 = \frac{1 - \tau}{\phi(\sigma)}, \quad \Pi_3 = (1 - \tau)(W - \bar{l})$$

$$\Pi_4 = \frac{(I + G_I)\mu\sigma}{\lambda^2\phi(\sigma)}, \quad \Pi_5 = -\frac{X_1\sigma}{\lambda^2}$$

(8.64)

Remembering that the dynamic variables W, σ and ρ are constant, and so too are f and $\bar{r}$, we discover that upon total differentiation of equations (8.51)–(8.54), the short-run multipliers are given by the solution to this system, whose Jacobian we assume has a positive determinant Δ.[5]

$$\begin{bmatrix} 1 & -C_1 & -C_2 & 0 \\ \gamma_1 & 0 & \gamma_3 & -1 \\ L_1 & 0 & L_2 & 0 \\ \Pi_2 & \Pi_1 I_1 - 1 & \Pi_3 + I_2\Pi_1 & 0 \end{bmatrix} \begin{bmatrix} dQ \\ dY^D \\ de \\ dp \end{bmatrix} = \begin{bmatrix} dG_d + \Pi_5\,d\lambda \\ -\gamma_3\,d\lambda^* \\ d\bar{l} \\ -\Pi_i\,dG_I - \Pi_4\,d\lambda \end{bmatrix}$$

(8.65)

Therefore if we let $d\bar{l} = 0$, and so compare fiscal and commercial policies

$$dQ = L_2\{(\Pi_1 I_1 - 1)\,dG_d - \Pi_1 C_1\,dG_I$$
$$+ [\Pi_5(\Pi_1 I_1 - 1) - \Pi_4 C_1]\,d\lambda\}\,\Delta^{-1} \tag{8.66}$$

$$dY^D = \{[L_1(\Pi_3 + I_2\Pi_1) - \Pi_2 L_2]\,dG_d$$
$$- (L_1 + L_1 C_2)\Pi_1\,dG_I + [L_1\Pi_5(\Pi_3 + I_2\Pi_1)$$
$$- L_1 C_2\Pi_4 - \Pi_2\Pi_5 L_2 - \Pi_1\Pi_4 L_2]\,d\lambda\}\,\Delta^{-1} \tag{8.67}$$

$$de = L_1\{(1 - \Pi_1 I_1)\,dG_d + C_1\Pi_1\,dG_I$$
$$+ [C_1\Pi_4 + (1 - \Pi_1 I_1)\Pi_5]\,d\lambda\}\,\Delta^{-1} \tag{8.68}$$

and

$$dp = (L_1\gamma_3 - L_2\gamma_1)\,\{(1 - \Pi_1 I_1)\,dG_d + C_1\Pi_1\,dG_I$$
$$+ [C_1\Pi_4 + (1 - \Pi_1 I_1)\Pi_5]\,d\lambda\}\,\Delta^{-1}$$
$$+ \{\gamma_3 L_2[(\Pi_1 I_1 - 1) + \Pi_2 C_1]$$
$$+ \gamma_3 L_1[C_2(\Pi_1 I_1 - 1) - C_1(\Pi_3 + I_2\Pi_1)]\,d\lambda\}\,\Delta^{-1} \qquad (8.69)$$

In view of the signs of the partial derivatives of the behavioural functions, and the fact that Π_1 to Π_4 must be positive, we can deduce that $\partial Q/\partial G_d$ and $\partial Q/\partial G_I$ are both positive (see note 5). Additionally, $\partial Q/\partial\lambda$ ($= \partial Q/\partial t$) will be positive if this sufficient (but not necessary) condition is fulfilled

$$\frac{t}{1+t} > \frac{\sigma X_1 - (I + G_I)C_1\sigma^\delta\mu}{\mu\sigma^{1+\delta}I_1 X_1} \qquad (8.70)$$

We can state, however, that should all of the tariff revenue be dispersed to the non-government sector $\Pi_1 = \Pi_4 = 0$ and $\partial Q/\partial t$ is positive.

We can also check that our model is consistent because equation (8.68) informs us that movements in the rate of depreciation of the home country's exchange rate e are in the same direction as those in output Q. This is the result that changes in the short-run money demand equation (8.53) indicate must happen. With a fixed real stock of (domestic) money, an increase in output can only be financed by an expected appreciation (here, devaluation) in the exchange rate, which will bring about a reduction in the demand for money (via the increase in the domestic rate of interest) which will accommodate the increased transactions money demand arising from the increased output.

As far as the rate of inflation of the consumer price index is concerned we can draw the following observations. If the behavioural properties of the domestic macroeconomy are such that an increase in government expenditure on domestically produced goods raises output, it must also raise the rate of price inflation. Likewise, equations (8.66) and (8.69) also indicate that if the tariff or its increase, boosts domestic output, then the conditions which permit such an outcome to emerge, also produce an increase in inflation.

An increase in government expenditure on imports will always raise the rate of inflation in the short run. This consequence arises from two effects: the change in expenditure gives a spur to domestic output and it also increases the rate of appreciation of the exchange rate. These effects reinforce each other in increasing the rate of inflation. Essentially, however, it is the impact of the increase in the government's expenditure on imports on the exchange rate which generates the output, inflationary-reinforcing, effects, via the direct stimulus it produces to the demand for domestically-produced output through exports and the indirect stimulus it provides by causing domestic residents to switch demand away from importables. Additionally, if $\partial\lambda^*/\partial\lambda > 0$, this will provide further inflationary impulses.

Equations (8.66)–(8.69) highlight for this dynamic model one of the results obtained for our static and pseudo-dynamic models, namely that there will exist, in principle, a trade-off between policy measures if the authorities should seek to shift output and inflation to particular levels. Additionally, nested within that proposition is the notion, familiar from the literature on 'targets and instruments' (see, for example, Tinbergen (1952) and Theil (1961)), that the authorities should employ as many instruments as they have targets. Thus, if it is their desire to raise output by $d\bar{Q}$ in the short run in this model, they can select arbitrary values for any two of dG_d, dG_I and $d\lambda$ and set the remaining instrument at its implied appropriate level, employing equation (8.66) and using the preassigned value of $d\bar{Q}$ and the two arbitrary policy instruments. But, should their objective be to produce a desired vector of target variables, such as $[d\bar{Q}, d\bar{e}$ and $d\bar{p}]$, then the authorities should use equations (8.66), (8.68) and (8.69) to select dG_d, dG_I and $d\lambda$ given the target vector.

8.3   The Steady State

The steady state is the more interesting state in which to consider the implications of various forms of economic policy and especially the use of a general tariff. The steady state is described by the short-run behavioural and market clearing relationships epitomized in equations (8.51)–(8.55), with, we recall, $d + k$ set equal to $\bar{l}$, and b replaced by $W - \bar{l}$; together with the dynamic equations (8.56)–(8.58) set equal to zero. Clearly, the economy cannot be in its steady-state configuration unless the 'drive' variables are themselves at rest. In that case, we have both stock and flow equilibrium with steady-state rates of growth of inflation and of the appreciation of the exchange rate, accompanied by steady-state levels for output, real disposable income, the terms of trade, real wealth and the real stock of money.

The conditions that ensue from our having set the dynamic equations to zero are then inserted into equations (8.51)–(8.56) to yield this steady-state system

$$Q = C(Y^D, \bar{r} - f - \lambda^*, \sigma, W) + X\left(\frac{\sigma}{\lambda}\right) + G_d \tag{8.71}$$

$$(1 - \gamma_2 - \gamma_3)(f + e + \lambda^*) = \gamma_0 + \gamma_1(Q - \bar{Q}) \tag{8.72}$$

$$\bar{I} = L(Q, \bar{r} - f - \lambda^*, -(f + e + \lambda^*), W) \tag{8.73}$$

$$Y^D = (1 - \tau)\left[\frac{Q}{\phi(\sigma)} + (\bar{r} + e)(W - \bar{I})\right] - (f + e + \lambda^*)W$$

$$+ \frac{\mu\sigma(\lambda - 1)}{\phi(\sigma)\lambda}(I + G_I) \tag{8.74}$$

$$S(Y^D, \bar{r} - f - \lambda^*, W) = 0 \tag{8.75}$$

with $I(.)$ given in equation (8.55), wherein $\bar{r} - f - \lambda^*$ replaces $\bar{r} + e - \rho$ by the steady-state properties of the model (see equations (8.6), (8.30) and (8.31)).

The steady-state comparative statics follow from differentiation of equations (8.71)–(8.75) and (8.55). We note in equation (8.74) that we need to differentiate the terms in σ now, which, *ex hypothesi*, was not necessary in obtaining the short-run comparative statics results. To do so we shall assume that in the initial steady state $\sigma = 1$, so that $\phi'(\sigma) = (1 - \delta)$.

The differentiation yields this system

$$\begin{bmatrix} 1 & -C_1 & -C_4 & -(C_3 + X_1\lambda^{-1}) & 0 \\ -\gamma_1 & 0 & 0 & 0 & 1 - \gamma_2 - \gamma_3 \\ L_1 & 0 & L_4 & 0 & -L_3 \\ \Pi_6 & \Pi_7 & \Pi_8 & \Pi_9 & \Pi_{10} \\ 0 & S_1 & S_3 & 0 & 0 \end{bmatrix} \begin{bmatrix} dQ \\ dY^D \\ dW \\ d\sigma \\ de \end{bmatrix}$$

$$= \begin{bmatrix} C(dr - df - d\lambda^*) + dG_d + \Pi_5\, d\lambda \\ -(1 - \gamma_2 - \gamma_3)(df + d\lambda^*) \\ d\bar{I} + (L_2 + L_3)(df + d\lambda^*) - L_2\, d\bar{r} \\ \Pi_{11} \\ S_2(df + d\lambda^* - d\bar{r}) \end{bmatrix} \tag{8.76}$$

where

$$\Pi_6 = -\lambda^2(1-\tau)$$

$$\Pi_7 = \lambda^2 - \mu\lambda(\lambda - 1)I_1$$

$$\Pi_8 = [\lambda^2(f + e + \lambda^*) - \lambda^2(1 - \tau)(\bar{r} + e) - \mu\lambda(\lambda - 1)I_4]$$

$$\Pi_9 = -[\mu\lambda(\lambda - 1)][I_3 + \delta(I + G_I)] - \lambda^2(1 - \tau)(\delta - 1)Q$$

$$\Pi_{10} = [\lambda^2(1 - \tau)\bar{l} + \lambda^2\tau W]$$

and

$$\Pi_{11} = -\lambda^2(1 - \tau)(\bar{r} + e)\,d\bar{l} + \mu(I + G_I)\,d\lambda + \mu\lambda(\lambda - 1)\,dG_I$$

$$+ [\mu\lambda(\lambda - 1)I_2 + \lambda^2(1 - \tau)(W - \bar{l})]\,d\bar{r}$$

$$- [\mu\lambda(\lambda - 1)I_2 + \lambda^2 W]\,df - [\mu\lambda(\lambda - 1)I_2 + \lambda^2 W]\,d\lambda^*$$

The multiplier effects on output are

$$\frac{\partial Q}{\partial \lambda} = \frac{-(C_3 + X_1\lambda^{-1})(1 - \gamma_2 - \gamma_3)S_1L_4\mu(I + G_I)}{|J|}$$

$$- \frac{\Pi_5\Pi_9(1 - \gamma_2 - \gamma_3)S_1L_4}{|J|} \tag{8.77}$$

$$\frac{\partial Q}{\partial G_d} = \frac{-(1 - \gamma_2 - \gamma_3)S_1L_4\Pi_9}{|J|} \tag{8.78}$$

$$\frac{\partial Q}{\partial G_I} = \frac{-\mu\lambda(\lambda - 1)(1 - \gamma_2 - \gamma_3)(C_3 + X_1\lambda^{-1})S_1L_4}{|J|} \tag{8.79}$$

$$\frac{\partial Q}{\partial \bar{l}} = \frac{-\lambda^2(1 - \tau)(\bar{r} + e)(1 - \gamma_2 - \gamma_3)(C_3 + X_1\lambda^{-1})S_1L_4}{|J|}$$

$$\tag{8.80}$$

Now it is not possible to sign $|J|$ the determinant of the Jacobian of equation (8.77) uniquely, solely on the basis of the information we have about the signs of the parameters in the economic system. But suppose that it is negative, this would have been a necessary condition for stability had the equations for the steady state not been derived from an explicitly dynamic system.[6]

With $|J| < 0$, the signs of the partial derivatives of the behavioural equations determine that, in the steady state, the level of output will respond positively to a small increase in the general tariff, provided $(\gamma_2 + \gamma_3) < 1$ and τ, δ are sufficiently small to render Π_9 negative. If we let e be zero so that we are in a fixed exchange rate regime, without a tariff, $(\gamma_2 + \gamma_3) < 1$ increases output, as can be seen quite straightforwardly in that case. Fiscal policy operating via an increase in government real expenditure on domestically produced output will have a favourable effect on the level of that output in the steady state, provided this time that Π_9 is positive.

The government importables-expenditure to output multiplier is positive definite if $|J| < 0$. In such a situation we might surmise that the effect of the government's higher propensity to import is that the foreign exchange rate appreciation increases and the terms of trade worsens (σ rises), so causing exports to be stimulated and the domestic demand for home goods by domestic residents to increase. If $|J| < 0$ and $(\gamma_2 + \gamma_3) < 1$, an increase in the real stock of money must produce an expansion of domestic output. The fact that $(\gamma_2 + \gamma_3) < 1$ means that any increase in demand in the system will not be dissipated in inflation. In effect, any inflationary pressures generated by, say the increased tariff, will not be passed on fully into the consumer price index, and hence fully into money wages, so that there will be some incentive for firms to increase the production of the domestic economy's basket of goods. If $\gamma_2 + \gamma_3$ summed to one, then the impact of the sudden increase in the tariff would be absorbed totally in a rise in the inflation rate of the consumer price index (equal to the domestic price inflation in the steady state). There can be no trade-off between output and inflation.

Should that trade-off be present then it can be exploited by commercial and monetary policy. However, an extra side condition has to be imposed to render the effects of fiscal policy as beneficial as those of commercial and monetary policy. There can be differences, therefore, between policies in the steady-state version of the dynamic model. There might exist a trade-off beween types of policy, so that even in this world of 'certainty' a real, meaningful choice of policy can occur. The optimal strategy depends upon the model's parameters and the objectives of policy, for example, if the notion is to raise output by a specified amount some policies will not be feasible and others, as in the situation here, such as an increase in a general tariff or an increase in the real stock of money, can be used as alternatives.

The same considerations apply *mutatis mutandis* to changes in the exchange rate appreciation rate in the steady state. Movements in that rate mirror those in output: again for the same reasons as they had to in the short-run version of the models. Yet again, by extension, should the government wish to design a policy package to meet a policy target vector we would find from the solution vector of equation (8.76), for all of the appropriate elements of the target vector, that some policy combinations are now feasible whilst others are not. This amplifies the difference between the dynamic full information model and the static models of similar versions.

There is little that could be gained by our grinding out all the solutions for the differentials contained in equation (8.76). Even this comparatively small model is so complex that we can unscramble very few of the equations to produce anything resembling a result that can be signed and evaluated intuitively. However, before completing this section we might mention that when the model is solved for the change in the quantity of imports in the steady state, consequent upon the increase in the general tariff, it is feasible for them to exhibit an *increase* in accordance with the CEPG's propositions.

8.4   *Stability and the Time Paths of the Endogenous Variables*

To repeat them for ease of reference, the economic system consists of these equations

$$Q = C(Y^{\mathrm{D}}, \bar{r} + e - \rho, \sigma, W) + X\left(\frac{\sigma}{\lambda}\right) + G_{\mathrm{d}} \tag{8.81}$$

$$p = \gamma_0 + \gamma_1(Q - \bar{Q}) + \gamma_2\rho + \gamma_3(f + e + \lambda^*) \tag{8.82}$$

$$l = L(Q, \bar{r} + e - \rho, -\rho, W) \tag{8.83}$$

$$Y^{\mathrm{D}} = (1 - \tau)\left[\frac{Q}{\phi(\sigma)} + (\bar{r} + e)(W - l)\right]$$

$$- \rho W + \frac{\mu\sigma(\lambda - 1)}{\phi(\sigma)\lambda}(I + G_{\mathrm{I}}) \tag{8.84}$$

$$\dot{W} = S(Y^{\mathrm{D}}, \bar{r} + e - \rho, W) + (\rho - p)W \tag{8.85}$$

$$\dot{\sigma} = [(1 - \alpha_3)(f + e + \lambda^*) - \alpha_0 - \alpha_1(Q - \bar{Q}) - \alpha_2\rho]\sigma \tag{8.86}$$

$$\dot{\rho} = \theta(p - \rho) \qquad (8.87)$$

with $I = I(Y^D, \bar{r} + e - \rho, \sigma, W)$ and $\phi(\sigma) = \sigma^{1+\delta}$.

To examine the stability of this system necessitates our solving it in the short run for Q, p, e and Y^D, in effect for given values of the dynamic and the exogenous variables. That procedure yields, in general, these solutions

$$x_i = \Omega_i(W, \sigma, \Pi, z), \quad i = 1, 2, 3, 4 \qquad (8.88)$$

where x_i denotes the vector of endogenous variables, Q, p, e and Y^D, in numerical order; and z represents the vector of exogenous variables. When the solutions for the x_i are inserted into equations (8.85)–(8.87) we have a third-order differential equation system

$$\dot{W} = F(W, \sigma, \Pi)$$

$$\dot{\sigma} = \psi(W, \sigma, \Pi) \qquad (8.89)$$

$$\dot{\rho} = \chi(W, \sigma, \Pi)$$

The condition for stability is that the characteristic equation of the Jacobian of equation (8.89) be such that its three roots (β_i) all be negative. From those roots and the initial conditions of the model we will have solutions, naturally, of this form for the dynamic variables

$$W(t) = \bar{W} + k_0 \exp(\beta_1 t) + k_1 \exp(\beta_2 t) + k_3 \exp(\beta_3 t) \qquad (8.90)$$

where t now denotes time, the k_i are constants dependent upon the initial conditions in the model and $\bar{W}$ is the steady-state solution.

Evaluation of the $\Omega_i(.)$ does not permit us to unscramble anything (remotely) useful in terms of the β_i and hence in respect of the general solution for the time paths of the variables W, σ and ρ; and so by implication in regard to the time paths of the other endogenous variables Q, p, Y^D and e. It would be useful to examine those time paths for restrictive commercial policy and fiscal policy regimes. However, the only means by which this is feasible is by a numerical model, and this is the only method by which the stability of the model could be tested since a Liapunov function could not be discovered for the system (8.89) (see note 6).

8.5   A Numerical Model

The model utilized in previous sections was linearized, and it was solved for the short-run and for the steady state to investigate the effects of a general tariff on the economy. Additionally, the dynamic paths of the variables Q, Y^D, e, p, ρ and W were obtained to permit the transition path from one steady state to another to be analysed. The values of the parameters, partial derivatives and control variables used are listed in the accompanying note.[7]

The short-run results are portrayed in tables 8.1–8.4. These tables indicate in every case that an initial tariff (even as high as 10 per cent) will raise output in the short run; besides increasing the inflation of the consumer price index, real disposable income and the depreciation of the exchange rate. The movements in the inflation of the CPI and the depreciation in the rate of exchange are correlated positively, as required by economic intuition, so much so that the faster is the rate of depreciation of the home currency as the tariff heightens, the faster is the rate of inflation of the CPI. The faster is the growth in output as the tariff increases, the faster we would also expect the inflation of the CPI to be, since output proceeds above $\bar{Q}$ and inflationary pressures from domestic prices *per se* feed into the inflation of the CPI.

TABLE 8.1

t	Q	Y^D	e	p
0	13.2569	14.4659	2.92846	5.07554
0.1	14.0246	17.1529	3.31232	5.68971
0.2	14.8913	20.1863	3.74567	6.38307
0.3	15.8775	23.6378	4.23873	7.17196
0.4	17.0095	27.6000	4.80476	8.07762
0.5	18.3225	32.1955	5.46126	9.12802
0.6	19.8636	37.5893	6.23180	10.3609
0.7	21.6978	44.0091	7.14892	11.8283
0.8	23.9177	51.7786	8.25885	13.6042
0.9	26.6590	61.3733	9.62952	15.7972
1.0	30.1301	73.5220	11.3650	18.5741

$\tau = 0, \mu = 1.0$

TABLE 8.2

t	Q	Y^D	e	p
0	13.2569	14.4659	2.92846	5.07554
0.1	13.6113	15.7061	3.10563	5.35901
0.2	13.9510	16.8953	3.27551	5.63082
0.3	14.2771	18.0365	3.43855	5.89168
0.4	14.5903	19.1327	3.59514	6.14223
0.5	14.8913	20.1863	3.74567	6.38307
0.6	15.1809	21.2000	3.89047	6.61475
0.7	15.4597	22.1758	4.02987	6.83780
0.8	15.7283	23.1159	4.16417	7.05267
0.9	15.9873	24.0221	4.29364	7.25982
1.0	16.2371	24.8964	4.41853	7.45965

$\tau = 0, \mu = 0.5$

TABLE 8.3

t	Q	Y^D	e	p
0	9.29161	0.58731	0.94581	1.90329
0.1	9.36057	0.82866	0.98029	1.95846
0.2	9.43045	1.07325	1.01523	2.01436
0.3	9.50128	1.32114	1.05064	2.07102
0.4	0.57307	1.57240	1.08653	2.12845
0.5	9.64584	1.82710	1.12292	2.18667
0.6	9.71961	2.08531	1.15981	2.24569
0.7	9.79441	2.34710	1.19720	2.30553
0.8	9.87025	2.61255	1.23513	2.36620
0.9	9.94716	2.88173	1.27358	2.42773
1.0	10.0252	3.15474	1.31258	2.49013

$\tau = 0.25, \mu = 1.0$

As again is to be expected on a priori grounds, the higher is the marginal tax rate τ, the smaller is output at any given τ. The bigger is τ and the smaller is μ (the larger is the slice of tariff revenue that accrues to the government), the smaller is the impact on output and inflation of any level of tariff. This is because, in the short run, the levels of government outlays on imports and domestic goods is assumed fixed; the government's budget can

TABLE 8.4

t	Q	Y^D	e	p
0	9.29161	0.58731	0.94581	1.90329
0.1	9.32434	0.70184	0.96217	1.92947
0.2	9.35426	0.80659	0.97713	1.95341
0.3	9.38174	0.90276	0.99087	1.97539
0.4	9.40705	0.99136	1.00353	1.99564
0.5	9.43045	1.07325	1.01523	2.01436
0.6	9.45214	1.14917	1.02607	2.03171
0.7	9.47231	1.21975	1.03615	2.04785
0.8	9.49110	1.28552	1.04555	2.06288
0.9	9.50866	1.34697	1.05433	2.07693
1.0	9.52510	1.40451	1.06255	2.09008

$\tau = 0.25, \mu = 0.5$

then be in surplus if it imposes a general tariff and claws back most of the revenue for itself. This puts less pressure on the home market, but especially on the foreign exchange market, so reducing e and hence p. In the long run (the steady state), naturally, the government's budget must balance *ex definitione*; and any changes in its expenditures are investigated by implication in the analysis of the dynamic paths of the endogenous variables, which will indicate if the steady state is a stable position, such that sudden changes in the level of government economic activity will propel the system in one direction or another, but will never cause it to oscillate away from a steady-state solution.

The solutions for the steady state, where the variables being solved for are now Q, Y^D, e, σ and W (the level of real wealth which adjusts to maintain the government's budget in balance) are presented in tables 8.5–8.8. The pattern of results contained in these tables is similar to that revealed by tables 8.1–8.4, but they are far less accentuated. The general tariff increases output in the steady state in the four cases of (τ, μ) illustrated, but it does so only marginally and smoothly. The biggest impression on output is made if, when the general tariff is introduced or raised, the government sets τ to zero and μ to unity. Since it cannot survive without some revenue if it wishes to play any part at all of a macro- or of a micro-allocative role in the economy,

TABLE 8.5

t	Q	Y^D	W	σ	e
0	9.84492	4.10335	6.10348	1.50073	2.38000
0.1	9.87297	4.08468	6.08468	1.50815	2.49189
0.2	9.89624	4.06917	6.06917	1.51429	2.58497
0.3	9.91588	4.05608	6.05608	1.51947	2.66353
0.4	9.93268	4.04488	6.04488	1.52390	2.73073
0.5	9.94722	4.03519	6.03519	1.52774	2.78886
0.6	9.95991	4.02673	6.02673	1.53109	2.83965
0.7	9.97110	4.01927	6.01927	1.53404	2.88440
0.8	9.98103	4.01265	6.01265	1.53666	2.92411
0.9	9.98990	4.00673	6.00673	1.53900	2.95962
1.0	9.99788	4.00141	6.00141	1.54111	2.99154

$\tau = 0, \mu = 1.0$

TABLE 8.6

t	Q	Y^D	W	σ	e
0	9.84492	4.10335	6.10348	1.50073	2.38000
0.1	9.85898	4.09401	6.09401	1.50445	2.43593
0.2	9.87064	4.08624	6.08624	1.50753	2.48257
0.3	9.88050	4.07067	6.07967	1.51013	2.52199
0.4	9.88893	4.07404	6.07404	1.51236	2.55574
0.5	9.89624	4.06917	6.06917	1.51429	2.58496
0.6	9.90263	4.06491	6.06491	1.51597	2.61052
0.7	9.90826	4.06116	6.06116	1.51746	2.63305
0.8	9.91327	4.05782	6.05782	1.51878	2.65307
0.9	9.91774	4.05484	6.05484	1.51996	2.67097
1.0	9.92177	4.05216	6.05216	1.52102	2.68706

$\tau = 0, \mu = 0.5$

it is clear that it should choose to set τ at low as possible. However, if it raises τ and μ, it has the policy option of increasing its expenditures G_d and G_I. In this dynamic model it might be more appropriate for it to retain some proportion of the tariff revenue but to spend it predominantly on importables. This is because there is now the increased possibility of the government's levering up the inflation of domestically produced goods, since it has

TABLE 8.7

t	Q	Y^D	W	σ	e
0	9.43473	4.37684	6.37685	1.39250	0.73896
0.1	9.45812	4.36125	6.36125	1.39867	0.83250
0.2	9.47762	4.34825	6.34825	1.40382	0.91049
0.3	9.49412	4.33725	6.33725	1.40817	0.97648
0.4	9.50826	4.32782	6.32782	1.41190	1.03305
0.5	9.52052	4.31965	6.31965	1.41514	1.08207
0.6	9.53124	4.31250	6.31250	1.41797	1.12497
0.7	9.54071	4.30620	6.30620	1.42046	1.16283
0.8	9.54912	4.30059	6.30059	1.42268	1.19647
0.9	9.55664	4.29557	6.29557	1.42467	1.22657
1.0	9.56342	4.29106	6.29106	1.42646	1.25367

$\tau = 0.25, \mu = 1.0$

TABLE 8.8

t	Q	Y^D	W	σ	e
0	9.43473	4.37684	6.37685	1.39250	0.72869
0.1	9.44643	4.36905	6.36905	1.39559	0.78572
0.2	9.45617	4.36225	6.36255	1.39816	0.82470
0.3	9.46442	4.35705	6.35705	1.40033	0.85770
0.4	9.47149	4.35234	6.35234	1.40220	0.88598
0.5	9.47762	4.34825	6.34825	1.40382	0.91049
0.6	9.48298	4.34468	6.34468	1.40523	0.93193
0.7	9.48771	4.34152	6.34152	1.40648	0.95086
0.8	9.49192	4.33872	6.33872	1.50759	0.96768
0.9	9.49568	4.33621	6.33621	1.40858	0.98274
1.0	9.49907	4.33395	6.33395	1.40948	0.99628

$\tau = 0.25, \mu = 0.5$

a higher marginal propensity to spend than the personal sector has, and now excess demand will cause P_d, the domestic inflation rate, to increase. To generate economic activity the government might be better advised to attempt to increase the depreciation in e by spending more of its tariff proceeds on imports. In the numerical model we have presented here, government expenditure levels are, of course, fixed, or control variables. However, if they are altered they are likely to produce the kind of outcome just outlined heuristically, an outcome different from that obtained in the static models of earlier chapters for the simple reason that they *were* static models with properties which omitted movements in the price level of domestically produced goods. The steady state produces a non-linear system (because of multiplicative terms in the endogenous variables incorporated in the definition of real disposable income) and so cannot be solved in general, even given the parameters of the kind we have specified beforehand, for target packages of government policy, and the associated vector of instruments (including G_d and G_I). The system has to be solved numerically *in toto*. In the case of the short run, by way of contrast, if the behavioural functions are assumed to be linear (as we have so assumed they are), the delineations of the parameters will permit us, via equations (8.66)–(8.69) to solve for a set of policy strategies for a preassigned vector of policy targets (either in levels or changes). However, we shall not present the results from that exercise; it is left to the reader to do so by inserting the coefficients we have used (see note 8) to examine the trade-offs between τ, μ, G_d and G_I that might exist.

The dynamic properties of the system have also been investigated in full, for tariffs between 0 per cent and 100 per cent, for the combinations of (τ, μ) stipulated in tables 8.1–8.8 and for given values of the government's policy variables. Again we have not confused the text with the permutations that arise when the government's outlays are allowed to alter. But once more, as with the steady state, the dynamics cannot be solved analytically to enable us to see how, for given parameter values, amendments to the control variables will affect the transition path of the key endogenous variables. The dynamic paths of those variables can be obtained only by our employing a full numerical description of the model.

Even for the four combinations of cases of (τ, μ) used in tables 8.1–8.4 and 8.5–8.8 and for given G_d and G_I we have deemed it sensible only to provide a sample of the results found; since they are all similar for all t, we have chosen to portray the dynamic paths of the endogenous variables Q, Y^D, e, p, σ and W for values of $t = 0$ and $t = 0.10$. We then do this pictorially since that is a far more efficient way to do so; as the variables tend to require 25 time periods before they stabilize on their steady-state values. The four pairs of graphs of the variables for the specified τ, μ and t are portrayed on figures 8.1–8.4: the scales of the variables

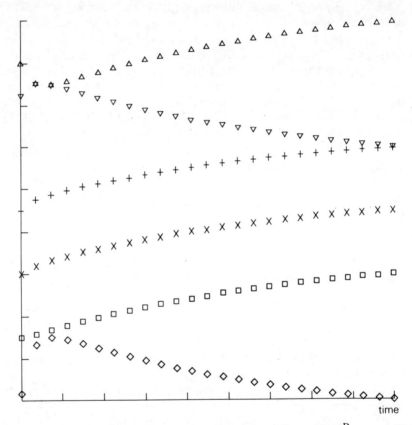

FIGURE 8.1(a)   Reading from the top the curves refer to Q, Y^D, e, p, σ, W, for the values $\tau = 0.000$, $\mu = 1.000$, $t = 0.000$

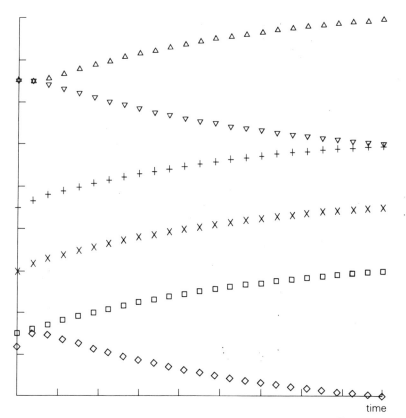

FIGURE 8.1(b)   Reading from the top the curves refer to $Q, Y^{D}, e, p, \sigma, W$, for the values $\tau = 0.000, \mu = 1.000, t = 0.100$

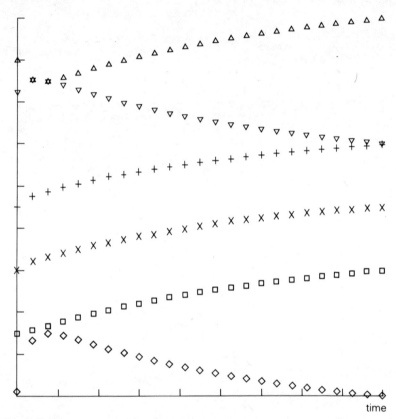

FIGURE 8.2(a)   Reading from the top the curves refer to Q, Y^D, e, p, σ, W, for the values $\tau = 0.000$, $\mu = 0.500$, $t = 0.000$

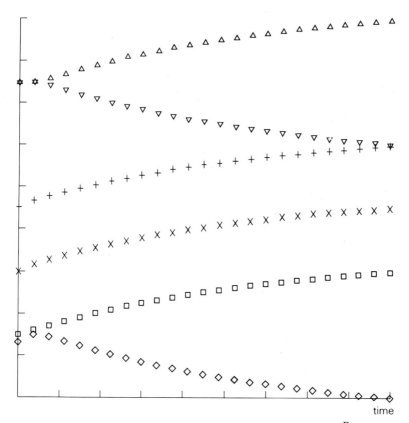

FIGURE 8.2(b)   Reading from the top the curves refer to Q, Y^D, e, p, σ, W, for the values $\tau = 0.000$, $\mu = 0.500$, $t = 0.100$

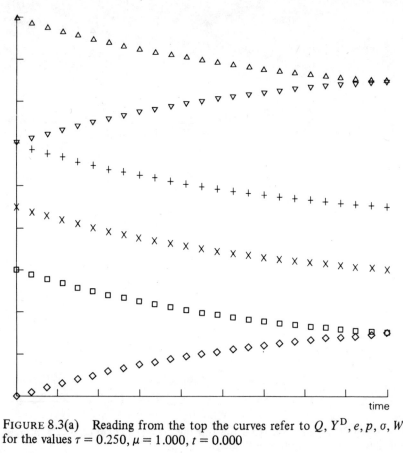

FIGURE 8.3(a)   Reading from the top the curves refer to Q, Y^D, e, p, σ, W, for the values $\tau = 0.250, \mu = 1.000, t = 0.000$

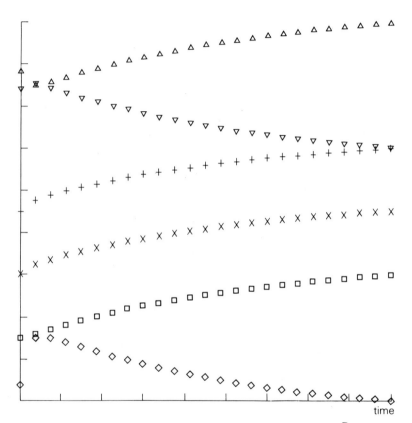

FIGURE 8.3(b)   Reading from the top the curves refer to Q, Y^D, e, p, σ, W, for the values $\tau = 0.250$, $\mu = 1.000$, $t = 0.100$

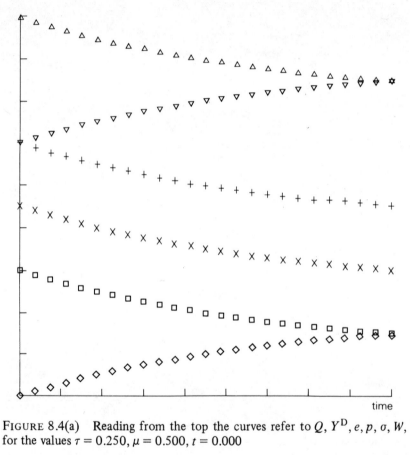

FIGURE 8.4(a)   Reading from the top the curves refer to Q, Y^D, e, p, σ, W, for the values $\tau = 0.250$, $\mu = 0.500$, $t = 0.000$

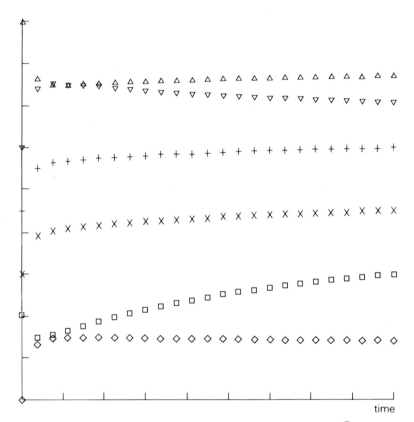

FIGURE 8.4(b)   Reading from the top the curves refer to Q, Y^D, e, p, σ, W, for the values $\tau = 0.250$, $\mu = 0.500$, $t = 0.100$

COMMERCIAL, MONETARY AND FISCAL POLICY

have not been plotted since the objective is to illustrate their dynamic paths in a comparative fashion. The phase diagrams for all pairs of variables have not been included since their structure (usually proportionately linear, in fact) is obvious from a glance at the time paths of the individual variables. If these time paths had included oscillatory periods then phase diagrams would have been invaluable in deciphering the relative movements in the endogenous variables.

Notes

1 Additionally, in a model of fixed exchange rates, or of a 'marginal float', the government might decide to intervene in the market for foreign currency in an attempt to sterilize increases in foreign reserves, consequent upon the emergence of a balance of payments surplus.

2 The model we shall be employing is a mere extension of those already set forth in this book. It is one that is composed of what have long since become standard elements; but it has been exploited most by Turnovsky (1976, 1977) upon whose constructs we rely heavily. We have also used some of his notation, but we have attempted to retain as much as possible of the notation we have adopted throughout the previous chapters.

3 R follows from the fact that $FE/P = \sigma/\phi(\sigma)\,\lambda$.

4 Note that

$$W = \frac{\mathrm{d}}{\mathrm{d}t}\left(\frac{L+B}{P}\right) = \frac{\dot{L}+\dot{B}}{P} - pW$$

Thus if we divide equation (8.28) by P and deduct $-pW$ from the resulting expression we end up with equation (8.29), in which we have made use of the definition of σ, the terms of trade. Also we should point out that the tariff revenue PR in equation (8.24) is in domestic prices since we have defined R per se to be real revenue measured in terms of P. That is it is revenue in domestic prices deflated by P.

5 The conventional, Routhian, stability conditions are not really of any assistance to us in a truly dynamic model. Δ can, in fact, be negative or positive. The conditions that help to make it assume the one sign or the other also affect the numerators of the relevant multipliers in like manner. So we could assume that Δ was negative instead and still obtain our conclusions. In signing Δ and the multiplier effects we have assumed that $L_2 < 0$ and $\mathrm{II}_1 I_1 < 1$; this last would be guaranteed if $\sigma \leqslant 1$.

6 The Jacobian for the steady-state model is also not nested uniquely within the set of Routhian conditions that must hold if the model is to be stable and so the dynamic paths of the variables converge on their (new) steady-state values as the exogenous variables alter. Strictly, for a model which is

explicitly dynamic, its stability can be assessed either by finding the solutions to the system given by equations such as (8.90) or by examining whether or not a Liapunov function can be discovered for the differential equations system *per system* epitomized in equations such as (8.89). But (except in trivial circumstances) a search for such a function can only be carried out when the differential equations are written in numerical form. If such a function can be located then the system is stable; and this circumvents the need to solve explicitly for equations like (8.90). In our case, despite deriving the coefficients for equation (8.89) from the parameter values specified in note 7 below, it proved impossible to derive a Liapunov function. In fact, the only way that we could investigate stability was through a complete numerical analysis of the model, solving for the actual values of the endogenous variables for a given set of parameters and tracing out their time paths. (On Liapunov functions see, for example, LaSalle and S. Lefschetz (1961).)

7 $c_1 = 0.3$; $c_2 = -0.1$; $c_3 = 0.1$; $c_4 = 0.1$; $\gamma_0 = 0.4$; $\gamma_1 = 0.4$; $\gamma_2 = 0.1$; $\gamma_3 = 0.8$; $L_1 = 0.2$; $L_2 = -0.4$; $L_3 = 0.3$; $I_1 = 0.55$; $I_2 = -0.2$; $I_3 = -0.05$; $I_4 = 0.05$; $G_d = 1.0$; $G_1 = 1.0$; $\bar{r} = 3.0$; $X_1 = 4.7$; $Q = 10$; $f = 1.0$; $\lambda^* = 0$; $\bar{\lambda} = 1.1$; $\delta = 0.5$; $S_1 = 0.15$; $S_2 = 0.15$; $S_3 = -0.15$; $\theta = 0.5$; $\alpha_0 = 0.5$; $\alpha_1 = 0.8$; $\alpha_2 = 0.2$; $\alpha_3 = 0.6$.

Note that the requisite adding-up constraints are satisfied. The values of γ chosen are such as to guarantee a positive effect on output of a general tariff in a fixed exchange rate world. In the case of the steady state we have not set the initial σ at unity as we have done in deriving the analytical results in the main text: it was not possible to do this for computational reasons. The solution vector is for a once and for all tariff.

9
Concluding Observations

Intellectual and academic tradition has generally been anti-protectionist, and has not favoured the imposition of tariffs and quantitative restrictions even for specific countries. Political opinion has oscillated sharply between support and opposition (although there has always existed a strong protectionist lobby in the US). An assessment of the economic effects of protection for the domestic economy generates a lot of heat, and occasionally some light.

Neville Chamberlain was the Chancellor of the Exchequer when he introduced protectionist legislation in Britain in the early 1930s. Eight years later this is what he had to say on his earlier measures: 'We recognise that for the full development of international trade it must flow along multilateral channels, and that we must put an end to that vicious policy of economic nationalism and autarky which did so much to upset the last great peace settlement.' (Quoted by Capie (1983).) Note that the statement was being made during the Great War and, implicitly, protectionism was partly held responsible for the war!

Assessing the economic history of Britain during the inter-war years, with special reference to the depression and protectionism, Capie (1983) concludes:

> Lessons from the past ... are far from unambiguous, but the experience of the inter-war years adds to our general understanding of the issue of protectionism and its course and outcome. The principal causes have again been seen to be war and economic depression, ... there is little evidence that protection has ever done anything to promote economic growth and welfare, and the inter-war experience provides further evidence of that. Indeed, the growth of protectionism has invariably gone hand in hand with developing rationalism, and imperialism, and resulted in dismal consequences.

216

Criticizing the Cambridge Economic Policy Group's call for commercial policy-induced protection for the British economy, Krugman presents a series of analytical models to conclude: 'If there is only one England, New Cambridge policies may succeed; but in a world of Englands, they must fail.' Krugman's (1982) discussion on real wage resistance contains this observation.

In part the critics are well intentioned. There can be little doubt that if one country imposes trade restrictive policies and retaliation follows, literally, from the rest of the world, then the volume of international trade will definitely decline. If *everyone* protects we all lose.

However, there are three good reasons why this should not be so. Firstly, the share of the small open economy in total world exports is expected to be relatively low. Thus import controls in a small economy, and for a temporary period, may not be significant enough for the rest of the international economy to follow suit immediately. Secondly, as we have shown earlier, if commercial policy is expansionary, then domestic output and disposable income will rise. This may increase the volume of imports, thus aiding world trade and reducing the possibility of retaliation. Thirdly, protection is not being advocated for all countries and at the same time. Certain countries, principally those where conventional demand management policies have failed to stimulate the economy, need protection more than others. Commercial policy, in conjunction with other measures, can be used as a short-run stabilization instrument to rejuvenate the economy. If this increases output, causes structural change and raises disposable income, then after the removal of protection, it will be in a position to import more from other economies. Domestic demand diversion to local products and possible productivity increases on the supply side can also reduce export dependence. The next set of countries, in the pecking order of needs, can then follow with their commercial policies. Of course, policy co-ordination is paramount, but at an analytical level the possibilities exist.

The argument can be explained further by means of an analogy. The post-war period has seen a number of 'export miracles'; Germany and Japan in the 1950s, the 'Gang of Four', South Korea, Taiwan, Hong Kong and Singapore from the late sixties. But a major part of the success story is related to the intention and ability of the rest of the world to absorb the production surpluses of these countries. After all, world trade must balance, so that a trade surplus for some must be a trade deficit for others. In a sense, if *all* countries of the world wished to have a trade surplus and enjoy the benefits of the export multiplier, the 'miracle' would become a 'myth'. Economic experts exhort countries to follow an export oriented growth strategy and run up a trade surplus which has a positive effect on domestic output. But this will only work if some countries are willing to *import* and have a trade deficit. It has been claimed, and rightly so, that if every country protects, the world trading system will break down. But then it is equally valid to say that if every country desires to have a trade surplus then the system will be (by definition) un-workable. The macroeconomic implications are similar. Yet protectionism raises the spectre of calamity, while export promotion is praised by all.

We now discuss, briefly, some of the implications of the trade-theoretic literature for our macroeconomic analysis of protection. Trade theory demonstrates[1] that tariffs reduce domestic real income and welfare for a small country. This is because the economy has no influence on the world price, exogenously given, thus a tariff cannot change the terms of trade. This potentially welfare-improving channel is therefore blocked. On the other hand, higher prices of importables, may lead to a fall in imports and this will cause a loss, in terms of foregone opportunities; alternatively the domestic economy will have to pay more for its imports compared to free trade. Overall, welfare declines. In the large country model, as the theory of optimal tariffs suggests, the position is reversed. The improvement in the terms of trade (a decrease in the relative price of imports in the world market), consequent on the domestic economy imposing a tariff and thus reducing its demand for importables, increases welfare. Starting from a zero tariff, a large country always gains after its imposition. If the foreign country's demand for its own imports (home country's exports) is inelastic then, given trade balance, a tariff causes the domestic economy's imports to rise. This is welfare augmenting once again. Alternatively if the foreign demand elasticity is greater than unity, we have the standard result on the optimum tariff, which sets the upper bound, above which real income will start declining.

The macroeconomic model that we have discussed, though always called the 'small' open economy, is actually 'large' from the point of view of trade theory. Given flexible exchange rates, and complete specialization, the terms of trade are endogenous and can change in response to domestic policy. Thus with the imposition of tariff, the (real) exchange rate falls and the improvement in the international terms of trade leads to welfare increases. The fall in imports, if it takes place, can have the opposite effect. As we have seen, if the export elasticity of the small open economy is less than one, but the propensity to import is sufficiently large, in that the Metzler paradox does not hold, then a tariff may have a Pareto superior effect. Domestic output may expand, both in the rigid real and nominal wage models, and the value of imports, at world prices, will also rise (provided, of course, we have trade balance). Thus a discussion of tariffs, in a small open macromodel with flexible exchange rates, tends to be consistent with the trade literature.

Quite often trade intervention has been justified in terms of domestic distortions. But it has also been shown that restrictive trade policies tend to be 'second best' in the sense that appropriate taxes and subsidies could remedy the distortions more usefully. We have met examples of this argument in chapter 7. Again the justification for tariffs is that it is possible to combine them with tax/subsidy measures without giving rise to budgetary imbalances. At the aggregate level, raising or lowering taxes requires concomitant changes in the budget which are not usually discussed at the more microeconomic levels of trade models. Without a formal analysis it is not always possible to say that a tariff cum tax (subsidy) cum balanced budget policy is superior or inferior to one where there are production taxes financed by budgetary accommodation.

International trade theory emphasizes the Pareto optimality of free trade, thus from the world's point of view a tariff is suboptimal. However, results in this area are almost always based on the assumption of full employment of available resources. For example the standard diagrammatic presentation of the effect of tariffs on world production in a two-country two-commodity model always presupposes that the countries are on their production possibility schedules. But the transformation functions are drawn on the basis of full capacity utilization of the factors of production. If the countries are *inside* the production possibility set, then it is difficult to give a precise meaning to the usual marginal conditions. The slope of the transformation curve tells us what happens if resources are released from one sector and fully employed in another. Since macromodels inevitably deal with unemployed labour and under-utilized capital stock, again, the usual assignments may be inapplicable. Thus the Pareto superior movement, implied by a removal of tariffs, cannot be easily justified in the type of models that we have discussed.

As we noted in chapters 1 and 2, the economic implications of the British general tariff of 1932 has been a subject of great discussion and of even greater controversy, and it might be of interest at this point to mention briefly some of the studies that have been made of it.[2] Reference has already been made in chapter 2, to the study of Eichengreen, which is a formal analysis of the macroeconomic effects of protection as opposed to the inter-industrial studies done by others. His main conclusion from the historical data, though not necessarily from his theoretical model, is that the general tariff was indeed expansionary. The improvement in the terms of trade, attributable to the tariff itself, was substantial; this managed almost to neutralize the rise in the domestic price of importables. In spite of this, absorption rose and went even above aggregate output; this of course, contrary to expectations, produced a current account deficit. The increase in aggregate expenditure (absorption) raised output. Foreman-Peck (1981), on the other hand, emphasizes the traditional expenditure-switching arguments by which local demand for domestic goods increased at the expense of importables and the consequent multiplier increased aggregate output. Both estimate that GDP was 2.3 per cent higher in 1938 due to the presence of the tariff – a not inconsiderable amount. The formal modelling of the British historical experience adds considerably to our analytical understanding of the possible expansionary effects of tariffs.

In the preceding pages we have made occasional empirical references where these have seemed especially germane. However, we have not strayed too far from the theoretical analysis of commercial policy. Our preference rests with tackling first of all the theoretical issues that emanate from the introduction of that type of policy. Others clearly prefer a direct empirical assessment of their effects; but, *de gustibus non est disputandum*. However, even bearing in mind the British general tariff of 1932, there is little evidence of substance upon which a macroeconomic evaluation of protectionism can be founded, so that we probably do have to fall back on analytical enquiry.

In that regard, we can now usefully summarize some of the results we have obtained. At the most general level we have demonstrated once more the oft-found conclusion that propositions or hypotheses in economics are not of universal validity. Those propositions are not 'model free'. This is frustrating but it is ineluctable.

It has enabled us to demonstrate that the opinion that, in a regime of freely floating exchange rates, protectionism is to be avoided at all costs is not one that can command universal support. Furthermore, it has permitted us to deduce that protectionism can have advantageous repercussions on the domestic macroeconomy, amplify the output-generating effects of conventional monetary and fiscal policies and provide a direct stimulus to the economy of the rest of the world.

We have also been able to show that the prevailing orthodoxy on protectionism can be challenged in a variety of characteristics of the macroeconomy. However, in line with our previous comments, whether the orthodox conclusions hold or are refuted depends upon the precise assumptions that are made concerning the behavioural properties of the respective models (e.g. about the price and income propensities to import, the price elasticity of export demand, the degree of capital mobility that is allowed, etc.).

Across a range of macroeconomic models our analyses make it possible to answer questions 1–12 posed in chapter 1. The reader is referred to pp. 8–9 of that chapter. In very bald terms we can reply to them as follows:

1 Yes; there will be many such models.
2 Not necessarily; in certain cases there will be equivalence, but the general tariff can boost imports in the long run, whereas a binding and effective quota cannot do so, *ex definitione*.
3 No; as we have just reminded ourselves.
4 Yes; but flexibility in money wages and prices that result in a fixed real wage for the domestic economy need not prevent a general tariff (or a general quota) from instigating macroeconomic recovery.
5 Not necessarily.
6 Yes.
7 Yes; it is more likely that commercial policy will be an enhancement to monetary and fiscal policies, rather than vice versa.
8 This question has not been accorded a comprehensive treatment in the book, but the answer is ambiguous.
9 Yes.

10 Yes; it is possible that even if output would not be boosted by a general tariff the government could alter that outcome by its spending some or all of the revenue itself.

11 Yes; the domestic economy's level of 'welfare' can also be enhanced by the adoption of protectionist policies.

12 The maximum revenue and optimum tariffs of the pure theory of international trade can be incorporated into the macroeconomic analysis of commercial policy; but they play only a minor role.

Naturally, in reality, the macroeconomic structure of even 'small' open economies will differ in detail from the models we have portrayed. Nevertheless, if we believe that there is a role for 'aggregate economics' then in particular situations the models we have analysed might well paint a broad picture of the characteristics, rather than just a caricature, of macroeconomies. Thus, if it is felt that it is a reasonable approximation to assume that the price of domestically produced goods is fixed (up to, say, some full employment level), that the essence of the financial market can be captured by a money and a bonds world, that there is capital mobility between the domestic economy and the rest of the world, a model such as that detailed in chapter 5 will provide at the least some insights into the likely qualitative implications of the domestic government implementing a protectionist strategy. Some proximate econometric estimates of the economy's behavioural functions will provide some quantitative assessment of the repercussions of protectionism.

Notes

1 See Caves and Jones (1977) for an excellent discussion.
2 Capie (1983) is a strong critic and also provides a good overview.

References

References

Arrow, K. J. and Kurz, M. (1970) *Public Investment, The Rate of Return and Optimal Fiscal Policy*, Baltimore: Johns Hopkins Press.

Bhagwati, J. (1965) On the equivalence of tariffs and quotas, in R. E. Baldwin *et al.* (ed.), *Trade, Growth and the Balance of Payments*, Amsterdam: North-Holland, 53-67.

Bhagwati, J. and Johnson, H. G. (1961) A generalised theory of the effects of tariffs on the terms of trade, *Oxford Economic Papers*, 13, 225-53.

Blinder, A. S. and Solow, R. M. (1973) Does fiscal policy matter? *Journal of Public Economics*, 2, 319-37.

Blinder, A. S. and Solow, R. M. (1974) Analytical foundations of fiscal policy, in A. S. Blinder *et al.* (ed.), *The Theory of Public Finance*, Washington DC: The Brookings Institute, 3-115.

Boyer, R. (1977) Commercial policy under alternative exchange rate regimes, *Canadian Journal of Economics*, 10, 218-32.

Branson, W. H. (1979) Exchange rate dynamics and monetary policy, in *Inflation and Employment in Open Economies* (ed. A. Lindbeck), Amsterdam: North-Holland.

Brock, W. A. (1975) A simple perfect foresight monetary model, *Journal of Monetary Economics*, 1, 133-50.

Calvo, G. and Rodriguez, C. (1977) A model of exchange rate determination under currency substitution and rational expectations, *Journal of Political Economy*, 85, 617-25.

Capie, F. (1983) *Depression and Protectionism: Britain Between the Wars*, London: George Allen & Unwin.

Caves, R. E. and Jones, R. W. (1977) *World Trade and Payments*, Boston: Little, Brown and Co.

Chan, K. (1978) The employment effects of tariffs under a free exchange rate regime, *Journal of International Economics*, 8, 415-24.

Cripps, F. and Godley, W. (1976) A formal analysis of the Cambridge Economic Policy Group model, *Economica*, 43, 335-48.

Cripps, F. and Godley, W. (1978) Control of imports as a means to full employment and the expansion of world trade: the UK's case, *Cambridge Journal of Economics*, 2, 327-34.

Dickinson, D. G., Driscoll, M. J. and Ford, J. L. (1982) Protection, the value of imports and optimal trade-restricting policies, *Weltwirtschaftliches Archiv*, 118 (2), 317-31.

Dornbusch, R. (1976) Expectations and exchange rate dynamics, *Journal of Political Economy*, 84, 1161-76.

Dornbusch, R. (1980) *Open Economy Macroeconomics*, New York: Basic Books.

Dornbusch, R. and Fischer, S. (1980) Exchange rates and the current account, *American Economic Review*, 70, 960-71.

Driscoll, M. J. and Ford, J. L. (1983) Protection and optimal trade-restricting policies under uncertainty, *The Manchester School*, 51, 21-32.

Eichengreen, B. J. (1979) Tariffs and flexible exchange rates, Unpublished Ph.D. Dissertation, Yale University.

Eichengreen, B. J. (1981) A dynamic model of tariffs, output and employment under flexible exchange rates, *Journal of International Economics*, 11, 341-59.

Fetherston, M. J. and Godley, W. (1978) New Cambridge macroeconomics and global monetarism: some issues in the conduct of UK economic policy, in K. Brunner and A. H. Metzler (eds), *Public Policies in Open Economies, Carnegie-Rochester Conference Series on Public Policy*, vol. 9, Amsterdam: North-Holland.

Findlay, R. A. and Rodriguez, C. (1977) Intermediate imports and macroeconomic policy under flexible exchange rates, *Canadian Journal of Economics*, 10, 208-17.

Ford, J. L. and Sen, S. (1984) Tariffs can increase output under flexible exchange rates: a critical exegesis and extension of the Mundellian analysis, paper presented at the *European Meeting of the Econometric Society*, Madrid.

Foreman-Peck, J. (1981) The British tariff and industrial protection in the 1930s: an alternative model, *Economic History Review*, 34, 132-39.

Friedman, M. (1953) *Essays in Positive Economics*, Chicago: Chicago University Press.

Godley, W. (1979) Britain's chronic recession – can anything be done? in *Slow Growth in Britain*, Oxford: Clarendon Press.

Godley, W. and May, R. (1976) The macroeconomic implications of devaluation and import restriction, *Economic Policy Review*, 3.

Gylfason, T. and Helliwell, J. F. (1983) A synthesis of Keynesian, monetary and portfolio approaches to flexible exchange rates, *Economic Journal*, 93, 820-31.

Harberger, A. C. (1950) Currency depreciation, income and the balance of trade, *Journal of Political Economy*, 58, 47-60.

Hindley, B. (1979) Rigid real wages and international economic policy, in J. P. Martin and A. Smith (eds), *Trade and Payments Adjustment under Flexible Exchange Rates*, London: Macmillan.

Houthakker, H. S. and Magee, S. P. (1969) Income and price elasticities in world trade, *Review of Economics and Statistics*, 51.

Johnson, H. G. (1972) *Further Essays in Monetary Economics*, London: George Allen & Unwin.

Keynes, J. M. (1936) *The General Theory of Employment, Interest and Money*, London: Macmillan.

Kimbrough, K. P. (1982) Real disturbances, the current account, and the exchange rate, *Journal of International Economics*, 13, 291-300.

Kouri, P. J. K. (1978) Balance of payments and the foreign exchange model, Cowles Foundation Discussion Paper no. 510.

Krueger, A. O. (1983) *Exchange Rate Determination*, Cambridge: Cambridge University Press.

Krugman, P. (1982) The macroeconomics of protection with a floating exchange rate, *Carnegie-Rochester Conference Series on Public Policy*, vol. 16, 141-82, Amsterdam: North-Holland.

LaSalle, J. and Lefschetz, S. (1961) *Stability by Liapunov's Direct Method with Applications*, New York: Academic Press.

Laursen, S. and Metzler, L. (1950) Flexible exchange rates and the theory of employment, *Review of Economics and Statistics*, 32, 281-99.

Levari, D. and Patinkin, D. (1968) The role of money in a simple growth Model, *American Economic Review*, 58 (4), 713-53.

Mangasarian, O.L. (1966) Sufficient conditions for the optimal control of nonlinear systems, *Journal of Society for Industrial and Applied Mathematics (Control)*, 4, 139-52.

Metzler, L. A. (1949) Tariffs, the terms of trade, and the distribution of national income, *Journal of Political Economy*, 62, 1-29.

Modigliani, F. and Padoa-Schioppa, T. (1978) The management of an open-economy with '100% plus' wage indexation, *Princeton Essays in International Finance*, No. 30.

Mundell, R. A. (1961) Flexible exchange rates and employment policy, *Canadian Journal of Economics*, 27, 509-17.

Mundell, R. A. (1962) The appropriate use of monetary and fiscal policy for internal and external stability, *IMF Staff Papers*, 9, 70-9.

Mussa, M. (1976) The exchange rate, the balance of payments and monetary fiscal policy under a regime of controlled floatship, *Scandinavian Journal of Economics*, 78, 229-48.

Obstfeld, M. (1982) Aggregate spending and the terms-of-trade: is there a Laursen-Metzler effect? *Quarterly Journal of Economics*, 97, 251-70.

Ott, D. J. and Ott, A. F. (1965) Budget balance and equilibrium income, *Journal of Finance*, 20, 71-7.

Patinkin, D. (1965) *Money, Interest and Prices*, New York: Harper and Row.

Persson, T. and Svensson, L. E. O. (1984) Current account dynamics and the terms of trade: Harberger-Laursen-Metzler two generations later, *Institute of International Economic Studies Seminar Paper No. 277*.

Robinson, J. (1964) *Economic Philosophy*, Harmondsworth: Penguin.

Routh, E. J. (1955) *Dynamics of a System of Rigid Bodies*, New York: Dover Publications.

Samuelson, P. A. (1947) *Foundations of Economic Analysis*, Cambridge, Mass: Harvard University Press.

Samuelson, P. A. and Swami, S. (1974) Invariant economic index numbers and canonical duality: survey and synthesis, *American Economic Review*, 64, 566-93.

Sohmen, E. (1958) The effect of devaluation on the price level, *Quarterly Journal of Economics*, 72, 273-83.

Sohmen, E. (1969) *Flexible Exchange Rates* (revised edn), Chicago and London: University of Chicago Press.

Svensson, L. E. O. and Razin, A. (1983) The terms-of-trade and the current account: the Harberger-Laursen-Metzler effect, *Journal of Political Economy*, 91, 97-125.

Theil, H. (1961) *Economic Forecasts and Policy*, 2nd edn, Amsterdam: North-Holland.

Tinbergen, J. (1952) *On the Theory of Economic Policy*, Amsterdam: North-Holland.

Tobin, J. (1980) *Asset Accumulation and Economic Activity*, Oxford: Basil Blackwell.

Tower, E. (1973) Commercial policy under fixed and flexible exchange rates, *Quarterly Journal of Economics*, 87, 436-54.

Turnovsky, S. J. (1976) The dynamics of fiscal policy in an open economy, *Journal of International Economics*, 6, 197-215.

Turnovsky, S. J. (1977) *Macroeconomic Analysis and Stabilisation Policies*, Cambridge: Cambridge University Press.

Turnovsky, S. J. (1981) The effects of devaluation and foreign price disturbances under rational expectations, *Journal of International Economics*, 11 (1), 33-60.

Varian, H. (1984) *Microeconomic Analysis*, 2nd edn, New York: W. W. Norton and Company.

Weitzman, M. L. (1974) Prices vs. quantities, *Review of Economic Studies*, 41, 50-65.

Wilson, C. A. (1979) Anticipated shocks and exchange rate dynamics, *Journal of Political Economy*, 87, 639-47.

Yohe, G. W. (1977) Towards a general comparison of price controls and quantity controls under uncertainty, *Review of Economic Studies*, 229-38.

Young, L. (1980) Optimal revenue-raising trade-restrictions under uncertainty, *Journal of International Economics*, 10 (3), 425-39.

Index